The Return of the Feathered Serpent
Shining Light of 'First Knowledge'

Survival and Renewal at the
End of an Age, 2006-2012

by
JC Husfelt, D.D.

authorHOUSE™

1663 LIBERTY DRIVE, SUITE 200
BLOOMINGTON, INDIANA 47403
(800) 839-8640
WWW.AUTHORHOUSE.COM

First published by AuthorHouse 2/2/2006

ISBN: 1-4259-0546-3 (sc)

Printed in the United States of America
Bloomington, Indiana

This book is printed on acid-free paper.

For my family—
Sherry, Jamie and Jessie
The Bee Clan

Acknowledgements

I would like to express my gratitude and appreciation to my family for their love, spirited companionship, support, help and belief in my quest. I would also like to express my sincerest appreciation to Jane Justice for her untiring editing while balancing a new-born in one hand and my manuscript in the other—thank you. And to her husband, Ian Owens, who assisted not only with their son John, but also with my book.

My wife and I would like to thank all the indigenous teachers and mentors who have shared their 'jewels' with us over the years. In addition, I would like to thank our 'adopted son,' Jo-Jo for his suggestions.

I would also like to thank Jim Kalnins for his unintentional photo of an Archangel and two Assisting Angels that is the cover photograph. Finally, I would like to thank our Apprentices, Personal Apprentices and all of our students who have supported us over the eighteen years of our Apprenticeship Program.

Contents

Title and Cover Photograph

The Return of the Feathered Serpent refers to the prophesized return of the 'messenger.' The prophetic theme of a returning cultural hero is one of the most enduring myths known to humankind. At all times its impact and importance is due to the message of hope and renewal that the hero brings to a gloomy world locked away, as always, in the shadows ruled by fear. In a monumental and epic time of need, the hero re-appears. To the Mesoamericans, their returning prophet or cultural hero was known as Quetzalcoatl—the Feathered Serpent.

Even though the Feathered Serpent imagery is basically Mesoamerican, the concept is worldwide. Whether we are discussing the return of Christ at the 'second coming' or the white prophet, the prophesied future Buddha, the Hawaiians' returning prophet-god Lono, the Inka's Viracocha or the return of King Arthur, the message is still the same—in the darkest of times, a light will arise—a 'wayshower' to love and equality, peace and oneness. The returning hero will bring a message of love, equality and oneness. This prophet will bring light—a light that will dispel the dark despair of humanity just as the Morning Star brings the light of dawn out of the darkness of the night.

In addition, the returning hero has always brought a consistent teaching. This is the teaching that 'you, and no one else, must do the work.' The returning hero is only the messenger and the guide; the ones who listen and hear the message must do the spiritual work.

Certain New Age authors and gurus preach that magically at the end of this Age, all will be elevated to a higher plane of being, a higher consciousness—all will be enlightened through an increase in the vibrational frequency—no war, no need for power or material possessions. It might sound good and easy but isn't that also the message of the church—believe in us, have faith, pay us and you too (of course only Christians), will spend an eternity in heaven.

In my opinion, this doesn't make common sense. A seed in nature does not automatically vibrate into a flower—it struggles to reach the light. It needs water, nurturance and 'feeding' to break through (the earth) and to develop into a beautiful flower, blooming perhaps for only a short period of time. Just like nature, this book is not a quick fix, but it is a life-guide to healing, love and oneness.

The second part of my title, *Shining Light of 'First Knowledge,'* refers not only to the foundation spiritual knowledge of various indigenous cultures world-wide, but in addition, it acknowledges the significance of the cover.

It is a photograph of an Archangel and two assisting angels!

I tell the story of the visitation in the final segment of the Feathered Serpent Chronicles, which you will find after Chapter 6. My wish is that this light will help provide hope and comfort for you in any time of need; and additionally, to remove any doubt that we are ever alone in our journey through life.

I have written the story of the visitation, my vision as being the Morning Star plus two other personal true adventures, in what I call 'Mythic Prose.'[1] Each tale, which I call The Feathered Serpent Chronicles, is true but is written in a mythic way to do justice to the actual Otherworldly events and experiences witnessed not only by myself, but most importantly, by others. In addition, my words are not 'channeled,' they are my words from my own heart and mind.

Foreword

The knowledge contained within this book has been accumulated from over 25 years of my 'looking, listening and learning' from indigenous elders and shamans from all over the world. It also emanates deeply from my own soul wisdom. In addition, the teachings are not just limited to the traditions of Mesoamerica but also include the indigenous knowledge and teachings that I have received directly from the East (Japanese) to the West (Celtic), the North (Northwest Coast First Nations People) to the South (Incan) and finally, the Pacific Basin (Hawaiians).

Even though the Feathered Serpent imagery is basically Mesoamerican, the concept is worldwide and refers to our dual nature—divine and human, which is not separate but is one. The knowledge contained within this book is what I refer to as the 'first knowledge.' It is knowledge that is weaved throughout and found in all the 'first people' indigenous spiritual/religious traditions on this earth before it was changed to suite the ruling religious leaders as their own dogma and doctrine.

In 1993, the day after a ceremonial 'feeding of the ancestors' and the morning of my vision, I was told by a Native Hawaiian healer friend that during the ceremony, a Hawaiian ancestor in spirit form had come to him with a message for me: 'that I was at the level of a *kahuna*[2] and that I was bringing back the old knowledge that had been forgotten, lost or corrupted. And that I must not identify it as being Hawaiian or any other culture's knowledge, which only separates people and does not unite them.'

Thus, I call this old knowledge, 'First Knowledge.' The purpose behind this book, my teachings and my message is to educate. It is to give a different perspective from what you can get from the New Age people, Self-help gurus and the religious ruling elites—who keep you subservient and in fear. In addition, it is to 'open the eyes' of all people to the knowledge that we are divine (feathered) as well as human (serpent)—that all things are divine as well as having their own very special intrinsic form. This is the knowledge of the interconnectedness and the Divine Oneness of all things.[3]

Let it be known that there is not just one divine 'sacrificed person who died for our sins.' Each one of us is divine and each one of us must 'sacrifice' our own egotistical illusion to 'see truth;' the truth that each one of us is truly divine—a sun of God and that every part of nature is as well divine and—a sun of God.

This book will not make you a shaman (*curandero* or a *kahuna*). There are already too many New Age people with little experience, little knowledge and very little, if any at all, sacrifice through stringent, hard training who call themselves such. A shaman may be 'made;' but the majority of true shamans, who are beyond doubt powerful healers and ceremonialist, have a gift—it was a major piece of their soul that was brought in at birth and is a defining part of 'who they are.'

If it is not a part of your soul's evolution, you may still heal yourself of the past woundings, and through this healing, help others in their own healing. Remember, even the ones with a gift must still do their spirit work and train hard.

What glory is there in getting up a few hours before first light, driving to an ice-covered stream all alone in zero degree temperature, and then giving prayers and a song to open the stream before taking your clothes off, submerging not once but four times in the stream, singing your spirit song and then coming out with final prayers of completion, a closing song and a gifting, attempting to dress when you have no feeling in your body except for the remnants of the icy-fire that had surged throughout your body while in the icy waters and then meditating, for who knows how long, under a blanket and finally returning home, hopefully safe?

Doing this, there are no labels attached by others calling you master, just hard spirit training. Winter after winter, this was just one part of my spiritual training at least once a week. It was not until I was fifty-five that I felt I had achieved a level of mastery (after more than 25 years) that justified others referring to me as a master.

But very few are willing to attempt such a training regime. I had one person contact me wanting to know if I taught Eagle Medicine. It seems that he had attended a neo-shamanic workshop and someone had retrieved an eagle guardian for him. And of course, he now wanted to learn Eagle Medicine.

First off, you do not choose 'medicine,'[4] it chooses you; and only after you have proven yourself through hard spirit training. Please be discerning if you choose to study with a 'shaman,' or attend a workshop. Focus not on the external of others but focus on your own healing of your heart and mind. Remember, it is the journey that is always most important not the arrival.

Even though I discuss the full pathway of the Feathered Serpent Medicine Wheel, this book only covers the first two directions—the South and the West. The South is the path of personal healing where we learn to shed the past and release the emotional entanglements of anger, resentment and guilt. In the West, we face our symbolic death of the 'old self' and step beyond the fear, uncertainty, and doubt that lives within us. This is not the immediate illusionary fix of New Age programs. It takes time and effort to work through these first two directions and to heal and transform one's heart and mind.

The final three directions of the Medicine Wheel, North, East and the Center, will be presented in my forth-coming book 'Further Teachings of the Feathered Serpent,' to be released during the fall of 2006.

For now, let the present journey begin.

Rev. Dr. JC Husfelt
The Morning Star
Ahzab Kab Ek—"the star that awakens Earth"

The Importance of Nature

*In the light of the past and the present unbridled
destruction of the earth's biosphere, it is essential for all
people to acknowledge that nature is divine—a living
existence in which everything has life and consciousness
shared in common with all human beings.* JC 2004

There is one key element and one very important concept that permeates the belief and philosophy of this book, indigenous cultures and Divine Humanity. This is the belief in the importance of nature; not the dominance and/or stewardship of it as believed by the Christian Religion, but a partnership and a oneness with nature—a nature that is divine, alive, conscious and responsive. Nature is the holy grail of healing and the secret to the maintenance of wholeness and wellness for all individuals, communities and nations. Nature is without a doubt *Kulana Huli Honua.*[5]

Humanity in partnership with nature is essential for the survival and the renewal of the human race. In addition, a oneness with nature is primary in becoming a Feathered Serpent. The Church, Science, Capitalism and our consumer society have supported and encouraged the superiority of humanity over nature. In their self-serving views, they have promoted a separation paradigm as proper, biblical, justifiable and necessary for the progress of the human race.

In their arrogance, they have basically stirred up a hornet's nest. In their egotistical self-importance, they say: global warming—so what, as long as the few can greedily increase their wealth at the expense of the poor and the earth. The masses, being the masses, follow as sheep being led to the crumbling edge of an unstable mountainous cliff.

As I write this, the wrath of Mother Nature in the form of Hurricane Katrina has devastated the gulf coast of America. Nine months earlier, the South Asia Tsunami changed the face of that part of the world. A recent quote from the *Seattle Times* indicates the mind-set of the ones in charge:

> Homeland Security officials defended their agency's response to Katrina and its ability to combat terrorists and Mother Nature....[6]

Combating, not harmonizing, Mother Nature reveals an underlying mindset of our culture in its separation from the essential paradise that has provided, and so far still provides, humanity with food, shelter and beauty. Why do so many go along with this separation paradigm?

As a child, I remember lying in the grass while looking up at the immense sky; it was so majestic in its blue tinged beauty. Then I fondly recall rolling over onto my stomach, smelling the earth and its life-force while gazing at the greenness of the love that the earth shares with all of her creatures.

I remember the magic of chasing lightning bugs in an attempt to capture their light for just a brief moment before letting them go on their way into the night. Even at a young age, I was ever seeking the light. I know that I am not alone in these memories of happiness when our hearts, not our minds, beckoned us to be a part of and connected to the earth. As children, from the depths of our hearts and souls, we recognized nature's wisdom as a gift to be shared by all. Many of us saw and lived in a garden paradise that provided the adventures and magic of life that only nature can provide.

My parents, on the other hand, had seemed to lose sight of this simple truth, nature's wisdom. Possibly, it was due to their excessive work habits in their effort to 'provide for me.' But it was my great uncle who fostered and nourished in me the uncomplicated facts of life and the beauty and wisdom of the fruits and flowers of creation. He would let me help him while he tended his concord grape vines and nurtured his pride and joys, the bright flowers with the sword-shaped leaves—gladioluses. Picking a grape and holding it between his thumb and forefinger, he once spoke these wise words to me:

> "Jimmy, this is the perfect color of purple; if you pick the grape when it is a lighter color, it will rob the vine of its gift. And if it is a deeper bluish-purple, you will have dishonored the vine by letting the grape stay on too long."

I must ask where our elders have gone. Are they just riding around in their RV's and SUV's? And the children, what has happened to them? It is a tragic legacy that our culture has promoted in its capitalistic technological gold-rush. The closest that children seem to come to nature is virtually; this is through such on-line games as EverQuest. Their 'character' does walk virtually through a forest, but it involves searching or hunting for other characters to kill or monsters to 'hack up.' This is far from becoming one with nature.

Perhaps a good example of children's mindsets today may be summed up by a thirteen year old's comment, a son of one of our East coast apprentices visiting our home in Washington State. I asked him, "How do you like it out here?" And his response, in all seriousness—"too much nature!"

Too much nature—I would have to counter that statement with my own of 'not enough nature.' It's rapidly disappearing; this has a direct effect on children's lives, causing epidemic dysfunctions such as Attention Deficit Disorder (ADD). As I stated in the very beginning—nature is humanity's holy grail.

There is a belief within some indigenous cultures that for every 'ill' of humanity, there is the subsequent 'cure' within nature. I also believe this. Not only have I seen the positive healing effects that nature has provided for our students and others, but a simple example of the 'ill' and the 'cure' is the remedy for the sting of nettles. Wherever there are nettles, close by to them, you will find the natural antidote to their sting.

As a society, we need to get our children away from the computer/TV screens, cell phones and iPods. All people, but especially children, need to spend as much time as possible in nature—not trying to conquer or exploit it, nor to use it for recreational purposes that pollutes and tears up the earth, but to become one with nature.

Everyday as I gaze at the Pacific Northwest beauty that lies before me, I feel a constant oneness with the tall cedars and the misty mornings; a joy to behold, a feeling to cherish and the smell—fresh, alive and mysterious—one of the gist's of life. Why do people react so negatively to an over-cast misty morn? Does it sub-consciously vibrate their own inner over-cast and possibly darkened heart? Tomorrow may bring a sun filled view of the cedar trees—the darkness gone, the mist a memory. What about the darkened hearts of people? Does the sun ever metaphorically shine within them?

Separate from nature, many walk through life as in a bubble—possibly seeing a flower and possibly even smelling its beauty but with a heart and mind separate from the truth of the flower and the experience of nature as their home. We lock ourselves away within the protective walls of a human-made structure, spend the majority of our waking hours commuting and working inside, separate from the rain, the sun and as the days darken, even the moon. And for what, I ask?

Of course, the answer is more and more and bigger and bigger things, a security based on fear, a life based on the future not the present and of course, the 'Great American Lie' (not dream). Not only do we suffer with this mindset, but more importantly, our children and the earth suffer.

The mantra alive today is: Make More Money. It does not matter if making money destroys the earth or other human beings, what matters is making money. What is your philosophy—Make Money? Or Catch Fish? (Please see Appendix 2)

Please, wake up and help others wake-up to the present reality. As I stated in the title, *Survival and Renewal at the End of an Age*, we are at the end of the Fifth Sun—it is a time of purification. This end time began with the Venus Transit of June 2004 and will complete in 2012. Since the Venus Transit, in just a little over a year, we have seen two major cataclysmic responses from nature—accounts of 'wrath and fury.' And this is just the beginning of the earth changes.

But do not despair. It is a necessary cleansing that has occurred before and will occur again. The secret, and everyone always wants the secret, to the coming earth changes is a strong, pure and loving heart and mind; and becoming one with nature, not separate from it.

The end of this Age is a cleansing, not a total destruction of the earth and humanity. It is a time of the Return of the Feathered Serpent. It is a time of returning to the values of family, peace, love and oneness; a oneness not only with each other as Divine Human Beings, but also with nature and all the things of the earth.

Guidelines—Oneness with Nature

- Acknowledge and believe that all things, including nature, have a consciousness and are alive and responsive.
- Spend consistent alone-time just being with nature, not in a separate way but as a part of nature.
- See and acknowledge the beauty of nature and its children (creatures).
- Listen to a tree and converse with it.
- Talk to the winds and the winds will talk back.
- See the oneness and beauty of even the smallest creatures of earth.

- Walk softly over the earth and consciously harm no things.
- Have pets if possible.
- Let your yard grow naturally; do not use chemicals on it and do not make it a miniature golf course.
- Before cutting trees (only if necessary) or picking fruit off the vine—ask permission and give blessings.
- Have as many plants and flowers as possible in your living space.
- Garden—tend to flowers and plants with loving care.
- If possible, have a vegetable and/or herb garden.
- Eat organically and pressure society to make organically grown food affordable for all people.
- Eat locally grown or raised food as often as possible.
- Walk often and be with nature.
- Bless the overcast sky as well as the clear blue sky; bless the sun and the moon; bless the wind and the rain.
- Spend time with your family in nature.
- Daily bless nature and its importance to all.
- Increase the time that you would normally spend outdoors
- Walk barefoot on the earth.
- Forgo a hat or umbrella during rain and experience heavens tears on your head—No rain/no Rainbows.
- Look, listen and learn from nature.
- Be one with the ocean and the sea.
- Embrace the *Aloha* Spirit.

The *Aloha* Spirit

It is a matter of no small importance in the rating of a people to take account of their disposition toward nature….[7]

Of all the greetings and partings found spread throughout the earth, I believe that the Hawaiians *aloha* has the most depth and multitude of feeling and meaning. It is a right brain solution to a left-brain manipulated and controlled world. *Aloha* means that I acknowledge the 'spark or sun of God' within you as you acknowledge the 'spark or sun' within me. *Alo* means 'in the presence of' or 'to be with' and *Ha* is 'the breath of life.' *Aloha* Spirit is the spirit of oneness and the love that is the breath of the soul. It is a loving state of mind where hate has no resting place. To the Hawaiians, *aloha* represents love. All of life is founded on this love, the love of the sea, the love of the sky and the love of the *'āina* (land), and all its inhabitants.

Ha is the secret key within *aloha*. It is the breath that we all share. It is the life-force and consciousness that connects us all. It carries our words, words that may create or destroy throughout the world. To the wise ones of old, words were no less powerful than deeds.

Breath is life, a life that is pure. But the loving breath that enters us may leave our bodies tainted and shallow with various materialistic thoughts that decay and separate people from the essence of the land and sea. Let your breath be pure. The following may help you embrace the *Aloha* Spirit:

> To bring *aloha* into your life, you must practice the *aloha* spirit. One way of describing these qualities is using the very letters of the word *A-L-O-H-A*.
>
> *Akahai* (Gentleness) Be loving by showing others kindness. Helping not only those close to you, but those who are not. This connects you to the *'āina.*
>
> *Lokahi* (Unity) Be in harmony with yourself, your family, all people, and the world. Feel the interconnections of everything. To find pleasure in life, bring pleasure into life.
>
> *'Olu'olu* (Pleasantness) Be a pleasant person who gets along with all people and the *'āina.* You must forgive those who you feel have wronged you—including yourself.
>
> *Ha'aha'a* (Modesty) Be humble about yourself and not egotistical or self-centered. Be concerned of other's feelings as much as your own.
>
> *Ahonui* (Patience) Be happy white what we have now rather than impatient with what we want in the future.
>
> Once you master all of these and bring *pono* (balance) into your life, you must bring awareness of *aloha* to others and help them achieve the same balance, for the final part of living *aloha* is to share the breath of life with everything. The more we do this the more *aloha* there is in the world and the more *aloha* there is in ourselves.[8]

Human's Current Relationship to Nature

The loving embrace of *Kane*[9] is warmth that words can never really properly describe but at all times must be experienced. The *Ha*, the breath of life, warmly courses throughout my body and soul. In front of me is a seascape that a human artist could never fully replicate. Turquoise-studded thundering waves, crashing but then receding, are interlaced throughout with the beautiful songs of our winged relations. This for me is the symphony of life, a life that resonates so deeply within the core of my heart, a heart that is extremely fulfilled and happy at this moment.

The introduction to this book was written while I was on the Belizean shores of the Caribbean in 2004; another land of rainforest and sea that resonates so deeply within me. Now it is September of 2005 and my wife, Sherry, and I have returned to the Big Island of Hawaii after an absence of 11 years. And it is here where I am writing this commentary.

My heart is extremely happy to be back on the island where I had my vision in 1993 and an island that speaks so deeply of my own soul and personality. My fiery side has been known to break down the inner wounded structures of others. This is not to hurt them but to provide fertile ground for new inner growth. Many times the ones who are on the receiving end of my fire are resistant to losing their known structures, painful as those may be, because they fear the unknown more than the known.

The energy of the Big Island is likewise very intense. It mirrors the fiery awesome power of the tempestuous volcano goddess, Pele. On this island, she is known as *Pele ai honua*—'Pele who eats the land.' One of my most vivid memories being on this island in 1992 was seeing and experiencing Pele's life blood flowing into the ocean—creating new land; a new birth, which I deemed 'baby earth.' If a person truly believed and trusted, lying on this newly formed 'baby earth,' could, I believe, go a long way in healing a person's ills, possibly even cancer—radiation kills cancer cells, why couldn't Pele's 'baby earth energy' transform and heal the cells? At the very least, it would be a memory that would last a lifetime.

My heart, on the other hand, was deeply saddened by the greedy materialistic changes that have occurred on this island over the past 12 years. Development everywhere and the destruction of nature have taken hold on this island.

The Aloha Spirit is the spirit of the Hawaiian Islands. It is the spirit of nature—a reverence and respect for all things and the 'garden' that surrounds us. Only a fool would think that we have been "kicked out of this 'garden.'" But then, if you believe that nonsense, it would justify behaviors of destruction—it's not our garden any longer, so let's ravage and destroy it. That is just what is happening.

I experienced this same story of spiritual desecration and nature's destruction four months earlier when I had returned with my son and a group of our martial art students to Koyasan, Japan. In 1987 I had experienced on Koyasan the transformational energy of the esoteric Buddhist deity—Fudo Myoo through a 'descending spirit exorcism.'

A Japanese esoteric shaman priest had conducted this ceremony at midnight in front of the great Kōbō Daishi mausoleum, the originator of Japanese Shingon Esoteric Buddhism. Eighteen years later, this great mountain of Kōbō Daishi's and his temple city, in my opinion, had been corrupted into one of materialistic greed—the spiritual essence had been sucked dry.

And so it seemingly goes all across the earth, the destruction of nature, and the spiritual energy and power that goes along with it, all in the name of 'development,' 'progress' and even for the superficial needs of 'New Age people.' When I had walked the Incan trail, the Royal Path, to Machu Picchu in the 1980's, we were the only ones on the trail. Now supposedly, there are showers and even permits are needed as it is so crowed with people.

Compared to Koyasan and other likewise desecrated sacred areas on this most beautiful earth, the mana (spiritual power) is still strong on this island—Pele's island. But still, the land and the sea, the ancestors and the Native Hawaiians are crying their tears of sadness for what has been lost. Houses and condos are built everywhere, even on agricultural-zoned land. Money talks for most people louder than the spirit does even when the benefits of not developing are known:

> ..."Benefits like clean water, fire suppression, climate stabilization, reasons people consider Hawaii paradise and go to great trouble to come visit—all of these things flow from the land and all are greatly threatened today."[10]

The 'tech boom' made millionaires out of many people. This led to more development and destruction of nature to further the egos and fervor of investors. Most people jumped at the chance to reap, or was it rape, the benefits from tech stocks. Then came the bust.

But never fret; there are always ones to fuel the next money craze. To keep the economy from 'tanking'—war was the first priority and then low interest rates were offered on home mortgages. Consumer credit caused the frenzy for building houses and more houses; buy up the land and build, build and build: not what is necessary in square footage, but larger and larger homes (all of course with three-car garages). One home seems not to be enough—second homes, retirement homes; it doesn't matter just more, more and more.

This moneymaking ploy of developers has ultimately harmed the environment long-term and hastened global-warming, resulting in rising sea levels. I wonder how many of these homes will be destroyed by the forces of nature over the coming decade?

Just think for a moment about the amount of trees that have been slaughtered, the total land raped while destroying the natural habitat, all in the name of greed. It doesn't stop there; we now have TV's and computer monitors encased in wood—what does the slaughter of more trees mean to materialistic egotistical people?

> Holzkontor, a designer of wood peripherals, has hand-carved monitors in 39 wood species, from ash to zebrano ($5,800-$8,900)....
>
> *Home* spotlights the marriage of technology and wood in the magazine's September issue. "People are going for a polished, glossy wood look so they can get the high-end feel of the electronics with a more natural look," senior editor Nicole Sforza says.[11]

What's next: designer **wooden** jeans! But it is never too late. I am just the messenger; I need your help in righting these wrongs and re-establishing *pono* (balance/harmony) on earth. You can make a difference, but it begins with your own state of heart and mind. This book is a guide to help you heal and to become *pono*, where your 'heart becomes your face.'

As I have emphasized, nature is extremely important. In my opinion, religion and spiritual teachings can never be separated from nature—the primary teacher is always nature. Religion and spiritual studies are supposed to explore and seek knowledge about the mysteries of life, death and creation. This seeking of truth, about these mysteries and the pursuit of a fulfilled life and happiness, cannot be found in a book, no matter if some human says it is the 'word of God;' nor can it be found within human made structures—it can only be found in nature and our relationship to the earth and to the heavens. The true foundation of any church or religious structure is the green earth with the roof being the blue sky above.

Books written, degrees held or clothes worn do not impress nature. Nature only responds to one's heart and mind. And it is the heart (body) and the mind that this book focuses on and is based on.

Introduction

On that day, a cloud arises,
On that day, a mountain rises,
On that day, a strong man seizes the land,
On that day, things fall to ruin.... (Chilam Balam)[12]

As darkness turns to light, the sun once again returns to the central lands of the Americas. The crystal blue tapestry of sky is studded through-out with various shaped, billowy white clouds as if they are the discarded pillows of the gods and goddesses. But at another time, an age that the indigenous people wished had never happened, there appeared low on the horizon white clouds as well. In the dawn light, these clouds never rose higher into the sky, but only came ever-closer to shore. That morning, as the winds blew in off of the sea, what thoughts, feelings and wishes were in the hearts of these people? These lands were home to an advanced civilization that lived in harmony with nature. Perfect they were not. But the 'slavers' who were approaching were even further from perfection. In their lust for power and gold, they transformed this land forever—and not for the better.

Hernando Cortéz and his Spanish conquistadors, who set foot on the sands of the Americas that sad morning, were 'slavers,' though not in the usual sense. Bolstered by their sense of righteousness and doing the 'work of God,' the work of the Catholic Church, they brought with them a slavery of the heart and of the mind. With fire, brimstone and smiles, the spirit was ripped from the deepest, inner core of these native people, resulting in a life of economic inequality and fear-based religious practices. Through their greed and materialism, these conquerors have left a legacy of death and destruction, which is most evident today in the on-going devastation of the rainforests and the ecological biosphere.

Instead of oneness and love, the Church and the conquistadors brought separation and fear. And this same story has been repeated many times over across the landscape of this beautiful planet; a Mother Earth gives beauty, love and life to her children, and in return, receives only disrespect, abuse and destruction from the ruling elitist patriarchal sons and daughters.

With wide-eyed innocence, these indigenous people welcomed the strangers; not with fear but with love and the belief that these strange ones were the people of their returning man-god prophet—Quetzalcoatl—the Feathered Serpent, they thought. The Plumed Serpent, as he was also known, had returned. In each of our hearts, I think that we can feel the simplicity, and then the terror of truth unfulfilled, that these people felt. It is a theme replicated many times over in our so-called progressive world.

The Mesoamerican people, in the most inner recesses of their consciousness, were ever aware of the anticipated return of their cultural hero—Quetzalcoatl. In their myths, and in a distant time, he had brought wisdom as well as peace, knowledge and equality to the people. In his wake, he had substituted a 'burning,' or a gifting to the spirit-world of quail, rabbits, snakes and butterflies, for the priestly controlled brutal feeding of the gods—the blood sacrifice of human beings.

This prophetic theme of the returning cultural hero is one of the most enduring myths known to humankind. At all times its impact and importance is due to the message of hope and renewal that the hero brings to a gloomy world locked away, as always, in the shadows ruled by fear. To the Mesoamericans, their white prophet or cultural hero was known as Quetzalcoatl, the 'Morning Star.'

Symbolically, the return of the hero represents the spiritual concept of the infinite cycle of death and re-birth. But it also represents the return of light or enlightenment to a world void of love and a humanity that has darkened once again through materialistic greed, dogmatic religious beliefs, war and inequality.

The Morning Star

The spiritual histories of many cultures portray the morning star, the planet Venus, in the same emblematic role as the returning hero. Why Venus? There are a multitude of reasons that stretch as far back as ancient solar mythology where the returning hero time and again is also portrayed as the born again sun-god:

At dawn, as soon as the brightening morning star in the east announced that the sun was rising, the priest called his assistants together and kindled the fire upon a mound of earth by rubbing together two sticks in which the God was supposed to be hidden. As soon as the spark shone in the 'maternal bosom,' the soft underpart of the wood, it was treated as an 'infant child.' ... There is no doubt that we have before us the Vedic Agni cult the original source of all the stories of the birth of the Fire-Gods and Sun-Gods....[13]

Venus and the Sun are intertwined in an immortal dance of re-birth. As the morning star, or the light coming out of the dark of the night, Venus announces the arrival of the Sun. It is the harbinger of the day to come. It stands at the breaking of dawn as the last star to disappear into the glory of the Sun.

Since Venus is the brightest heavenly body apart from the sun and the moon, its brilliance has always symbolized enlightenment as well as the journey to bring this light to the world. Venus spends part of its time as being either the morning star or the evening star. This perception of Venus as being 'twins' and the significance of its luminosity underscores the mythological religious ideals of many cultures. The 'twins' designation symbolizes the dual forces manifested in humans and the dualities of life, the light and the dark, male and female which contain the potentiality for a unified balance of wholeness or oneness—non-dual interpenetration. For that reason, Venus is viewed as being the bridge-builder between pairs of opposites, specifically spirit and matter. This is also the role of the returning hero who teaches that equality and balance are of the utmost importance in achieving spiritual transformation.

To some the morning star was 'God's Eye' positioned between darkness (ignorance) and light (knowledge), but always the wayshower to understanding and wisdom. The great Lakota Black Elk spoke of the importance of the morning star as follows:

Morning Star, there at the place where the sun comes up, you, who have the wisdom which we seek, help us in cleansing our-selves and all the people, that our generations to come will have light as they walk the sacred path. You lead the dawn as it walks forth, and also the day which follows with its light, which is knowledge. This you do for us and for all the people of the world, that they may see clearly in walking the holy path, that they may know all that is holy, and that they may increase in a sacred manner.[14]

Venus rules Libra, which is symbolized by the sign of the scales representing balance. According to a friend, Elizabeth Van Buren, in her wonderful book, *Lord of the Flame*:

> ... a special feature of the root, heart and brow chakras is that an inverted triangle lies at their centre. Inside these are three knots or granthis; the kundalini breaks these as it passes through them. These knots are called respectively the knot of Shiva, the Knot of Vishnu and the knot of Brahma. Since Brahma is the Universal Father-Mother, Vishnu the son born of the two-in-one and Shiva, the third member of the all-male trinity, god of the lower world, this symbolism seems to confirm that the son of God who has entered the Earth-plain many times to redeem the planet is represented by the heart chakra and is the balance, the scales his emblem.[15]

Even though Elizabeth refers to the Cultural Hero as the son of God, the enduring teaching and message of each returning 'sun of God' was focused on achieving a balance between spirit and matter with the additional knowledge that we are all a child of God, divine as well as human. To the returning hero, separateness is the illusion; oneness is the reality—all existences interpenetrate radically non-dualistically (non-dual interpenetration - Oneness).

Accordingly, the secret to life was achieving oneness through balance and interpenetration of our non-dualistic divinity and humanity. The Mesoamericans' Quetzalcoatl, known as the morning star, represented the symbolic teachings of death and resurrection as well as characterizing the knowledge of oneness, balance and harmony. As an archetype the Plumed (Feathered) Serpent or Quetzalcoatl represented human beings' true nature: the feathers stood for our divine or spiritual nature (the Father) and the serpent represented our humanity or connection to physical creation (the Mother).

Venus also figured prominently in the prophecies of the Maya:

> The Maya of Central America believe that the present Earth cycle will end between December 21, 2011 and June 6, 2012. During this period, they predict, an interesting planetary alignment will occur. Venus will pass in perfect alignment between Earth and the sun, with the transit lasting approximately 8 hours.... For centuries, our ancestors have associated Venus with the culture hero, the bringer of peace and tranquility to a cycle previously dominated by chaos.... The Hopi prophecies also speak of the "lost

white brother," Pahana, the culture hero who is the equivalent of Mesoamerica's Feathered Serpent.... The peace star is the sign of the culture hero, Pahana. This is the planet Venus, the bringer of all things to the center.... Venus/Quetzalcoatl, the Morning Star of enlightenment, rises in the east, and the shore where the ocean meets the dawn sky—the mouth of the dragon—is symbolic for the New Age. When the old cycle was over, it was said, Venus/Quetzalcoatl would return reborn in the jaws of the dragon.[16]

Even in the fiction of J.R.R. Tolkien's *Lord of the Rings*, we discover Venus, star of hope, as being symbolized by Eärendil, the half elf (divine-angel) and half human:

... Hail Eärendil, star most radiant, messenger most fair! Hail thou bearer of light before the Sun and Moon, the looked-for that comest unawares, the longed-for that comest beyond hope! Hail thou splendour of the children of the world, thou slayer of the dark! Star of the sunset hail! Hail herald of the morn![17]

In addition, it is interesting to note that the morning star rises in the darkest part of the night and is seen by only a few who are awake (awakened) at a time when the majority of others and the world are asleep. The morning star is like the thief in the night. For that reason, the return of the hero is noticed by only a few.

Many have not understood this connection between the returning hero and the morning star. And as a result, in the past thousand years, the false return of the cultural hero has tragically resulted in the destruction of two different cultures. The white sails of Captain Cook's ships spoke of the return of the Hawaiians' white prophet Lono. Not only was Cook not the returning hero, but he also betrayed the trusting and spiritual Hawaiians, which eventually lead to the introduction of venereal disease and the coming of Christian missionaries and their poisonous message of separation and original sin. And as we have seen, the same catastrophic event occurred to the Mesoamericans with the appearance of Hernando Cortéz and his Spanish conquistadors.

Even though both cultures had lost sight of their original spiritual base of peace and love and had reverted to war-like behavior and the resultant human sacrifice, the false prophets opened the doorway to the introduction of Christianity and to an even greater sacrifice: the one of heart and mind, unity with nature and the freedom of belief:

It would not do for us to brush aside contemptuously the notions held by the Hawaiians in religion, cosmogony, and mythology as mere heathen superstitions. If they were heathen, there was nothing else for them to be. But even the heathen can claim the right to be judged by their deeds, not by their creeds. Measured by this standard, the average heathen would not make a bad showing in comparison with the average denizen of Christian lands. As to beliefs, how much more defensible were the superstitions of our own race two or three centuries ago, or of to-day, than those of the Hawaiians? How much less absurd and illogical were our notions of cosmogony, of natural history; how much less beneficent, humane, lovable the theology of the pagan Hawaiians than of our Christian ancestors a few centuries ago if looked at from an ethical or practical point of view. At the worst, the Hawaiian sacrificed the enemy he took in battle on the altar of his gods; the Christian put to death with exquisite torture those who disagreed with him in points of doctrine. And when it comes to morals, have not the heathen time and again demonstrated their ability to give lessons in self-restraint to their Christian invaders?

It is a matter of no small importance in the rating of a people to take account of their disposition toward nature....

The poetry of ancient Hawaii evinces a deep and genuine love of nature, and a minute, affectionate, and untiring observation of her moods, which it would be hard to find surpassed in any literature. Her poets never tired of depicting nature; sometimes, indeed, their art seems heaven-born. The mystery, beauty, and magnificence of the island world appealed profoundly to their souls; in them the ancient Hawaiian found the image of man the embodiment of Deity; and their myriad moods and phases were for him an inexhaustible spring of joy, refreshment, and delight.[18]

The End of an Age

The light in the deepest dark of night, this is the herald of the sun, the morning star, proclaiming to all creatures of the earth, the return of light. The earth is a reflection of the heavens and the heavens are a reflection of the earth. Or in other words, what is above is below and what is below is above. Down through the millennia, this statement has been recognized as a philosophical spiritual truth. If this is in fact truth then humanity, in this early part of the 21st century, is in the deepest dark of the night as evidenced by the events of the past and the events of the present.

The world is ruled by a materialistic elitist cadre of political/religious/corporate scavengers that bottom feed off of the fear-soaked blood of their people. One time in Central America I happened to be talking to a British woman who was the executive secretary to the head of a worldwide management consulting company. After a few minutes of the usual polite 'chit chat,' she began to open up to me her suppressed feelings about her boss. Undoubtedly his work and home life is so much easier because of her diligence in handling his financial and personal affairs. In a world guided by light, we would anticipate respect and kindness in return for her unwavering efforts. But in a world governed by greedy egotistic darkness….

After a few minutes, she finally poured out her true feelings to me. I was a stranger, but a safe one, reflecting a feeling within her heart that I would listen to her unconditionally while making no judgments or assumptions about her. Always guarded in her work-life and presenting an image—a false face—that was expected of her, she truly had no one to talk to about her resentments, angers and frustrations. The following are a few of her comments paraphrased:

> I know everything about my boss—his financial affairs, even his dosage of blood pressure medication, but do you suppose that he knows anything about me… no…. He's rude to me… even one time he told me that I wasn't being paid to think….

How sad, but on the other hand, how angering that one human being, so giving and loyal, would be treated as such by another human being. And to make things even more out of balance and worse, her boss is the CEO of a company that helps other companies manage their people—the greatest and most precious resource that any company can have are its people; not just the elitist at the top of the pile, but every employee is equal and worthwhile and deserves respect and a caring attitude—except in today's world. Capitalism is a scourge on the earth. It will be viewed as the darkest of the dark paradigms that have ever occurred on this earth.

Inequality, war, habitat change, warmer oceans, global heating up and melting down—this is the legacy of Capitalism. In the name of profit and Capitalism, "things that normally happen in geologic time are happening during the span of a human lifetime."[19] And this forebodes the foretold 'earth changes.'

The 'religious right' has to acknowledge the past destruction of the earth through the 'flood.' It's stated in the bible. But the bible is not the only book or legend that tells of the earths past destruction by ravaging waters.

Greek mythology relates to a 'flood' as well as the destruction of Atlantis by its 'sinking into the waters.' Hawaiian legend also tells of a flood:

> Nuu was of the thirteenth generation from the first man. The gods commanded Nuu to build an ark and carry on it his wife, three sons, and males and females of all breathing things. Waters came and covered the earth. They subsided to leave the ark on a mountain overlooking a beautiful valley. The gods entered the ark and told Nuu to go forth with all the life it carried. In gratitude for his deliverance, Nuu offered a sacrifice of pig, coconuts, and awa to the moon, which he thought was the god Kane. Kane descended on a rainbow to reproach Nuu for his mistake but left the rainbow as a perpetual sign of his forgiveness.[20]

To the Mesoamericans we are living in the Fifth Age or Fifth Sun. Each of the previous Ages ended with the destruction or death of the 'old,' which then allowed the re-birth of the next or 'new age.' As in other myths from around the world, they also recognized the destruction of their Fourth Age by water:

> The First Age, called Sun 4-Tiger, was brought into order out of primordial chaos. Then a struggle between the gods ensued, resulting in a collapse of the cosmos and, according to one tradition, its reorganization by the winning deity, Tezcatlipoca. The beings who lived in this era were eaten by ocelots. This process of order and collapse was repeated four times. The Second Age was called Sun 4-Wind, and the beings who lived there were carried away by wind. The Third Age was Sun 4-Rain, and fire rained on people and they became turkeys. The Fourth Age was Sun 4-Water, and water swallowed the people and they became fish. Then, the present age, Sun-4 Movement, was created out of the sacrifice of a large number of deities in Teotihuacan, or elsewhere, depending on the tradition. It was believed that this age would end in earthquakes and famine.[21]

Hindu texts teach that the world is periodically destroyed by either fire or water. In shamanic lore, these are the two elements that purify and bring transformation to individual human beings as well as humanity as a whole. In my estimation it does not take much foresight or visionary skill to see that our world, as it stands in this early part of the 21st Century, needs purification and that this cleansing of peoples and governments is closer than many realize. The world is out of balance and as the myths of the past tell us, the balance will be restored.

Over the years, I have been privy to prophecies from various cultures related to me by medicine elders, shamans, or wise men if you will. One of these was Vince Stogan, a Salish Indian Doctor. He didn't call himself a shaman, but if you needed a label, he preferred to be called an Indian Doctor. However, he did refer to his uncle, alive during the early part of the 20th Century, as a shaman. In fact, a 'strong' shaman was his term as in 'strong heart, strong mind and strong hands for healing.'

My wife, Sherry, and I had apprenticed with Vince and his wife, Mom Stogan, after they had observed us doing healing work. They had taken us aside and said, "We see ourselves in you; we want to pass our ways on to you; do you want to learn them?" We were very privileged and honored to have been asked and then to have worked so closely with them. After many years of apprenticing, untold pre-dawn bathings, assisting in burnings and healings, they at last transmitted and passed on their knowledge, ceremonies and traditions to us with the authority to conduct these ourselves.

Like all orally transmitted knowledge, we could not write anything down while they were teaching us. They taught like all true shamanic traditions teach by the process of 'look, listen and learn.' The following is from Sher's notes after listening to Vince talk about the prophecies of his uncle—the 'strong' shaman:

> … My uncle predicted all the events that would happen and they all have been/come true (bombs, WWII, TV, cars & styles, etc.). If things don't calm down over in the Middle East, it will be another war that will be big, WW III – a part of the earth changes. Uncle said it would be like a little boy picking on another little boy then one of their big brothers will join in – and then another member until the whole family is fighting and it will spread to everybody joining in and choosing sides.

This account was written in the early 90's and it upset Vince to talk about it. He was reluctant to tell us as much as he did. Both Sherry and I knew that he was probably keeping other more horrific things to himself. The point being is that the earth changes will occur and that there will be turmoil during the transition from our present age to the next age whether we call it the Sixth Sun or the Age of Aquarius.

Most Westerners are more familiar with the Ages of the humanity based on the 12 constellations such as our current Age of Pieces and the forthcoming Age of Aquarius rather than the Fifth or the Sixth Sun of the Mesoamericans. It is interesting to note that each Prophetic or Zodiacal Age[22] is under the influence of not one, but of two heavenly constellations: the Ascendant Cardinal House Constellation as well as the more widely known Vernal (spring) Equinox Constellation.

This revelation goes a long way in explaining the 'why' behind the war-riddled Age of Pisces. Aries is the Ascendant Cardinal House and is ruled by Mars—the archetypal planet of war and destruction. Therefore, during the past two thousand years (approximately), not only Pisces has influenced us, but also, Aries has had an unkind impact on us as a whole. For students of ancient mythological religious history, this knowledge explains the 'why' of the prolific worship of the calf (i.e. Moses' Golden calf) and the bull (i.e. Bull symbology of Assyria and Babylonia)) during the Age of the Ram—Aries. Taurus—the Bull was the Ascendant Cardinal House. Further in the dust of the past during the Age of Gemini—the Twins, we discover the beginning of fertility cult worship connected with a reverence for the moon and for the earth mother. The Ascendant Cardinal House was Cancer—ruled by the moon and dedicated to fertility.

In this coming new time of Aquarius, the energy and influence of Pisces will not disappear. Without the above knowledge, the supposed 'Enlightened Age of Aquarius' would seem on the surface to lack the Piscean qualities of compassion, forgiveness and divine love, essential for 'light', as they would be of the preceding Age of Pisces. Clearly, we can now see the truth—Pisces will, on the contrary, exert a great beneficial influence during the coming Aquarian Age. In fact, without the undue influence of martial Aries, the most positive qualities of Pisces will surface from the depths of the sea to provide a fertile seascape of spirituality.

The sea (Piscean energy) and its resources will be of the utmost importance to our future well-being, as well as the worldwide magic of the Internet (Aquarian energy), as it opens the capstone to the well of knowledge for a thirsty, parched humanity. The twin dolphins (an ancient symbology) of Pisces swim in the ocean of life providing us with a feeling of the interconnectedness of all life on earth. In addition, the angelic cupbearer of Aquarius, an air/mind sign, provides a mental connectedness to humanity. In the future what a dance we each have to look forward to between this dolphin of the turquoise crested seas and the angel of the emerald-edged clouds. But what about the transition time, which is the time between the end of Pisces and the beginning of Aquarius? And what is in store for us with the ending of our current age, whether it be called Pisces or the Fifth Sun?

According to the Maya calendar, we are in the last *katun* period of the Fifth Sun of the Maya Great Cycle. This began on April 6th, 1993 (my vision of being the morning star occurred in October of 1993). A *katun* is about 20 years in length, and there are 260 *katuns* in a Great Cycle of 13 *baktuns* (about 5125 years). The Fifth Sun by all accounts ends on the winter solstice of 2012. The Dresden Codex, a Maya text that survived the Spanish conquest, refers to the beginning of the Great Cycle as the Birth of Venus on the 12th of August 3114 BCE.

During the last eight years of this Fifth Sun, Venus again shines out of the darkness with two rare passages across the Sun called transits. The first transit occurred on June 08, 2004 and the second will happen on June 06, 2012. Transits of Venus across the disk of the Sun are some of the most extraordinary planetary events. Normally when Venus switches from its position in the heavens as an evening star to its role as morning star, it disappears for a period of approximately 8 days. From a mythological viewpoint, this was seen as the hero's journey through the underworld with the hero's resurrection days later as the morning star.

From the divine perspective Venus is the 'sister' of the earth and may be viewed as a cosmic mirror for the earth. It is under these circumstances that the Venus passages across the face of the sun are dramatically important to the earth. During a Venus transit, the light of the sun sends the energy of Venus to the earth and foreshadows future events of cosmic proportions. June 8, 2004 began the final 8-year period that will complete the Age of the Fifth Sun. This is the 'time of the Morning Star—the Return of the Feathered Serpent—Quetzalcoatl:'

The start of the last Mayan Age was the Birth of Venus, the Quetzalcoatl star on 12 August 3114 BC. On the last day of the age, 22 December 2012, the cosmic connections between Venus, the sun, the Pleiades, and Orion are once more in evidence. For just as Venus was indeed 'born' on the earlier date, it's rising just before the dawn being heralded by the Pleiades at the meridian, so it now symbolically 'dies.'[23]

Thus ending the Age of the Fifth Sun. So what does all of this foretell? Is 2004 – 2012 a turning point in World History? Are you awake or are you still self-absorbed in your own materialistic rat-race?

Survival and Renewal

Have you ever been truly hungry without enough food to eat? Have you ever been truly thirsty without enough water to drink? For many on this earth, this is a common occurrence. However, as a reader of this book, you probably answered "no" to the food and water question. But what about the future?

The ecological biosphere is in sad shape. With war and terrorism as an on-going and common occurrence, fear is rampant; add to this toxic and explosive mix the vast chasm that has widened between the "haves" and the "have-nots" on this earth. We are as far from peace and unity as we have ever been in the written history of humanity. Separatism rules the day—and its name is fear. Fear separates and generates conflict. Our culture and society are based on fear—the fear of terrorism, the fear of aging, and the fear of strangers, whether from another culture or our own. These are just a few of the fears that thunder through people's minds. And our dysfunctional society does not stop there. In addition, people act and react from their ego-based selves—and the ego-based self is ruled by the male-dominated—left sided brain—patriarchal paradigm. This paradigm spreads a message that 'might is right,' 'big is better,' 'the male aspects of life are superior,' 'money rules' and 'fear motivates.' Over the next six years, war as a protection from terrorism will rule the day. Peace will be but a faded memory as the male-dominated egotistic paradigm runs berserk over the earth.

Do not lose hope. The return of the Feathered Serpent is the return of Oneness—a unity of heaven and earth—a time of peace, freedom and societal-economic-species equality. One teaching that I emphasize and one to keep in mind is that a 'person of power' does not protect or hide himself or herself from life but accepts life with open-arms no matter what life throws at them. This is the reality of life lived as love not as fear. The second part of this teaching is how do we respond to what life presents to us, whether that is a spiritual happening or a traumatic event. This book will help you survive and renew during the next six years and beyond, no matter what life bestows on you. The feathered-serpent (divine human) ideal and path will help guide you in becoming this 'person of power,' known throughout history as the shaman.

The Shaman

A shaman is a person with the ability to connect the profane or earthly existence to the sacred, the heavens and thus provide a link between heaven and earth. He or she is a visionary and what I call a 'pathfinder to the soul.'

Shamans are dreamers, philosophers and nondogmatic religious guides and teachers. But they are probably best known as healers, specifically wounded healers; which means that the shaman has been doing their own healing of their past woundings. Even though a Shaman is a healer, not all healers are Shamans. A Shaman is also a 'person of power' who dream-voyages to the Otherworld for knowledge and freedom. This is the freedom from our ego-self. The Shaman helps others, and themselves, escape from the imprisonment of anger, guilt, resentment and greed. This gives one freedom to love and to be loved.

For eons, shamans have been the keepers of the various cultures' sacred traditions. Humans have often looked to these dreamers for guidance and knowledge about the inner, invisible world of power and healing. Shamanism is a journey of the soul conducted by the shaman known as a master of the spirits. The shaman adventures consciously among ancestor or creator gods and goddesses, spirits, and energies on other planes of reality, and returns with sacred knowledge that will be a benefit to themselves and others. The original shaman was not only a healer, but also fulfilled and performed the role of priest, wizard and spiritual leader. In addition to achieving and maintaining harmony within their community, the shaman was burdened with the task of opening and healing the hearts of their people.

The Heart that Sees

The shaman-priests of Mesoamerica brought a concept to their people called *Ollin*. It symbolizes the 'motion principle' in Mesoamerican thought, but in addition, it has the meaning of a purified heart or a 'heart that sees' through the illusions of life. This is the *Ollin* heart. And this type of heart is a microcosm of the 'heart' of the universe that maintains balance and harmony through its constant motion or movement, whether it is expansive or contractive.

With an *Ollin* heart, we are able to discover our true path in life and follow it. We discover joy in our true identity as we fulfill our destiny in life. With a 'heart that sees,' everything in life is sacred and every action that we take is hallowed. There is no stagnation in our life, only movement. This movement is always towards destiny and away from the mediocrity of a life that has been lived in self-blindness.

With an *Ollin* heart, we bring our inner self out into the world for all to see who we are. This is a concept that is foreign to our culture and society. Many live a lie, but few live truth. We are taught to hide 'who we truly are' from others, including our co-workers and neighbors. We present falsehoods and false faces to the world. And depending on the circumstance or the environment, we even wear different false-faces—one face at work, another face at home, and still yet another face alone. With the 'heart that sees,' there is only one face—our true heart-face—this is the 'heart' of Quetzalcoatl and the heart of Oneness:

> The Nahua peoples believed that we are born with a physical heart and face, but that we have to create a deified heart and a true face. The ordinary word for heart was *yollotl*, a word derived from *ollin*, movement. Thus the ordinary human heart is the moving, pumping organ that keeps us alive; but the heart that can be made by special efforts in life is called *Yoltéotl*, or deified. The phrase used to describe the face that we must make if we are to be truly men is *ixtli in yollotl*, which signifies a process whereby heart and face must combine. The heart must shine through the face before our features become reliable reflections of ourselves.
>
> Thus heart-making and face-making, the growth of spiritual strength, were two aspects of a single process which was the aim of life and which consisted in creating some firm and enduring centre from which it would be possible to operate as human beings. Without this enduring centre, as the Nahua poet tells us:

> … you give your heart to each thing in turn.
> Carrying, you do not carry it.
> You destroy your heart on earth.
> Are you not always pursuing things idly?

> If we are unable to create this second heart and face, we are merely vagrants on the face of the earth. The idea of vagrancy is expressed in the word *ahuicpa*, which means literally 'to carry something untowardly' or without direction. There is another word, *itlatiuh*, which means to pursue things aimlessly. *Ahuicpa tic huica* means 'carrying, you do not carry it'- and this directionless carrying was believed by the Nahuas to be typical of man's ordinary state on earth. By accident we do not achieve direction, any more than we can be sure of traveling from London to Edinburgh by going to a station booking office and asking for the first ticket that comes to hand, or by thoughtlessly boarding the first bus that comes along because it happens to be moving.[24]

Ollin, in addition, means earth-shaking or change. *Nahui Ollin*, 4-Movement, is the name of our present age, the Age of the Fifth Sun. This symbolizes the four previous ages or Suns synthesized into the present fifth age, the Fifth Sun. According to Aztec legend, these four historical ages corresponded to the elements of earth, wind, fire and water and each were destroyed by a cosmic cataclysm. From this point of view the four elements of the previous four ages are integrated into the current Fifth Age or fifth element, the element of spirit. According to myth, the Fifth Age's destiny is destruction by earthquakes as corresponds to its name: 4-Movement. On the other hand, is there something more, such as a hint of survival and renewal, hidden within the inner secrets of these Mesoamerican myths?

The Aztec calendar Sun Stone is a visual representation of Mesoamerican myth and their cosmogonic concept of cyclical space and time. In its center is pictured a human face, *Tonatiuh*—Sun God, shown within the symbol of *Ollin*, symbolizing our present age of the Fifth Sun:

> The face of Tonatiuh is surrounded by a large *Ollin* symbol (movement or earthquake), occupying the central position in the Sun Stone because it is the dominat (sc) one in the epoch of the fifth sun, the era in which the Aztecs considered themselves to be living.
>
> In the four square composing part of the symbol itself are carved the dates in which the four previous epochs ended....
>
> **4 Jaguar.** The first and most remote of the cosmogonic epochs is represented by *Ocelotonatiuh*, Jaguar god. During that epoch lived the giants that had been created by the gods but were finally attacked and devoured by the jaguars.
>
> **4 Wind.** The second epoch is represented by a crocodile head, *Ehecatl*, god of the air. During that period the human race was destroyed by high winds and hurricanes and men were converted into monkeys.
>
> **4 Rain.** The third epoch is represented by the head of rain and celestial fire. In this epoch everything was destroyed by a rain of lava and fire and men were converted into birds to survive the catastrophe.
>
> **4 Water.** In the fourth epoch, represented by the head of *Chalchiuhtlicue*, water goddess, wife of Tlaloc, destruction came in the form of torrential rains and men became fish in order not to perish by drowing (sc).[25]

The fifth epoch, our present one, was mythically birthed at the 'place where one becomes a god.' This place was Teotihuacan, a grand and mystical city that was a ceremonial and spiritual/religious center located northeast of present day Mexico City. This happened to also be the home of the prophet Quetzalcoatl and his religion of 'equality, flowers and songs'—a religion of the heart. According to legend, it is here where wisdom flourished and the arts and sacred science originated so many thousands of years ago.

The key to renewal and survival over the next six years and beyond is secreted within the meaning and the symbology of *Ollin*. According to Frank Waters in his Mexico Mystique:

> The Nahuatl concept of movement as a fundamental motivation of all life is symbolized by one of the key hieroglyphs and day-signs, *ollin* (movement)....
>
> All symbolize the interlock polarities of earth and sky, light and darkness, male and female....
>
> The Fifth Sun, the Sun of Movement, held for the Nahuas the added significance of being the unifying center of the four directional suns which had preceded it....
>
> Yet within the Fifth Sun, world, or era, lay another synthesizing center—the soul of man. Writes Leon-Portilla: "The profound significance of movement to the Nahuas can be deduced from the common Nahuatl root of the words movement, heart, and soul. To the ancient Mexicans, life symbolized by the heart (y-ollo-tl), was inconceivable without the element which explains it, movement (y-olli).
>
> The meaning, the challenge is plain. The movement taking place in man's heart between the two opposite polarities must be harmonized if man is to assume his greater role in the pattern of Creation.[26]

As we have seen, 2012 is calculated as the end date of the fifth epoch, the Fifth Sun. What then does this ending hold for us? I believe that there will definitely be great earth changes. But from the 'death' of our current age must come the birth of the new age—the golden age—the Age of the Sixth Sun; where each human will take his or her place as a Feathered Serpent—a Divine Human—a Sun of God.

The Feathered Serpent—a Sun of God

The Feathered Serpent is symbolic of the unity and equality of heaven and earth energies. Its imagery portrays a serpent, usually a water serpent of the earth, ascending to the sky where it achieves knowledge, power and wisdom, symbolic of the feathers and wind.

The Feathered Serpent is the archetype of a divine human. It is the union of heaven (divine) and earth (human), the divine-human. I call this concept of the divine-human, Divine Humanity. This is the belief that each one of us has an immortal 'spark' (metaphorically a miniature sun) within us. We are each a sun of God.

Each person is divine. And each person is human. And each person has an intrinsic worth/identity. This makes us all the same, but not the same. In addition, this belief includes all of nature and the earth and the heavens. Every part of creation has a 'spark' within itself as well as having an intrinsic quality/identity and a consciousness.

When we awaken to our true divine nature; when we recognize the two as one and the one as two; when we see past the trap of dualism that separates into opposites such as wind and water—heaven and earth; when we embrace the unifying heart wisdom that sees past the separating illusionary dualism of life to the complementary dualities of existence—a radical non-dualism;[27] when we live the 'I' in the 'We' and the 'We' in the 'I'; it is at that moment when we become 'feathered' (a metaphor for light) or as is more commonly known—enlightened.

Historically, there was an actual person who was called the Feathered (Precious) Serpent or the Plumed Serpent. His name was Quetzalcoatl. As a spiritual teacher and leader, Quetzalcoatl brought to the Mesoamerican people the teaching and knowledge of enlightenment through a process of symbolic death and re-birth utilizing ritualistic water immersions.

In addition, he was seen as the 'once and future king' destined to return when the world was at its darkest. The word Quetzalcoatl is derived from Quetzal and Coatl - literally Quetzal Serpent. A Quetzal is a brightly plumed tropical bird with brilliant bronze, green and red plumage:

> Coatl is the sacred snake whose movements mirror the way that Kundalini energy moves up the spinal column awakening the wheels of light that surround each of the major body centers. When this serpentine energy reaches the crown chakra at the top of the head, we are one with the Universal. Quetzal is the sacred bird that connects Earthly power with the Heavenly realms of the universe. Together the Quetzal and the Coatl are the creatures that are closest

to the earth and heaven as well as representing the sacred balance of female and male.[28]

Quetzalcoatl was also known as the 'Precious Twin,' Kukulcan by the Mayas, Viracocha by the Inkas and Gukumatz by the Quiche Maya. Each was associated with Venus, the Morning Star. Once again according to Frank Waters:

> Quetzalcoatl was a uniting symbol achieving union of opposites: heaven and earth, morning and evening star, matter and spirit... the transcendental meaning of this great myth is clear. It is an expression of the universal doctrine of sin and redemption, of death and resurrection, the transfiguration of man into god... this myth, in the broadest possible terms, enunciates the principle of all Creation: the incarnation of divine light, purity, and spirituality into gross matter; and then the agonizing redemption of matter by spirituality—the immortal theme of all world religions.[29]

This is our journey of *Ollin*; a pilgrimage of spirit to achieve a sacred balance of energies that will unite us in a state of oneness—internally as well as externally. This book will help us begin our journey and guide us in awakening as a Feathered Serpent—a Sun of God—an awakening to our own intrinsic divine nature. And this awakening is the very key to survival and renewal at the end of this Age. In fact, it is also the secret to a happy, loving, powerful and satisfying existence—in this moment and in every moment of life.

Awakening

From the very core of my soul, I believe in my message that each one of us is divine—a spark/a micro-star/a micro-sun within our hearts. Everything has this spark—trees, animals and even black holes. In addition, everything has an intrinsic identity and value. Therefore, trees are not only divine, but are also intrinsically unique and may provide for us such things as shelter and food.

Humans are divine as well as intrinsically unique in all facets—some may choose to fish and some may choose to build bombs. Still, our divinity is within our heart, but remains hidden. This is diametrically the opposite of Christianity where each individual is intrinsically sinful. If you are a Christian and have 'faith' in the dogma and doctrine, there is no way that you would believe in divineness within; much less would you attempt to awaken it and work towards Divinehood, Buddhahood or Feathered-Serpenthood. However, I believe that even though we may have an imperfect and corruptible body-mind, it is still perfect and pure in its imperfections, which allows us to achieve Divinehood, or if you will, Feathered-Serpenthood now—in this body, in this lifetime.

If you believe in your internal light and pureness, then you must awaken this 'sun.' This is what I call the quickening of your Divinity; what Japanese Esoteric Buddhists call your Bodhicitta or awakening Mind. Are you ready to awaken?

The Feathered
Serpent Chronicles

My fellow pilgrims, we present to you the Feathered Serpent Chronicles as a gift to help guide you in your own spiritual awakening. There are many paths up the mountain of truth and only you can determine the one that is right for you. Hopefully these chronicles will help you discover your true path, one that is based on love, not centered on fear. Life is a mystery with a multitude of enigmas that provide an open gateway to the exploration of meaning, not in a profane manner, but in a spiritual way of love and power. We are all spiritual explorers on an adventure to discover the perennial wisdom that has flowed through all of the past ages of humanity.

The enlightened age is coming, to be known as the Sixth Sun—the Return of the Feathered Serpent. At this moment in history, however, we are in the transitional times, the changeover from our current Age of the Fifth Sun to this new one of the Sixth. It is an interlude between leaving the dark of the suffering and entering the light of the enlightened; a time anchored in spiritual awakening, but fastened to the old regimes of power and money.

Many know the Sixth Sun as the Age of Aquarius, the next stage in humanity's evolution. The symbolism of Aquarius is important. It is the archetype of the universal mystic, the seeker of truth, and is depicted as an angel—an immortal messenger—pouring water (consciousness) from an urn that is open at both ends. Its imagery signifies our human capacity to become one with the consciousness of the universe. It takes us beyond the egocentricity of the previous Ages and transports us to oneness of being, where we may directly access heavenly knowledge. It will be an Age of individualized religion, not dogmatic organized religion; a time to accept our divine side as well as our human side and to acknowledge our connection to, not separation from, all of creation.

We hope that what follows will be a stepping stone to bring you closer to your own truth and to provide further spiritual awakening during these transitional years. We are...

The Feathered Serpent (Dragon) Lord Regulus and Balamcoatl—the Morning Star[30]

The Awakening of Balamcoatl as the Morning Star

"Floating in that space between heaven and earth, I have a knowing of both. My soul's power suspends as a star in the luminous web of Oneness. I am divine and I am human, a child of God and a brother/sister to all creatures of the earth. A moment is an eternity as this knowledge engulfs my heart. Is it a dream? But isn't it all a dream? A scream and I awaken."

As my eyes slowly open, the portals to my soul gaze upon the surreal scene before me. A face, beautiful as the dew glistening on a lily, is now frozen into a mask of terror. It had been her scream that had brought me back; on the other hand, had I ever left? In a language not my own, the shaken Keko was stammering over the words to her master, the wizard-priest Sakura.

"Forgive me... master," said Keko. "I was afraid for him. His face was so red, just as the old texts portrayed. But the reality makes mere words pale in comparison; even when you are prepared for the possibility."

This part of the cemetery contained few stone lanterns. Only dim light was thrown on the humans gathered together in front of the Great One's mausoleum. The shadows, cased by what little light there was, heightened the mystical sense of wonder for the three, now drawn together as moths to a flame. The wizard-priest and his apprentice stood deathly still, surrounded by a silence that was deafening. Their questioning gaze centered on the one who would, in time, become known as the Morning Star. Surrounded by towering cedar trees, one could only guess whether it was night or day. But night it was, midnight in fact, a time of power; a time of opening between the worlds of matter and spirit.

This night, however, saw the presence of more than mere humans. In a reality far removed from the dreams of such beings, but as close as a drop of dew glistening in the dawn of a new day, moved the Plumed Dragon Lord named Regulus. Deep in observation and thought was he (or was it she?) of the messenger; incarnated once again as a human. But Regulus was not alone. Next to the dragon sat a *Myoo*—a Wisdom King. Surrounded by flames, this *Myoo* was called Fudo and was known to be the immovable one who would awaken a sentient being's heart/mind.

As the massive underside of the dragon rose and fell, the breath of excitement and joy spread throughout the cluster of stars and worlds known on Earth as the Milky Way. Reaching Earth in a time of no time, the breath of Regulus brought storm clouds out of cloudless skies, stirred the oceans into a brief tempest of fury and created a bolt of dragon lightning that streaked over the mountain of the Great One. So bright, yet it lit up the sky only for an instant.

"Does his partner, the faerie one, have any inkling of who he is?" asked Keko, questioning in her mind the meaning of the unearthly bolt of lightning.

Speaking in the tongue of his own people, Sakura replied, "She may have a slight knowing. But as his wife, she sees his very human side. Her heart may know, but her mind will deny the truth—it would be too unbelievable."

From a place of stillness, I silently watched the gestures and body language of the master and his apprentice; not knowing or in fact caring about the meaning of the words being exchanged. A moment ago, or was it an eternity ago? I was in a space of power. But no, I was the power. What does it all mean?

Six moons ago, while on a warrior pilgrimage—*musha shugyo*, my heart had brought me to this sacred mountain of the Great One. A coming home it was, from the first moment that I had breathed the mountain air. I had been here before; not in this lifetime, I knew, but in a previous incarnation.

"How do you feel?" asked Keko. As translator, she spoke my language while her Master did not.

"I feel awesome, powerful, but mystified," I replied. "Was I transforming into one of the guardians that serve the Great One—the Daishi?"

"Well, yes... but no. You may look at it as a merging of energies. Energies that few humans could accept, much less survive. It is the first quickening of your Bodhicitta—your Divinity. The others who were here will deny what happened, out of fear and envy. We sent them back to the temple," said Keko.

Her face was a canvas of shades, neither dark nor light. And her eyes were a sparkling tapestry of stars delicately etched within a bluish clad night sky. Sakura, on the other hand, was a vortex of power with eyes as dark as smidgens of coal. These eyes were not gazing on the beauty of Keko, but were intensely focused on Balamcoatl, the Morning Star. This meant the end of Sakura's search for the prophet—the one who would bring the message. He had finally found him.

"The gateway between the worlds is still open," said Sakura. "The energy of what just happened has vibrated through both worlds. The ones who still haunt this world have been awakened. Their attachment to materialistic life has kept them trapped on earth in death. Some of these specters increase their attachment to the earth through feeding on the life-force of humans. They are the ones who in life had darkened hearts, arrogantly valuing greed and materialism over love, family and spirit. They are the most dangerous of all the dead ones who still walk the earth; trapped between earth and heaven in a hell of their own making."

A strange wind rattled and whistled through the darkened cedar trees as Keko translated Sakura's words to me. The wind had come from the Northeast—the direction of demons.

Watching from the corner of the Great One's mausoleum was a transparent form cloaked in rotting robes; robes that at one time would have been worth a king's ransom. The specter's hunger-filled eyes, if you could call them eyes, were centered on Balamcoatl; whose life-force was even more powerful than the other male human, the wizard's life-essence.

"You are very open, Balamcoatl," said Sakura. "I must teach you a secret finger-intertwining and a spirit-shout."

As soon as Sakura had finished his statement, he noticed an icy twitching at the base of his neck. The air coming from the Northeast was suddenly cold and damp. This meant the presence of a dead-one. Without hesitation, Sakura turned and with a wrathful look, he twisted his fingers into shapes resembling miniature swords. With both hands held in front of his chest, Sakura sliced through the air shouting a sacred phrase out of a timeless past—an archaic magic that few knew and even fewer still practiced.

"To-yā; To," shouted Sakura. And with this, the specter was no more.

"My master says that we must leave now. We will be safer on the other side of the stream that separates the Great One's Mausoleum from the rest of the cemetery. Once we cross over the bridge, Sakura will tell you more and teach you the magic just used."

For a moment my mind flashed back to the moon month of the Virgin six years past. At that time I was exploring and seeking the Holy Cup in the Island Nation of the Dragon King. During an over-night respite, I had encountered a specter—a former monk who haunted the inn where I was staying. At that time I experienced an icy feeling just before seeing the glowing red eyes in my darkened room. It was the same feeling that I just had now. I wonder...?

In a some-what brief period of time, in another part of the cemetery, the three seated themselves on a centuries-old moss-covered bench: a resting place that had witnessed the endless passage of peasants, priests, monks, samurai and even Shoguns, all on their way to honor the Great One. Sakura taught Balamcoatl the ancient magic just used to disperse the evil one; an enchantment from a time no longer remembered. And now, all sat in silence.

Keko broke the stillness as her slender hand gestured to the path in front of them. "These cedar chips have felt the passage of thousands of my people on personal pilgrimages to honor the Daishi. Sakura and I brought you and the others here not only to honor the Great One, but to see if you were the one mentioned in the ancient texts."

The ancient texts... I was at a loss for words. I just sat there staring at the cedar-filled path wondering about the events that had just unfolded. The silence was deafening as no words were being spoken; even the winds were silent. Finally, I turned towards Keko and said, "What does all of this mean?" I let the question linger in the air, expecting a reply. But Keko just stared at me. No expression was visible, just her piercing eyes.

"Am I the one mentioned in the ancient scrolls? What does that mean? I'm just a simple spiritual seeker with a wife and two children."

With a slight smile and a brief nod of her head, Keko said, "You are the one who Sakura has been searching for... the one mentioned in the prophetic 'Plain of Heaven' scrolls of the Sun Goddess. It is your destiny to bring a message to humanity. Sakura can tell you no more than this... except for one thing. You must seek out the Wizard of the Four Winds in the Land of the Condor."

An owl cried in the distance while the wind kicked up. All of this happened, as sudden disbelief flooded my mind. It had been only two moons ago, during the month of the Ocelot, that I had been asked to join a pilgrimage to the Lost City. Supposedly it is located on a sheer mountain peak in the land that Keko had just mentioned. But how had Sakura known? Or had he? Could there be another explanation? Strange as it may seem, are unseen forces guiding my life?

JOURNEY TO AWAKENING

Chapter 1
The Journey to Become a
Feathered Serpent

Ce Acatl Topiltzin Quetzalcoatl upheld with the utmost
discipline the concepts of the god whose name he had adopted.
His people (serpent) aspired to divine existence (plumes-sky),
whilst at the same time believing that the divine descended
into the hearts of men (humans). The struggle between and the
union of opposites constituted the fundamental ideas on which
all laws, religious conduct and social habits were based.[31]

Life is a journey. For many it is clothed in the illusionary sweetness
of external power. Societies and institutions encourage this, realizing that
the weaker the people are internally, the greater the control that they will
have over them. Can you ever begin to imagine a society of evolved divine
human beings where equality and peace would rule the day? This is the
potentiality that the feathered serpent ideal presents to us today. To become
a Feathered Serpent, the archetype of a divine human, requires courage of
the heart and a pilgrimage of spirit. But how do we begin?

Out of the mists of time comes another archetype that will help guide
us and help us to take that first critical step on our journey of spirit. This
is the archetype of the warrior. The warrior ideal is not about the battling
of external foes, but it is about the struggle with the inner ones. It is here
that we face our anger, our fear and our doubt. The warrior journey is an
adventure into the underground caverns of self, ever-seeking the 'heart that
sees.' This is our quest to become a Feathered Serpent. This is our seeking

of our own personal holy grail. To the Japanese, a warrior pilgrimage is known as *musha shugyo*.

Musha Shugyo

There are many ways to describe the spiritual journey of the warrior. On the one hand, it is a search for truth as well as a quest for the ultimate reality of wholeness or oneness. And on the other hand, it is a passage into the unknown. Fittingly, it takes a key attribute that is part and parcel of the *musha shugyo*. That attribute is courage. It takes courage to step into the unknown and to think outside the box of mundane life. And then, it requires a courageous spirit to trust in a journey of life that few others are willing to take.

The Japanese term *shugyo* can be loosely translated as 'forging an impeccable spirit through an ascetic discipline,' or in other words—spiritual training. In reality *shugyo* is heart training—exercise of the heart, which is a path few choose because they have an un-enlightened or a 'covered' heart. This is a 'blind heart;' a heart that is fearful, spiritually ignorant, dogmatic, dualistic, egotistic and materialistic. By contrast, the ones who are fearless, open and striving towards an oneness of spirit have a 'heart that sees.' It is a heart that is crystal clear—a sparkling mirror that shimmers the spirit of heaven and earth. It is our inner still-pond, reflecting the moon of our souls.

Concurrent with this concept of dedicated ascetic training of the heart is the concept of *do/michi* or way/path. It is of utmost importance in life to have direction, a sense of purpose and an idea of one's destiny. Without this conscious compass, life takes on the characteristics of a dead leaf falling to the ground, pushed this way and that way by the prevailing winds of the past and the present.

Do you have direction? Have you ever considered what your purpose and destiny is here on earth? A path is vital for discovering your purpose in life and fulfilling your destiny.

The Feathered Serpent Medicine Wheel could become your path in life. The way is open to all. The path is before you. But you must take the first step.

The Feathered Serpent Medicine Wheel

Our *musha shugyo* takes us through the four winds or the four directions of the compass with our goal being the center or the fifth direction.

As 'masters of ecstasy and transcendence,' shamans from the Americas honored the earth with a cosmology centered on the four powers—the cardinal directions of the compass. This four-fold path to knowledge, power and healing, known as the Medicine Wheel, enabled the shaman to shed the past, face fear, step beyond death and achieve the mastery of vision—seeing with the heart.

Our four-fold pathway is known as the Feathered Serpent Medicine Wheel. However, there is a fifth direction—the Center—that makes our pathway a *Quincunx*. The quincunx is the most frequently occurring sign in the Mesoamerican symbolic language.

At the center of the medicine wheel, symbolizing the 'heart that sees' at the center of our being, resides the archetypal Feathered Serpent—the Divine Human. Each and every person has the potential to awaken as A Feathered Serpent—A Divine Human—A Sun of God.

1. **The Serpent Path of the South—Mastery of Release (Forgiveness).**

    This is the path of personal healing where we learn to shed the past and release the emotional entanglements of anger, resentment and guilt. We begin to walk in beauty by reclaiming our power, as we become the *wounded healer*. This is the realm of Forgiveness. Color symbology: Yellow.

2. **The Jaguar Path of the West—Mastery of Transformation (Death and Re-birth).**

    This is the path of the Mystic Warrior—the Luminous Warrior. Here we face our death and step beyond the fear, uncertainty, and doubt that lives within us. We are re-born as a Luminous Warrior. This is the realm of Divine Love. Color symbology: Black.

3. **The Hummingbird Path of the North—Mastery of Mind (Detachment).**

    This is where we learn the way of the Ancient Ones by stepping outside of time with the death of ego. We live in the timeless 'now,' in a state of awakening unfettered to

11

the past, to fear, or to death. This is the realm of Peace and Harmony. Hummingbirds are sun angels—messengers of light. As the teacher, we take our message of light (knowledge) to the ones shrouded in darkness (ignorance). Color symbology: White.

4. **The Eagle/Condor Path of the East—Mastery of Vision (Oneness).**

There is a prophecy from both North American and South American First Nation people: "When the eagle and the condor fly together, the Age of Peace will manifest." In the East, the Shaman learns to see with his or her heart. Here we see through the illusion of separateness to the reality of oneness. This is the path of the 'shining being,' known in old English as Elf. This is where you become '*Ollin*,' where your heart becomes your face. Color symbology: Red.

5. **The Center - The Fifth Direction: Feathered Serpent— Divine Human—Sun of God.**

It is in the East where we discover the gateway that leads into the center of the medicine wheel - the Fifth Direction. With an impeccable spirit, one must enter through this gate and travel to the center. It is only in the center where one may finally accept their mantle—as a child of the stars—an elf, a Sun of God—a Feathered Serpent. Color symbology: Blue/Green.

Archetypal Hero's of Myth and Legend

An archetype may be viewed as a universal theme. A universal theme may also be part of our own personal mythology. Pilgrimage and the heroic warrior are two archetypal personal mythologies of the feathered-serpent ideal.

Pilgrimage is one of the oldest endeavors of humankind. It may very well be triggered by a mysterious urge deep within our souls to follow in the footsteps of the ancestors. This inexplicable urge is felt by only a few of us. And of those, still fewer follow this heart-felt need to adventure into the unknown, not for riches and external power, but for purity of heart and soul and to answer the ageless questions of the meaning of our existence on earth.

Since the dawn of time, seekers of these questions have made pilgrimages to sacred sites pursuing true knowledge, wisdom and power. They always brought an openness of spirit to the potentiality of being in touch with the elements and becoming one with nature and the mysteries of life. To these spiritual adventurers, the mountains, jungles and the valleys facilitated a relationship with the Otherworld. Here they discovered inspiration, transformation and healing.

Musha shugyo is one of the corner-stones of developing the feathered-serpent ideal. Entering into the mountains, jungles and valleys, we become detached from the limitations of mundane time and space and the attachment to ordinary life. We step into the extraordinary and it is in this space that we develop and grow our ideal and the 'heart that sees.'

The way to true knowledge, power and wisdom is through direct and personal experience. The more that we can separate ourselves from the mundane world, the closer that we may then come to the realm of the divine. The magical mist that surrounds this sacred world stays hidden from the human ego, but will evaporate for the pilgrim who sincerely searches for the truth. It is possible to experience this sacred environment as an immortal human being, dwelling in the divine presence of the heaven and the earth.

To many it would only be the 'fool' who would sacrifice the known and comfortable for the unknown and metaphoric 'edge of the precipice.' But it is as the 'fool' that we begin our pilgrimage through our intuition and heart-felt innocence. Reason has no place in our decision when we choose a voyage into the unknown over safety and security.

What then may be an underlying influence that motivates us to choose a path that many others would view as foolish? May it partly be due to the inner need to walk in the way of the legendary ones—the heroes and heroines of myth and legend who have gone before us? Who among us has not dreamed of venturing forth as the fearless knight on a holy quest or as the wandering lone warrior—the samurai; or possibly as Brigid, the Celtic warrior goddess and protectress?

And who has not marveled, and possibly been inspired by the *musha shugyo* of the Fellowship of the Ring from J.R.R. Tolkien's trilogy, "The Lord of the Rings"? In addition, in the hallowed halls of extraordinary feats of sacrifice and courage, how can we ever forget the valiant defense of the 300 Spartans, who all gave their lives at the Gate of the Hot Springs—Thermopylae.

JC Husfelt, D.D.

The 300 Spartans at the Pillars of Fire—Thermopylae

I use Leonidas and the 300 Spartans as a paradigm of legendary heroic warriorship for very personal reasons. It was in 1962, as a young 16 year-old, that I watched a movie starring Richard Egan. This movie, **The 300 Spartans**, literally changed my life—a visual and soul rite of passage, so to speak. It vibrated a deep soul memory within the core of my being that has never left and has only grown stronger. It opened the gate for a birthing of a personal mythology of the heroic warrior that has taken me across the world seeking and searching for knowledge and power—my own personal *musha shugyo*.

Out of the archives of heroic courage and self-sacrifice march the ancient Spartans, saviors of Western Civilization through their heroic action at the Pass of Thermopylae known as the Hot Gates. This name was due to the sulfur springs in the area as well as the entrance into the pass that was narrow and felt like a passage through a gate.

In the spring of 480 B.C.E., King Xerxes of Persia set forth to achieve what his father (King Darius) had failed to achieve ten years previously in 490 B.C.E.—the conquest of the Greek city-states with the final goal being the whole of Europe. At that time, the Athenians valiantly crushed King Darius' empire-building desires on the plains of Marathon. The extremely religious Spartans, the most elite warriors of all the Greek city-states, missed the triumphant victory by arriving late to the battlefield due to their honor-bound observance of the feast of Carneian Apollo. Since the Persian defeat at Marathon, Darius' son, King Xerxes, had been amassing a titanic army of over 200,000 men as well as a massive fleet rumored to be close to 1,300 vessels. This time King Xerxes was not going to repeat his father's failure by invading from the sea, but was going to attack Greece by land. Just to move and supply such a massive force would be a feat in itself.

Once again the Persians were invading Greece and history seemed to be repeating itself—the Spartans, once more, were involved in a religious observation. This meant that, as before, the best warriors in Greece would arrive late. This time there was a difference: King Leonidas. His personal bodyguard of 300 was not honor-bound by the religious laws of Sparta. These laws kept the rest of the Spartan army from marching to battle, but not the King and his personal bodyguard. Aware of the Delphic Oracle that Sparta would be sacked or Sparta would mourn the death of a king from the house of Hercules (where Spartan kings claimed lineage), the Lion still went forth with his 300 to secure the pass at Thermopylae. True to their

14

honor and loyal to their king, the Spartans' sacrifice down to the last warrior at the 'pillars of fire' echoes throughout history as one of the foremost examples of bravery, courage and valor.

The following is a brief account of the defense of Thermopylae from an article that was originally written for the Alamo Journal, the official quarterly publication of the Alamo Society by Kevin Hendryx:

His name was Leonidas, "the lion's son," and we know very little about him, not even his age in 480 B.C., although it is likely he was in his fifth decade or even older. He had been king in Sparta for ten years, more or less, and left behind a young son as his heir....

Sparta's kings, holdovers from its archaic, tribal past, held little direct political power but were by law the generals of the army and held enormous influence and prestige. By taking command of the ad hoc Greek forces scraped together and sent ahead to the pass, Leonidas demonstrated a clear commitment to the cause of resistance... the Greek leaders may have underestimated the speed of the Persian advance. Leonidas could take only his personal bodyguard of 300 picked Spartans with him, plus small contingents from other cities collected en route. All told, Leonidas probably had about 7,000 men at his disposal once he encamped at the Hot Gates....

King Xerxes and his myriads.... reached the vicinity of Thermopylae in mid-August. Finding his progress blocked by Greek soldiers and ships, the Great King encamped just beyond the western reaches of the pass....

Leonidas appreciated the reality of the odds he faced. Only Spartans with living sons had been admitted to his bodyguard for this mission; the king did not want any Spartan line to die out....

Xerxes delayed four days while his fleet, battered by the seasonal mistral winds, was similarly bottled up. At last he ordered the pass taken by storm. The battle began August 18, 480 B.C.

The Persians came in waves beginning in the early morning. The Greeks met them in tight ranks before the repaired wall, in the narrow Middle Gate of Thermopylae....

When dusk approached, the defeated Persians gave up the attack.... Greek losses were very few, but Persian casualties must have been enormous....

On the next day the Persian onslaught was renewed. Xerxes sent forward picked men in specially formed units.... The Greeks appear to have been so fired up, in fact, that some battalions would not willingly give up their positions when it was time to be relieved.... The Persians fell in heaps, and they finally had to be forced into combat under the lash. At the end of the day, their energies spent, they limped away. It was a ringing victory for Leonidas and his men, while Xerxes faced the gloomy prospect of deadlock and acute supply shortages should his vast army become pinned down, laying siege, in effect, to the Hot Gates....

And then... 'the inevitable traitor appeared from the wings.' A man of the area... who knew of the hidden paths through the mountains went to Xerxes' tent and sold the information; moreover, he offered to act as a guide to show the way.... This outflanking move would place the Immortals in Leonidas' rear by morning, cutting him off and guaranteeing his destruction.

The Immortals... set out as night fell, and their way was made easier by a full moon.

Warning came to Leonidas before daylight...when... runners brought word that the Persians had broken through and would soon begin their descent, Leonidas knew that time was short. A last war council was called, and scholars have debated ever since over what exactly was said or decided.... What is most likely is that the Spartans stayed as a willing rearguard and that Leonidas accepted the Thespian and Theban volunteers but was not able or inclined to sacrifice the whole of the Greek army....

... The retreating hoplite contingents made their farewells and decamped, taking with them perhaps Leonidas' lesson that the Persians could be beaten. Those who remained made a hearty last meal to give them strength. Plutarch has preserved Leonidas' grim words: 'Breakfast well, for we shall dine in Hades.'

The death-struggle of the Greeks at Thermopylae was long celebrated by ancient historians.... The Spartans flung themselves at their enemies with reckless courage. Fighting with the foremost, Leonidas fell early, and a struggle worthy of Homer erupted around his body. Four times the furious Spartans drove the Persians back, and at last succeeded in dragging their king out of the churning fray... The Spartans and Thespians, now beset on all sides, continued to fiercely resist. When their spears were broken, they drew their short swords... and when these were lost or dulled, they used stones, or bare hands and teeth. Finally the Persians finished the last remnant with a shower of missiles.

... the name of every individual Spartan who died at Thermopylae was remembered for as long as ancient Sparta endured. They were engraved on a stone tablet in Sparta that could still be read over seven centuries later.... A monument was set up on the mound of the last stand-it has long since disappeared, but the recorded epitaph survives. One translation reads:

> *Go, stranger, and to the Spartans tell*
> *That here, obedient to their laws, we fell.*[32]

The glorious and fearless action of Leonidas and his three hundred Spartans, against overwhelming numbers and certain death, shines as a beacon of courage and loyalty for all of us who love liberty and freedom, while despising slavery and oppressive tyranny. This wise and noble conduct of the Spartans gives heart to all who strive to overcome adversity and provides a legacy of fearlessness that echoes for an eternity. They lived by the following:

> *A heart that sees death... but recognizes life*
> *A heart that sees life... but recognizes death*[33]

Mythology

Myths are our magic mirror into the life and the ways of peoples past. These legendary tales give us a glimpse into their hopes, their fears and their creative imagination. Myths transcend time and space by revealing to us the universal themes and life lessons that never become outdated. Myths are openings to the past that help us make sense out of the world around us. The old tales continuously seem to ring true within our hearts. And the lessons are always there, if we choose to look. Order evolves out of chaos; there is death and re-birth; ritual and sacrifice; a journey to the underworld and the return of the sun and the birth of the hero twins; dragons and the slayers of monsters; and in most cultures, the heroic quest, the cup or bowl of plenty. These are just a few of the many different mythic themes that we may look to for knowledge and guidance throughout our life.

Mythic Knowledge

Spiritual cleansing through the medium of water is one of the oldest known forms of purification recognized by humankind. Bathing under waterfalls, in streams and in the seas for purposes of purity and spiritual power is a universal standard, but stressed more so in some cultures than others. If you have ever traveled to Japan and spent any extended time there, you would have an understanding of the importance that purification plays in the Japanese mind and spirit. This emphasis on purification is partially due to Shintō mythology. One of their myths tells of a journey to the Underworld by the celestial deity Izanagi-no-mikoto, the male side of the primal couple that created Japan. His sister-wife, the goddess Izanami-no-mikoto, had died giving birth to the god of fire—Kagutsuchi. In his grief, at the loss of his sister-wife, Izanagi journeyed to the 'shadowy land of the dead,' called Yomi, to recover his mate. But he arrived too late to bring her back to the land of the living. Izanami had already eaten of the dark food of the Underworld thus connecting herself with the dead, not the living:

> Although Izanami tried to persuade the gods to allow her to return to the land of the living, they refused her request. Izanagi then stormed into the hall of the dead and, after lighting a tooth of his comb and using it as a torch, he saw Izanami. She was horribly transformed: her corpse was squirming with maggots and eight thunder deities had taken up residence in her body.
>
> Horrified at the sight of his wife, Izanagi fled back home. His behaviour infuriated Izanami, who sent the hags of Yomi… to hunt him down.
>
> At length, Izanami, who by now had herself become a demon, set off in pursuit of Izanagi. In order to block her way, her husband pushed a huge boulder into the passage that separated Yomi from the land of the living….
>
> The god then purified himself by washing in a river. When he removed his clothes, a new deity came into being as each garment fell to the ground. Finally, Izanagi washed his face and, in so doing, brought into existence the sun goddess *AMATERASU*, the moon god *TSUKIYOMI* and the storm god *SUSANO-WO*. Izanagi decided to divide his kingdom equally among these three deities.[34]

Think of the implications of this myth and the knowledge that it teaches. Of the primal couple that created Japan, one is now dead. The female is dead; the male is alive—death and life. Heaven and Earth—life in heaven and death on earth. And we learn of bathing in a river as purification from the icy fingers of death. But hidden spiritual knowledge is encoded in the act of removing his clothes and washing his face. See if you can discover this hidden knowledge in the pages to come.

Another myth from Japan called "The Lord of the Rice Bale" reveals some little-known spiritual knowledge that many may well overlook as they read the myth. This tale relates the story of the monster-slayer Hidesato. He was walking one day around Lake Biwa, Lake of Lute, near Kyoto. Approaching a river, whose source was the lake, he spied a sleeping dragon blocking the way across the river. Being of fearless spirit, he climbed over the dragon and continued on his journey. Within a very short period of time, he heard a voice calling out. Looking back he saw not the sleeping dragon but a wild-looking man with a crown on that was shaped like a dragon. This apparent human explained that he was the Dragon-King of Lake Biwa. He went on to say that he had a heroic task for Hidesato. At the approach of any human stranger, the king would assume the appearance of a fearsome dragon. Where so many others had fled, Hidesato had displayed his fearlessness and had not.

The task required of Hidesato was to slay a giant centipede that resided within nearby Mount Mikami. Daily it came down off of the mountain to eat one of the king's subjects. Agreeing to the task, Hidesato accompanied the king to his home beneath the lake. Hidesato was amazed at the opulence of the king's realm. As any proper host would, the king served Hidesato the choicest treats and the sweetest sake. Surrendering to the liquid embrace of the sake, Hidesato was suddenly startled back to full awareness by an earth-shattering thunderclap.

Where Mount Mikami had stood a few minutes before now undulated a gigantic centipede with fireballs for eyes—so large that it hid the mountain by its mass of thrashing coils. Being in the moment and without hesitation, Hidesato grabbed his bow and let fly an arrow to the beast. It hit its mark but, alas, bounced off harmlessly. Arrow after arrow Hidesato shot, to no avail. He had one arrow left. Before he loosened it, he suddenly remembered an old tale that had been told to him concerning the magical powers of saliva. With this in mind, he licked his last arrow and then let it fly. Straight and narrow it went and this time, it stuck fast. The monster shuddered and then died. The moment the light went out of the eyes of Mukade—the centipede, the sun darkened and fearful thunderbolts crashed throughout the sky as the earth trembled. Frightful as it was, the next morning the sun rose on a land of peace and beauty.

Hidesato was proclaimed saviour of the kingdom. For many nights and days, the Dragon King's people celebrated the victorious slaying of the monster. The sake flowed unabated until it was time for Hidesato to continue on with his journey. In gratitude the king presented him with a few gifts for a task well done. The gifts received from the Dragon King included a bale of rice, silk, two bells and a cooking pot. Hidesato decided to donate the bells to a local temple to commemorate his achievement. Of the other gifts, he kept them for himself. And magical were these gifts: the roll of silk was endless; the pot[35] would cook even though it was not near a fire and the rice yielded exquisite grain year after year with no signs of its depletion. And this is how Hidesato became known in legend as Lord of the Rice Bale.

Personal Mythology

Hidesato's quest and his fearless spirit speak to my own personal mythology. In addition, my mythology vibrates with the courage displayed by the indomitable spirit of heart and the strength of mind that allows a person to go and to stand where others will not. Sometimes the opportunity to exhibit the fearless courage that was displayed by the Spartans at Thermopylae may come unexpected as it happened to the 105 British Soldiers who repelled an attack of 4,000 Zulu warriors at Rorke's Drift. This legendary tale again demonstrates the indomitable spirit, not only needed by the British to resist overwhelming odds, but also required of the Zulus, when wielding their short stabbing assegais (spears) against the Martini-Henry rifle—at the time a weapon of mass destruction. Courage, an indomitable spirit against overwhelming odds, a fearless warrior on a holy quest, a mountain wizard schooled in the knowledge and wisdom of the ancients, a mystic shaman ever-seeking, a kahuna voyaging to new lands, these are just a few of the themes and the archetypes of my own personal mythology.

A personal myth is our inner galaxy that is a composite of our beliefs, images, life experience, our personal truth and our rules of life. At the center of our galaxy is a star that is a core theme around which our life evolves, develops and progresses. The brilliance of this star may enlighten us to the mysteries of the microcosmic and macrocosmic dimensions of life. In addition, revolving around this core star, and connected to it, are other stars that are our various themes and archetypes that reinforce our core mythic theme.

Life is mythic, metaphoric reality. To some people, a tree equates to money and that is how they view a tree. Their actions reflect their belief. But to others a tree is seen as a sacred being, to be respected and cared for in a ritualistic way. Why the difference? Where one person kills, cuts down a tree indiscriminately, another person honors and protects. Where does this difference in reality and behaviour originate? Could it be within a person's own mythology?

Institutionalized religion is dangerous. It may justify a person's action in a way that can cause ultimate harm to others and to the earth. One of the dogmatic beliefs that Christianity puts forth as ultimate truth is that humans are the stewards of the earth, superior to nature and all of its inhabitants. And humans, being superior, may do to the earth as they see fit. Kill and pollute, it doesn't matter; humans know what is best and have the 'god-given' right to do it!

There is no equality in this dogma of the church nor is there any reverence for the sanctity of life—that is all life, not just human life. But this dogmatic belief is a part of many people's personal mythologies. And their actions, based on this belief, have led to a potential ecological apocalypse that may occur on this earth in the not too distant future.

And how about you? Have you ever considered your own personal mythology? Do you know your rules of life? If not, then you may want to identify your personal mythology by accessing your own inner galaxy of beliefs and images. Begin by analyzing what your beliefs are, as well as your assumptions and expectations, concerning the following subjects:

- God/Creator/Great Mystery
- Goddesses and gods
- Heavenly beings such as angels and bodhisattvas
- Earthly beings such as faeries
- Mythic beings such as dragons and unicorns
- Myths and legends
- The earth and the heavens
- Women and men
- Magic
- Power
- Sex
- Competition
- War
- Peace
- Love
- Forgiveness
- Money
- Marriage
- Honor
- Family
- Ancestors
- Re-incarnation
- Death

These are just a few subjects that may 'prime the pump' in helping you understand yourself and your personal mythology. The next step involves discovering your core theme—the central star of your inner galaxy. As a reader of this book I would imagine that one of your inner themes might be the 'mystic shaman seeking knowledge.' Is this your core theme? If not, then spend some soul-searching time discovering the central theme of your personal mythology. Four questions may help you uncover your core mythic identity. These are: Who are you? What is the meaning of life? What is your purpose in life? How do you see yourself relative to all other things?

There are a few themes and beliefs that I feel are central to the development of a feathered-serpent ideal. These may also help you in the development of a personal mythology:

> **Divine Humanity**—as I stated in the introduction, this is the belief that each one of us has an immortal 'spark' (metaphorically a miniature sun) within us. Each person is divine. And each person is human. And each person has an intrinsic worth/identity. This makes us all the same but not the same.

> In addition, this belief includes all of nature and the earth and the heavens. Every part of creation has a 'spark,' divineness within as well as having an intrinsic quality. This belief is essential to the development of a feathered-serpent ideal for it means that the power is within us to achieve ultimate acts of power, as well as the ability to heal and to grow spiritually.

> This belief also provides us with the knowledge that we are one with nature, not separate from nature, but a part of nature. And our interaction with nature is an essential ingredient for becoming a Feathered Serpent. This common 'spark' means that all forms of creation are conscious and will respond to other consciousnesses. Without this belief, trees and animals, for example, would be unable to speak to us and thus we would be unable to learn their knowledge and wisdom.

> **Oneness**—the spiritual goal of a divine human is to achieve oneness with all things of creation. This is also the pinnacle of a feathered-serpent's achievement where there is no separation between object and subject—no conflict, in essence, no 'sword,' and no enemy. There is no place for the ego, which separates the 'I' from the 'we.' The ego works counter to the feathered-serpent ideal. The goal of a Feathered Serpent is to see with the heart the

'I' in the 'we' and the 'we' in the 'I.' This is the oneness that we seek.

We live in a dualistic world, which is a necessary spiritual illusion. It is our eyes that paint the canvas of this illusion of truth. We must not see with our physical eyes but with our heart. This is 'the heart that sees' the oneness of creation. This is 'the heart that sees' the beauty of creation. And this is 'the heart that sees' immortal love.

Nature (Life) as Dojo—a dojo is a school, a place of learning. It is a training place of the spirit. Its esoteric meaning is 'a holy place of learning and practicing the Way' and is viewed as a 'mandala of Awakening.' Based on these meanings, dojo is an appropriate term to use in our journey to awaken as a Feathered Serpent.

For us on this spiritual pilgrimage, the dojo is life—heaven and earth. First and foremost, the learning of spirit and oneness is conducted in and through nature. It is here in nature that we transform into the holy (whole) one—the Feathered Serpent.

The earth in all of its beauty is the primary source of our knowledge and power, while the heavens are the wellspring of that mysterious *force* that binds all together and is one of the most basic elements of the Creator and the created.

If you enter a dojo, can you feel the spirit? A true dojo is wherever the holy one decides to practice and share wisdom. This may be in a field or mist-covered mountain valley. The holy one and the dojo are one and the same. In today's merchant society, do not be fooled by large fancy buildings. The dojo is within the heart of the holy one, wherever the heart is, there you will discover the dojo.

Ritual

Mythology speaks of absolute reality. Mythology speaks to our minds and souls. What speaks to our body? Ritual does; it grounds our myths in mutual relationship, a practical relativity. But what is ritual and why is it so important to developing a feathered-serpent ideal?

Ritual is any set pattern of actions. These patterns of behavior can be performed either consciously or subconsciously. Our subconscious rituals are our mundane routine actions, such as smoking or driving a car, while our conscious rituals have a goal, such as exercising or achieving a black belt.

At this point, you may be asking yourself what is the difference between ritual and habit. Not much; the line between ritual and habit is very thin. Rituals may be cycles of your behavior. But what starts as a ritual can turn into a habit, if and when you lose sight of its inner meaning. The first puff of a cigarette can be an act of adulthood — a personal rite of passage. But this ritual, done mechanically and unconsciously, can turn into an addictive habit, and soon the original issue of becoming an adult is lost from sight. One Japanese esoteric priest that I studied with felt that many priests in Japan have lost sight of the inner meaning of their rituals and ceremonies. Now, he says, they are just conducting them out of habit!

Ritual is a part and parcel of life and is essential to the development of a feathered-serpent ideal. There are three stages to ritual—an opening, the body of the ritual and a closing. In addition, there are five basic components of what I would call effective sacred ritual:

Sacred Mind—refers to our pure intent and focus. We must understand any symbolism connected with our ritual and the meaning of any words or actions. Our focus is to achieve a state of no mind, which is still and un-chattering, as well as an immovable mind. An immovable mind is one that does not attach to the sensory input that is coming into the mind. The mind is totally aware of everything but not attached to anything.

Sacred Body—is the act of performing a ritual utilizing movement, sound, sight, and smell. Movements can be as simple as raising your arms to the heavens while speaking a prayer, or as complex as a set of prescribed dance movements (such as the Hawaiian Hula) or hand movements (i.e. esoteric Buddhist mudras). Sounds can include prayers, songs, chants, whistles, bells, horns (conch), flutes, drums, etc. The use of sight, or visualization, includes our sacred space, objects and our own internal visualizations. Smells can include the burning of incense or sacred plants. Sacred body also includes the use of special objects such as ritualistic clothing, food, staffs, vajras, drums and many other objects too numerous to list.

Sacred Space—may be as complex as a divine structure (temple) or as simple as a place in nature. It may already exist, or you may create it such as using an altar or the Japanese concept of kami-dana—spirit shelf. Even though all of the earth is sacred, there are certain spots that hold a special sacredness—not due to an institution's dogma, but from a sacred interaction of wind and water, heaven and earth. These sacred mountains, waterfalls, glens and so forth may be discovered intuitively by sensing their divineness. A space may be sacred or profane with some form of a 'gate' separating the two. In Shintoism the Torii, the gateway to Shinto shrines, and the sacred rope, shimenawa, are 'gates' that define and indicate sacred space where the kami (spirit) dwell.

Sacred Heart—is the opening and closing part of ritual. These are the prayers, the blessings, the meditation, the acknowledgements and the attitude, compassionate humbleness, of the one conducting the ritual.

Sacred Words—may be referred to as prayer. (Please see below)

Many times, it has been said that ignorance is bliss. This may be true but truer still is the fact that knowledge is power. There is an on going ritual in many martial arts schools that evidently confirms the saying that ignorance equates to bliss. This is the use of a ridiculous word, more often, though, a screech, 'Ossu.' It must be blissful because it is used so often. Possibly, even in the rest room! Surely the schools that use this vocalization are unaware of its meaning. The word, and I use that term loosely, is Japanese and the drunken and macho version of *Onegai shimasu*. *Onegai shimasu* basically indicates good will for the future between two individuals and is used in old school Japanese dojos with the meaning of 'please teach me.' The Japanese consider 'Ossu' impolite and not appropriate. Do not be ignorant, as it will inhibit your growth as a 'person of power'—a Feathered Serpent. Utilize ritual, but do it in a correct and knowledgeable way.

Prayer

To God—the Great Mystery—Creation, every word and every thought is a prayer that vibrates through the golden streams of time and creation. All things in the universe interpenetrate non-dualistically. All things have a consciousness and will respond accordingly.

The *kāhuna*, the shaman-priests of old Hawaii, deeply believed in the power of words, thought and prayer:

> Their prayers were the focus of force emanating from their being, perhaps from the conscious and subconscious mind and properly rendered were as effective for their purpose as a spear thrown in battle.

The above analogy is a good one for as the spear is a prayer (*pule*), the aim is concentration (*kia*), the strength of cast is desire (*kuko*), the direction is the objective (*makia*), confidence in ability is faith (*paulele*) and the lack of wind is no distraction (*malukia*). Just as all spears do not find their target in warfare, however, not all prayers command results either. Any of the former factors might be wanting or a new element might be introduced which could necessitate fundamental changes.

Of the mystical constituents in accomplishing a purpose through the power of words, desire was considered the most important. Intense desire might brush aside obstacles, make them inconsequential or even pierce them to achieve ambition.[36]

Prayer needs to be a natural part of living our daily lives. It is our connection with the Otherworld as well as with nature. Prayer needs to be from our heart; in the moment, with the intention that the prayer has already been fulfilled. To the rest of creation there is neither a past nor a future, just the now—this present moment. Pray not in the past or the future, but in the present. Pray for what you desire: 'my child lives' instead of 'please do not let my child die.'

Words have power. Blessing or praising is a form of prayer. Each morning we can pray by saying: "Greetings to the sun and the earth; I bless this day." My wife and I have studied with Auntie Margaret of the Big Island of Hawaii:

Prayer and the Hawaiian art of family mediation (*ho'oponopono*) are what Auntie Margaret considers her special ingredients for healing.

"We pray and sing every morning," she says of her massage students, "because I want them to empty everything in their hearts to be ready to help somebody. If you have problem, empty the problem out.

"I tell my students, when you go out to pick herbs, pray; when you prepare them, pray; when you give them, pray. Your patient going to get well.

"And the secret part of it is that before the sun goes down you *ho'oponopono*, you search your heart. *Ho'oponopono* meaning we empty all ourselves and ask for forgiveness before the sun goes down. You can't go to sleep with a troubled mind or troubled heart. You feel good because you're open minded."[37]

The Next Step

In this journey, prayer is important, but also important is the realization that we are never alone. Even deep in the mountains, we are never by ourselves. We not only have the companionship of nature, but we also have the companionship of 'guardians.'

Chapter 2
Guardians of Heaven and
Earth—Myth or Reality

There is an ageless spiritual belief that each and every baby born has a guardian. Whether it is called a guardian angel, a guardian animal or the Mesoamerican term, *tonal*, is unimportant. What is important is that this is a worldwide cross-cultural belief. Some traditions refer to this part of us as the higher self or our super-conscious self. Combined with this belief is the knowledge that every person throughout his or her life may also bond with one, or possibly more, spiritual guardians. This knowledge is a carry-over from the various shamanic cultures that dotted this earth millennia ago.

As a spiritual system of heaven and earth, shamanism is a journey of the soul conducted by the shaman, master of the spirit helpers. The shaman adventured consciously among ancestors or creator gods and goddesses, spirits, and energies on other planes of reality, and returned with sacred knowledge that would benefit themselves, others and the community. The earliest shamans had neither a patriarchal nor a matriarchal worldview, but recognized the oneness of all.

The shaman, as the intermediary between heaven and earth, communed not only with the spiritual entities of the heavens, but also of the earth. Today, the shaman is often put into a box of earthly dogma and is viewed as being strictly an earth-based practitioner. Shamans did look to the wisdom of the earth and nature, but not at the expense of the stars. The original shamans were balanced in their work of the heavens and the earth. The true shamans of old were not only healers, but were also priests, philosophers, astrologers, warriors and mystics—specialists and generalists in all spiritual aspects of the earth and the heavens. To view the shaman otherwise is ridiculous because the sole purpose of the shaman was to maintain harmony and balance within the people, the community and the land. And balance was only achievable through an equality of heaven and earth. This equality eventually leads to an oneness of self and community.

Shamans were able to retrieve knowledge and insight into the mysteries of heaven and earth by entering a trance-state, an altered state of consciousness. These ecstatic states were achieved through ascetic training; in other words, a form of *shugyo*. This type of *shugyo* could be repetitive movement (such as running), repetitive sounds (in the form of chanting or singing), ingesting hallucinogenic plants, fasting, isolation, and extremes of temperature (such as cold water immersion).

Wisdom of the Earth

As masters of heaven and earth, shamans were sensitive to the wood, the stone and all the elemental forces that surrounded them. They looked to the stars at night and to the four winds during the day. They listened to the magic roar of the streams and moaning surge of the oceans to learn the truth of the great mysteries of life. The shape of the clouds revealed the secrets of life and death. And the cry of the owl reminded them of their ancestors and the dark knowledge and wisdom of the earth.

This darkness is the realm of potentiality and growth, the womb that is the holy cup of all life. It is the deep dark soil that gives birth to a rose and the deep dark mysterious waters of the earth. It is the ground-spring of the shaman's power and our power—the feathered-serpent's power.

These physicians of the soul were known as the 'wounded healer.' Their ability and power to heal and perform feats of magic and psychic/ spiritual wonders was due to their own personal healing and ascetic training and sacrifice. Each and every one of the old shamans went on their own version of *musha shugyo*.

Having experienced their death and re-birth as well as the healing of their wounds through the earth, the shamans became the guardians and the protectors of the earth. The earth, the symbolic mother, is the teacher and the sacred source of vitality for the shaman as he/she develops a living, nurturing relationship to all of Mother Nature. The landscape of the great mother provided the shaman with the opportunities to face fears and to become a person of power. Questing in caves and purifying in streams and the ocean, the shaman experienced the death of the old self and the re-birth of the new as a child, guardian of the earth and a person of love and power. To the shaman, the veil between this world and the Otherworld was at its thinnest near running water. Being fluid, mysterious, purifying, life-giving as well as life-taking, living water was sacred and a source of spiritual power. This is the reason why one of the earliest forms of symbolic death and re-birth, full immersion bathing, was performed in swiftly flowing streams and rivers. This was the original type of spiritual baptism, not as membership into an organization such as the Christian church, but as purification through a symbolic birth from the 'womb of the earth.'

To these practitioners of power, nature was a magic looking-glass into the soul of the mysteries of heaven and earth. And it is through exploring and experiencing these mysteries that you will eventually become a Feathered Serpent.

A Sacred World

There is nothing more mysterious than the Otherworld—the world of spirit. This sacred world lies ever so close to our world of matter. Many do not realize that it is just a hair's breadth away. Most shamanic traditions view the Otherworld as having three different worlds—the Upper World, the Middle World or Middle Earth made famous by Tolkien's trilogy *Lord of the Rings*, and the Lower World.

This Otherworld is the sacred world of gods and goddesses, archangels, guardians, ancestors, spirits of the land—such as the faeries and the spirits known as elementals and many others known by different names from different lands. In addition, there are also much older energies that are very primal in their vibration and a force to be reckoned with when awoken. I remember one time when my wife and I assisted our teacher, an elder and Indian doctor, the late Vince Stogan, in conducting an 'animal burning' on one of the First People's Reserves in British Columbia. There had been unexplained accidents that had happened and the elders of the 'band' felt that they were rooted in a spiritual/shamanic cause. They needed Vince's help to set things right. Vince and his wife, Mom Stogan, were the carriers of the old shamanic traditions and were considered the most powerful elders alive.

An 'animal burning' is different from a traditional burning conducted for the ancestors, the ones who have passed over, the forgotten ones and the spirits of the land. It is conducted to feed the spirits of the animals, which also includes old primal spirits. It is considered more dangerous than a traditional burning as one of these primal spirits may 'show-up;' and one did—as we were assisting Vince in the ceremony. Once he had called in the 'spirits' to feed—an Old, Primal Sea Serpent came around the bend of the river. At that moment, it was time for us to leave. This is just one of many experiences that I have had with these primal vibrations—ones not to be 'fooled' with. The totality of the worlds—this world and the Otherworld—is sacred and needs to be respected and honored. When the harmony of both is destroyed, the fate of humanity will teeter on the sword's edge of extinction. Today, the harmony has been shattered and the results will be drastic and destructive at the end of this Age.

Guardians of Heaven

Of all the spiritual mysteries, one that has consistently fascinated and perplexed people is the existence of heavenly beings. And the question that is always posed: are they real or myth? What does your heart see: myth or reality? I will answer this question later in this chapter. But for now, let's explore these Otherworldly beings.

I use the term 'being,' although, 'energy' may be more appropriate. These beings take on various forms that are dependent on the culture and the underlying spiritual/religious tradition that claim them. It is a fascinating subject to explore; simple on the surface, but very complex underneath.

In the past, heavenly beings have been referred to as gods and goddesses, bodhisattvas, immortals and avatars, to name a few. Due to the complexity of our subject matter, we will simplify and limit ourselves to a brief discussion of four separate classifications of heavenly beings—Angels, *Myō-ōs, Akua* and Mesoamerican Deities.

Angels

Throughout time, humans have always identified with heavenly guardians—the higher light vibrations of creation. In some cultures and religious traditions, these guardians are viewed as messengers from above—angels. Angel comes from the Greek word *angelos*, which is the same as the Hebrew word for messenger—*mal'akh*.

Carvings of winged messengers date as far back as ancient Sumer in southern Mesopotamia—present day Iraq. Traces of the Sumerian civilization appeared as early as the 5th millennium B.C.E. To the Sumerians these beings were called *Anu-naki*, meaning 'of the heavens.' There is even evidence from excavations that Sumerian homes had personal altars to their guardian spirit. The early Hawaiians believed in the *awaiku*—the equivalent of angels. Their home was known by two names: *Lani keha* (Heavenly Breath) and *Kahiki Na* (Serene Spiritual Country of God in the East). The *awaiku* were not only messengers, but also guardians of nature:

Some *awaiku* listen to the prayers of *Kane's* children on earth, and convey their petitions to the divinities. Others among the *awaiku* play a variety of roles, such as the gods and goddesses of Nature under the supervision of the reigning deities, or as rainmakers who control the amount of water needed for the nourishment of crops, or as handlers of the bolts of lightning that flash from the skies during tempests by command of the storm gods, or as healing angels who assist the *kahuna lapa'au* by causing the divine healing power to flow from above into these spiritual healers, giving them the power to cure their patients.[38]

Similar to the Hawaiians, the Maya *Ch'orti'* believed that angels directed some of the forces of nature:

The *Ch'orti'* see lightning as the 'machete of god' (*umachit e katata'*) that is wielded by various angels (*anxerob' e katata'*) working under the auspices of god. Lightning is generally known as *jijb'ya'r*. However, special lightning bolts contain small, sharp stones on their tips so that when the angels of god throw them to the earth the *Ch'orti'* believe you can go to the strike spot and find the small flint point (also called "la hacha de dios"). These dangerous bolts are called *senteyo*, a term specifically used for the powerful, deadly lightning bolts that are accompanied by thunder (which, they say, is caused by the angels playing their drums or by angels chopping at the clouds with their machetes).

The angels who are given charge over lightning are known as "the first angels" (*e b'ajxan anxerob'*).... They are divided into two groups. The first are the "our older brother angels" (*e kasukun anxerob'*).... These angels "work" (*apatna*) from January to August but do their principal work between April 25th and May 5th since they are responsible for bringing the rain for spring planting.... Another set of angels, known as "the younger angels" (*e kumix anxerob'*) begin their work in September. The most powerful angel among this group is the "penultimate angel" who is known as Angel San Miguel or Angel San Gabriel. He begins to work on the first day of September and goes though the middle of November....

... The Ch'orti' also believe that one can get possessed by an evil spirit if lighting strikes close to where one is. A curandero must be called in order to rid one of this "*espanto*" (*b'aik'ut*), or "fright."[39]

In light of this quote, it is easy to consider that these winged messengers extend as far back as the earliest shamanic cultures. In fact, the shaman would be viewed as the angel of the community, for it was the shaman who could 'fly' to the heavens and return with a message—knowledge of the mysteries of heaven and earth.

Angels have often been referred to as 'morning stars.' This is symbolic of the light emerging from the darkness, being suggestive of the role that angels may play in our lives. These celestial beings are always around us and above us providing us with a link and ladder to the heavens. In the dark night of our soul, there is always the shining brilliance of our own angelic self, our guardian angel working towards the destiny of our soul's light evolution. We are all children of light, sons and daughters of Heaven and Earth, Feathered Serpents—suns of God.

Mikael

The principle angelic warrior guardian. Mikael, 'Who is as God,' is an elder archangel, meaning a preeminent or chief-angel, and is usually assisted by two warrior angels. Angels are androgynous. However, in Mikael's case I refer to this archangel's consciousness, spirit and energy as male even though all heavenly beings are one with creation and neither male nor female.

Mikael is the angel of fire, storm and the bringer of the rains. In Islam he is the angel of mercy, which in Arabic may also mean rain. It is a little known fact that Mikael was the messenger angel to the prophet Noah. In addition, he has assisted all of the other prophets since that time.

Mikael is the guardian of the Holy Grail and is acknowledged within Christian, Hebrew and Islamic lore. He also extends back through the mists of time and has been called by many different names in many diverse cultures. Two of these names were the Greek *Apollo* and the Celtic *Lugh*, both Sun Lords.

As the fiery warrior archetype, Mikael represents spiritual illumination as well as being the spirit guide for the dead, or what we would call the heavenly shaman—the psychopomp. As a psychopomp, he aids in the passing over of souls to the Otherworld and weighs the light of each soul's incarnation with his 'scales of truth.'

He is the angel of the sun, honored on Sunday and during the dog days of summer—the astrological sign of Leo. Mikael's honor day is celebrated as *Lughnasadh* on the first Sunday of August. His feast day, *Michaelmas*, is celebrated on September 29th in the sign of Libra, the sign of the scales and the ruler of Venus.

Mikael's symbology and iconology include: the laurel tree (*Apollo's* tree according to the Greeks), feline energy, the dragon-slaying sword—the 'sun sword,' the spear of truth—the 'sun spear,' serpents and dragons. He is the patron of warriors, swordsmiths and mariners as well as the great initiator into the Mysteries and the guardian of high places, spirals and labyrinths.

As the heavenly Prince of Light, Mikael pierces the dragon energies of the earth, thus forming the connection, union and oneness of Heaven and Earth. But Mikael, with his 'sun sword,' does battle with another dragon. This is the dragon of materialism, greed, and external power—the wingless dragon of the ego that stands in the way of achieving peace and unity on earth. In addition, this materialistic dragon blocks the path to our own spiritual power and the feathered-serpent ideal.

Myō-ōs

Many people seem to be aware of the Buddhist deities called bodhisattvas or bosatsus, but few seem to recognize the Japanese Buddhist *Myō-ō*. These vanquishers of evil stem from the Sanskrit term *vidyaraja*, meaning kings of wisdom. In Japan bosatsus are the gentle persuaders to salvation whereas the myō-ōs are intense 'in your face' enforcers of the spirit. These radiant wisdom kings are messengers of *Dainichi Nyorai* ('Great Sun')—the Cosmic Buddha of Shingon Esoteric Buddhism. The Shingon ('true word') sect originated by the saint *Kukai* especially reveres myō-ōs with the most famous being *Fudō Myō-ō*.

The knowledge and imagery of these esoteric Buddhist deities came to Japan in the 8th and 9th Centuries and were derived from Hindu deities. Fierce looking, these brilliant kings of knowledge strive to 'wake' us from the sleeping state of ignorance. Flames surround *myō-ōs* signifying their importance in helping people purify their hearts and minds by burning away their desire for material things and the greed that is attached to this desire.

Fudō Myō-ō

The warrior guardian of esoteric Buddhism and mountain ascetics, *Fudō Myō-ō*—Immovable Wisdom King—is known as the enforcer deity, the protector of Buddhism and the destroyer of the illusions of life. With a glaring countenance, *Fudō Myō-ō* (*Acala Vidyaraja*) guides us in achieving a mind that is unaffected by desires and the carnal temptations of life. As a messenger of *Dainichi Nyorai* (Cosmic Buddha), *Fudō* grasps the devil-slaying sword (*gōma no ken*) in his right hand, which symbolizes wisdom cutting through ignorance, while in his left hand the rope (*kensaku*) catches and binds the demons of desire, the obvious as well as the unseen.

Fudō Myō-ō is the best known and the central figure of the *Godai Myō-ō*—the Five Great Wisdom Kings. The other four are: *Gozanze* (East), *Gundari* (South), *Daiitoku* (West), and *Kongo Yasha* (North). Just as Mikael has two assisting warrior angels, eight child attendants often assist *Fudō*. The two most common that attend *Fudō* are *Kongara* and *Seitaka*.

Fudō Myō-ō is the purifier of our minds and hearts. Though compassionate, *Fudō-inu Myō-ō* (Immovable and Wrathful Mantra King) is the wrathful manifestation of *Dainichi Nyorai*. In some corners, he is considered the angry *myō-ō*. This is not the anger of emotional attachment to past chaos, but the anger of injustice and inequity—the anger that motivates us to right the wrongs, to lasso and bind the righteous ones who cause the destruction of order, the earth and other sentient beings. This is the passion of movement from an immovable place. This is the volcanic wrath that gives birth to new life.

Fudō's façade is fierce; a scowling grimace shadowing the eyes, one eye wide open and one half closed. His teeth are canine; one large fang pointing up and one pointing down. Eyes and teeth symbolize the sun and the moon, heaven and earth. And his hair, knotted in the way of the servant, signifies his service to *Dainichi Nyorai* and to all beings. But why the face of fury? Could it be to shake us up out of our spiritual complacency?

Steadfast in his determination to save sentient beings, *Fudō Myō-ō* guides us onto the path of self-control by cutting through the illusionary mind with his wisdom sword. And with his rope, he binds the un-serving passions that lead all astray. *Fudō*, as an unwavering state of enlightenment, is portrayed surrounded by flames that bring light and purification to the darkness of the deluded mind. And lastly, and possibly most importantly, he usually sits or stands on a flat rock symbolizing the concept of *fudōshin* —immovable mind, which eventually leads to *fudōchi*—immovable heart wisdom.

As I mentioned before, *Fudō Myō-ō* is the guardian of mountain ascetics—the *yamabushi*. These purveyors of power look to *Fudō* for their protection and knowledge. Suffering through cold-water austerities (*misogi*), which is one source of their power, the *yamabushi* see *Fudō* as a symbol of the generation of inner or internal heat—the key to spiritual power and enlightenment.

Akua

Akua (god/goddess/supernatural spirit) are the impersonal deities of the Hawaiian people. They may also be a Hawaiian's *'aumakua* or guardian spirit. The *Akua* exhibit not only divine traits and supernatural qualities, but much like Greek mythology, the Hawaiians' gods and goddesses express human frailties. The four major *Akua* are *Kāne, Lono, Kū* and *Kanaloa*. The *Akua* can also take different material forms such as an owl, shark, stone, a fireball or even an old woman such as the form sometimes taken by *Pele*—the volcano goddess. This ability is referred to as *kino lau* or changed forms.

Many people are unaware that each of the four major *Akua* above are also balanced by a corresponding goddess:

> Each of the four major male *Akua* — Ku, god of war; Lono, god of fertility and agriculture; Kane, god of sunlight and male essence; and Kanaloa, god of the ocean — had a female counterpart. These were Kuho'one'enu'u, war goddess of O'ahu island; Lonowahine, goddess of the Makahiki festivals; Kaneikawaiola, goddess of fresh running water; and Namakaokaha'i, goddess of the ocean.[40]

Prayer is common and plays an important role in Hawaiian life. Where there is prayer; there are the *Akua*:

> For the gods were ever present, guarding, guiding, warning, blessing, punishing. Supernatural spirits inhabited, and even assumed, the form of plant and animal, rock and stream.... They were visible in volcano flames. They whispered in the breezes; shouted in the thunder. Some of these spirits were distant and powerful *akua*, the impersonal gods. Some were *'aumākua*, family ancestors become gods. Some were *kūpua*, demi-gods and god-like spirits. All, even un-named spirits, were objects of prayer. For, one

theory holds, these nebulous "nature spirits" existed long years before the great gods, *Kū, Kāne, Lono,* and *Kanaloa* existed.

Therefore, what could be more natural than to pray to spirit, to *'aumākua,* to *akua*? To ask the help of *Lono* when crops were planted? For *Lono* was the deity of growing things. What could be more logical than to ask *Kāne* for clear water to drink? For *Kāne* governed stream and waterfall and even the drops that fell from the heavens. And what could be more fitting than to ask permission before taking fish from the sea? Forgiveness before stepping onto volcanic lava or digging in the earth?

Thus, the Hawaiian from early childhood acquired the habit of praying.

The pantheon to be prayed to was complex. Not the least of the complexities came in the belief that a single god had a dual nature. *Uli,* for example, was both the fear-instilling goddess of sorcery and the hope-inspiring goddess of resuscitation and restored life and health. *Laka* was the benign goddess of *hula*; she was also *Kapo,* goddess of poison and sorcery. *Kū,* the masculine principle, and *Hina,* the feminine, were individuals, and yet parts of the *Kū* -and-*Hina* godhead. For where *Kū* was, there was also *Hina.*

The same god-spirit might even exist in multiple forms or functions. *Kū* and *Kāne* and *Lono* had scores of named personalities. *Kū–kā'ili-moku* was the most warlike aspect of *Kū.... Kū-moku-hāli'i (Kū, the island-spreader)* was *Kū,* the beneficent god of forests and canoe makers....[41]

Kū and *Hina*

Kū ('rising upright') is guardian of the islands of Hawaii as well as the individual, family and farming. He is also recognized as the god of war, fishing, power, canoe making and the sunrise. He is the master martial god—the protector; his wife *Hina* ('leaning down') is the earth mother.

To the Hawaiians, *Kū* represents the East, or the sun rising, which indicates morning. *Hina,* his wife represents the West, or the sun setting, which indicates evening. *Kū* and *Hina* are representative of the balance that is needed for a person's well-being. *Kū* symbolizes the external while *Hina* is symbolic of all that is internal.

To the Polynesians who pre-dated the Hawaiian culture, *Kū* ('to penetrate darkness with light') was recognized as the morning star and his twin, his wife *Hina,* was the evening star.

Kanaloa

Kanaloa, companion and drinking buddy of *Kane*, is the *Akua* of the oceans while *Kane* is the exponent of fresh water:

> … Kane became the patron of fresh water and Kanaloa of the ocean, especially the deep ocean. Both are associated with canoes; Kane as builder and Kanaloa as sailor.…
>
> Individually, Kane is associated with sunlight, bamboo, taro, sugarcane… and coral; Kanaloa is associated with the ocean winds and bananas. Both are associated with red roosters and black pigs.[42]

Pele

Of all the volcano goddesses, *Pele* is probably the most well-known. Her myths and deeds have been told down through the generations of the Polynesian people. She is the goddess of Mount Kilauea on the Big Island of Hawaii and a goddess of fire and lightning:

> She is Pele-honua-mea, Pele of the sacred land. She is Pele-'ai-honua, Pele the eater of land, when she devours the land with her flames.…
>
> In folklore she may appear as a tall, beautiful young woman, or as an old woman, wrinkled and bent with age, sometimes accompanied by a white dog. When enraged she may appear as a woman all aflame or as pure flame. Her sacred name as a spirit is Ka-'ula-o-ke-ahi, the redness of the fire.
>
> To know Pele is to know the awe that the first Hawaiians must have felt when they came upon this huge island crowned with fiery volcanoes and trembling with earthquakes, an island so different from the smaller and more tranquil islands and atolls they had known in the South Pacific.…
>
> So long as the earth is alive with quakes and eruptions, Pele will live in Hawaiian hearts and minds as the personification of the natural phenomena of volcanic activity.…[43]

I've always felt a close connection with *Pele*—her power and energy. It is the power of destruction, but yet again, the power of creation—of new growth. It is the power that each of us has within us but many times deny.

Hers is the anger that may destroy. But on the other hand, it is the anger that may right the wrongs of the world—an anger that is needed more than ever in today's unjust world.

Mesoamerican Deities

As with many of the other indigenous cultures of the past, the Mesoamericans intimate relationship with nature is reflected within their cosmology. There are deities for fire, wind, lightning, star, corn and earthquake to name a few. Even the word for hurricane comes from the Mesoamerican god of thunderstorms and whirlwinds—*Hurakan*, which means 'one-legged.'

To the Mesoamericans all things are sacred and divine:

The Mesoamerican man, immersed in a sacred universe, discovered fully himself like *homo religiosus*. The superhuman forces and the powers represented by his deities transcend all his activities. The religious beliefs were all for him. Even the qualities groups, functions, processes and conducts were personified in his gods....

In this *numenístico*, deity organization scheme explained by the mythology, woman and man were stand over the same level. When Quetzalcoatl travels to the Mictlan to search the precious bones in order to create man, so much those of the woman as those of the man were contiguous; Quetzalcoatl bled his member on them and thanks to this sacrifice, joined by other gods, man and woman were born simultaneously.... But the myth is not only referred to the analogy between sexes; it also aim to the important and transcendent fact that the man as a creation occupies a superior level, since his birth happens as a consequence of the gods sacrifice, who gave him his essence in a completely hypostatic phenomenon, which implies the union of two natures: divine and human. According to this point of view the conception of the anthropomorphous pantheon finds its explanation, since man was created to the image and the likeness of the gods....[44]

Quetzalcoatl

Ehecatl-Quetzalcoatl is the wind and air deity who is solely mythical. *Topiltzin-Quetzalcoatl* is viewed as being more the historical person even though there are mythical accounts of his activities. The general name that is often used for both identities is simply *Quetzalcoatl*—the Feathered Serpent/Plumed Serpent/or Precious Twin:

> Even the origin of the mysterious figure of Quetzalcoatl is ambiguous. His name comes from the combination of the Nahua word *quetzalli*, which means "precious green feather," thereby alluding to a bird with brilliant feathers, and the word *coatl*, which means "serpent." In Mesoamerica, the bird and the serpent are symbolic representations of two regions significant to religious and cosmological thought: heaven and earth. In Mesoamerican symbolism, this double entity is a synthesis of opposites: it conjugates the destructive and germinal powers of the earth (the serpent) with the fertile and ordering forces of the heavens (the bird).
>
> The eternal battle between the creative and destructive forces gave birth to the image of the twins: two characters of similar appearance but endowed with contrasting powers. In Mesoamerica this symbolism is represented by the light of day and the darkness of night, the birth of life and fatality of death, the green season of sprouting plants and the somber days of dryness and sterility....[45]

Itzamna

The Maya consider *Itzamna* to be the creator of humanity:

> *Itzamna*, the celestial dragon, is one of the superior gods of the Mayan pantheon. He often appears on a celestial throne, ruling over the other deities....
>
> *Itzamna* is a heavenly god, however, in the dual thinking of the Mayan religion, where opposites agree, this deity brings together great cosmic opposites; he appears like the bird which represents heaven, and the serpent that personifies earth.
>
> In the central high-planes, this symbol of the god, represented with the figure of a feathered serpent, belongs to the god *Quetzalcoatl*, the same one that was integrated into the Mayan culture as *Kukulcan*....
>
> *Itzamna* is also associated to the Tree of the world, the central axle which united the sky, earth, and the underworld.[46]

The deity, *Itzamna*, is also considered to be the original and the greatest shaman of the Maya:

In antiquity *Itzam* generally meant "shaman," a person who worked with itz, the cosmic sap of the World Tree. Itzamna is the First Shaman and one of the gods who drew the images of the constellations on the sky at Creation.[47]

Earthly Spiritual Guardians

In addition to heavenly beings, there are also earthly ones. These are the spiritual entities that have a connection with the earth, nature and natural forces. They are known by many names depending on the culture. There are dragons, faeries, elves, gnomes, salamanders, mermaids, thunder beings, and tengu, to name a few. There is another classification of earthly spirit beings, which are ancestral guardians such as the Hawaiian *'aumākua*. I also include in this classification all forms of shamanic and guardian energies as well as the Mesoamerican concept of *nagual* and *tonal*.

Spirits of the earth are a mystery. Our linear minds cannot determine the scope or reality of such energies. To see within this mystery, as with any spiritual mystery, we must use our sixth sense, the intuitive side of our brain and refer to the myths and legacies of our ancestors.

One way to begin to understand and to connect with these earth spirits is through the province of wild and unspoiled nature. A wonderful and de-stressing exercise is to simply discover a field of wild flowers, walk through the field until you feel the urge to lie down. Then simply lie on the earth, breathe deeply and close your eyes. Be aware of all of your senses and feel the presence of the flowers. And just possibly you may be visited by a faerie. A 'person of power' always strives for balance in his or her life. These earthly energies may be a source of that balance. Never deny the worthiness of any energy that may connect with you.

Another way to enter the realm of these spirits of the earth is to become a confirmed dreamer. Dreams may unlock the mysteries within ourselves that our conscious mind is keeping hidden. And there is conscious dreaming, which is better known as 'going on a guided journey.' This is another source of the feathered-serpent's power.

And finally, read and delve through the pages of myths and legends, subjects that have fascinated humans for countless millennia.

Dragons

Once again the knowledge of these spiritual beings is a carry-over from ancient shamanic belief. In China, unearthed bronze vessels have revealed imagery of crude dragons. And these date from the Yin Dynasty over 3000 years ago. I choose to include dragons under earthly beings even though they have as much right to be included with the heavenly ones. Traditionally, the question of origin, heaven or earth, has intrigued the seekers of mystical knowledge and wisdom. Did humans first see the dragon in the stars, the constellation Draco? Or did the earthly dragon come first to be then transported to the stars? It does not really matter according to the ageless spiritual teaching: 'As Above, So Below, As Below, So Above.'

Traditionally, at least in the East, Dragons have been a source of inspiration, wisdom, fertility and immortality as well as, in many beliefs, the source of rain. However, in some myths and legends, dragons have not fared as well or have been held in such a high regard. In the West, primarily in Christian belief, they are viewed as a source of evil. If your organization was patriarchal, then any energy of the earth (matriarchal) would be deemed sinful and wicked.

Interestingly enough, enlightened and wise societies usually view the dragon negatively in only one guise. This is as the base earth dragon, the flightless dragon, which hoards wealth and exudes greed. This is the dragon of materialism and is the one that the Archangel Mikael slays.

Dragons are awesome. The Welsh word for dragon is *draig* and many times was used in the context of identifying a person as a warrior or leader—e.g. Uther Pendragon. As mentors for us, we also have a special kinship with them. Dragons may feed us inspiration to help us accomplish feats of wonder-working and magic that others would deem 'the stuff of dreams.'

Dragons on one hand may also be viewed as feathered serpents. At least, they are distant cousins. As we know, these 'bird-serpents' are a metaphor and a symbol of our journey to enlightenment—Divinehood. Being as wise as a serpent and as pure as a dove, the feathered serpent points the way to our internal rising of our serpent energy that lies dormant at the base of our spine. Arousing the serpent is a choice many deny—some out of fear and many out of ignorance. For the feathered-serpent ideal to be a reality, the serpent must be awoken out of its materialistic sleep—a sleep of spiritual death. When it is aroused, we additionally wake-up from our own self-induced illusionary ego. The awakening is not as difficult as it sounds. The most difficult, taxing and enduring aspect of this awakening is to stay awake and not be seduced into 'falling asleep' once again. Could this be the lesson in the importance of 'vigils' in spiritual initiation and training?

This energy that is trapped at the base of our spine is commonly referred to as the First Chakra. And the dragon, whose wings have not unfurled, may also symbolically represent this base energy. It is in this context that we become the heroic dragon-slayer. However, this name does not reveal its true meaning. What occurs is not a slaying, but a transmutation of the dragon or serpent energy. You can immediately see the confusion that this may cause and as a result, it sows fertile ground for religious dogma. This dogma, represented by the imagery of the slaying of the evil dragon by either Saint George or Archangel Michael, is not about dragons or serpents, but it is about the slaying and the suppression of all things female including nature and the natural energies of the earth.

The true treasure that the dragon guards is not the wealth and external power that goes hand-in-hand with that wealth, but life—the life that is everlasting—and divine wisdom. The earth is the womb and the dragon protects this precious treasure.

A Norse legend, the 'Volsunga Saga,' speaks about Sigurd, son of Sigmund. It was the heroic warrior Sigmund who drew Odin's sword from the tree Branstock. Sigmund's life, though, was fraught with sorrow and tragedy and in the end the magical sword shattered. However, the shards of Odin's sword were destined for his son—Sigurd, who it was prophesized, would win a prize greater than any mortal man.

Years passed, and finally, Sigurd's tutor, the master smith, Regin, helped to re-forge the sword, *Gram*, on the condition that Sigurd would slay a huge dragon for Regin. This dragon was none other than *Fafnir* whose cavern was deep within the dark forest of Mirkwood. In the legend, Sigurd defeated *Fafnir* and tasted the dragon's blood. As soon as the blood touched his tongue, Sigurd understood the 'language of the birds.' This was the angelic language of divine wisdom. Sigurd then proceeded to 'eat the heart' of the dragon. Thus the energy was assimilated within Sigurd transforming him into a 'person of power,' a feathered-serpent, with mastery over the lower/primal aspects of life.

Ancestral Guardians and Personal Guardians (Guardian Spirits)

Ancestral guardians are of the earth, and for some cultures, are an indispensable part of life. These guardians are the spirits of the family lineage that protect and guide the people as well as form a sacred bond between the land and the people. Ancestral guardians provide a legacy of sacredness that guides the people to a oneness of being with the earth, not separateness from the earth. Ancestral guardians connect people to the land. When this spiritual principle is not an integral part of a culture, the earth and its inhabitants are deemed expendable. This is exactly what has happened, and is happening today, resulting in an ecological catastrophe; the ramifications of which are still unknown. When people are separate and cut off from their ancestral lineage and heritage, the spirituality of the earth, as well as the values that such provides, become hollow, vague and in most cases, non-existent.

All is not lost if, and only if, we return to the sacredness of the land and look to the spirituality and values that are such an integral part of earth cultures—such as the Hawaiians where the elders (*kupuna*) were honored and revered. It was the *kupuna* who brought forth the voice of the ancestors. They were the well-source of wisdom and knowledge for the people of Hawaii. They taught the people and 'talked story' about the ancestral guardians (*'aumākua*), and taught that the ancestors could manifest in physical form (*kino lau*) such as the Hawaiian Owl or *Pueo*:

> The closest man-with-god relationship came in the *'aumākua*. The bond between human and *'aumākua* was very real....
>
> *'Aumākua* might take the animal form of owl, shark, lizard, turtle, caterpillar, eel, mudhen, or the indigenous field mouse.... Rocks might be merely sacred to a deity—but rocks might also **be** a deity.[48]

> *'Aumākua* may also be viewed as our divine self:

> ... the most important element in kahuna healing... is the god-self, *aumakua*, or, in simple terms, God. All healing, in the kahuna view, is really nothing more than the result of a natural communion with the god-self.... As taught by the kahunas, joyful cooperation with "god-in-everything" is the best medicine for all ills, the best solution to all problems, the best way to achieve personal fulfillment. To do this, however, takes a commitment to remind yourself constantly of the presence of God in all people, places, things and situations.[49]

In our journey to become Feathered Serpents, we need to embrace this knowledge of the *kahuna* and 'see' and remember that the divine is within all things of heaven and earth.

Ancestral guardians are distinctly different from a personal guardian, even though an *'aumakua* may be one's personal guardian. Personal guardians are usually referred to as *totems* or *power animals*. In our fast-paced, performance-oriented society, these Otherworldly energetic guardians have been trivialized in different ways, with one being the use of the term "power animals." A more appropriate name would be *guardian spirits*:

All spirit guardians belonged to the animate realm, or to what the Indians considered as animate; they all, that is to say, possessed vitality, for it was their vitality that conferred the blessing or power on the individual Indian. This animate realm included, in addition to animals, birds and fish, certain forces of nature, such as the winds and the thunder, which also had been human beings in the dawn of time....

West Wind.—Many coastal Indians in the State of Washington, but very few on the Frazier River, obtained this guardian spirit. Whoever succeeded, after long purification, in reaching its home became a great warrior, and by his prayers could ally a storm and bring fine weather.[50]

As we can see, guardians may take various forms other than animals. All indigenous cultures had a belief in spiritual guardians and in the importance that they played in the lives of their people. Guardian spirits, however, did not appear out of thin air; nor was it easy bonding with them, contrary to the ease of attaining power animals in New Age neo-shamanic workshops:

Each spirit... had certain powers or gifts that it could bestow, but it bestowed them in varying degrees, depending mainly upon the distance the man's vitality traveled to reach it, or, in other words, the amount of purification and fasting that he underwent. The medicine-man's guardian spirits—those that enabled him to cause and cure diseases—were in no respect different from others, but the majority dwelt much further away and were therefore less easily attainable.[51]

Personal guardians are powerful companions for us in our journey to become Feathered Serpents. These guardian spirits may help us become closer to nature and its seemingly wild and untamed forces. We are never truly alone in our journey of life. Our guardians are our constant companions as well as our helpers. A hummingbird guardian may help us move faster on our feet, whereas a serpent guardian may help us internally release/shed our past that is inhibiting our happiness and growth in the present. A jaguar guardian may help us in achieving a fearless state of mind, as well as giving us the courage to face our symbolic death so that we may be re-born as a 'person of power.'

Guardian spirits, including *'aumākua*, may also protect us and our loved ones and keep us safe, as well as at certain times provide us with supernatural abilities:

> Three enabling-strengthening concepts are associated with the *aumakua*: *kīheipua, ho'oūlu ia* and *noho*....
>
> *Kīheipua* comes by itself, the unsolicited gift of one's compassionate *aumakua*. A somewhat stronger possession that enables is *ho'oūlu ia*. This can be prayed for.
>
> *Ho'oūlu ia* is literally the "making to grow." Still far short of total possession, *ho'oūlu ia* is a kind of inspiration.... Laka, goddess of the hula and an *aumakua*, was invariably called upon to inspire the dancer to a better performance....
>
> A third type of possession is the total—but not permanent—possession called *noho* or *noho ia*....
>
> *Noho* by one's *aumakua* may supply the sudden burst of "superhuman" strength that enables a mother to lift a heavy log before it crushes her child, or the "second wind" that helps the exhausted swimmer make it to shore. In the benign *noho* of the *aumakua*, normal capability becomes spectacular.[52]

Medicine power comes from a strong mind and a strong heart. A strong mind and a strong heart come from hard training; ascetic practices such as fasting and extremes of temperature. The power of the shaman to heal only comes from strenuous training and suffering, and only in the same manner are shamanic guardians obtained:

> He Who Dwells Above... ordained that many creatures should never be visible to mortal eyes. They live in mystic... realms at varying distances from man, who knows of them through visions only, when his vitality leaves his body and travels to their homes. It is from these distant, invisible creatures, not from the common creatures around about, that man obtains really extraordinary power—power, for example, to cure diseases. The farther away they dwell, the greater the power they can bestow; but also the more difficult it is to reach them, because He Who Dwells Above will never allow a man's vitality or thought to travel to their homes until he has undergone a prolonged purification, and prayed and fasted unceasingly. Only one who has undergone this strenuous training, and suffered innumerable hardships, has ever become a real medicine-man... with power to cure human ailments. As Old Pierre

said: "Nowadays, I hear many of my friends say, 'I am a medicine-man; my power is latent in this knife.' But they do not speak the truth. They are not medicine-men; they have no medicine-power, but only the shadow of such power. Not one of them was willing to undergo the penance that alone gives admission to the really sacred realm, farther away than the realm of the ordinary guardian spirits, where dwell the spirits that give medicine-power."[53]

Guardians may well indeed 'stalk' us. This means that 'power' recognizes our quest to become Feathered Serpents and is 'waiting' to bond with us. To be worthy of being 'stalked,' our quest must include keeping ourselves in balance, or what the Hawaiians call *pono*; prayer, fasting and rigorous mystical disciplines including *misogi* (water purification); death and re-birth experiences and many other forms of *shugyo*—austere training .

All of these practices involve suffering and sacrifice. As a result of this training, a person will have accumulated a degree of spiritual/shamanic power and knowledge and the wisdom that comes from this practice and commitment.

There is no way around it. The earth, nature and *shugyo* are indispensable in our training to become Feathered Serpents. The training and commitment is not easy. It is tough and requires us to face the greatest foe that we have: ourselves. This type of training forces us out of the comfortable 'boxes' of our lives that provide for us a false sense of safety and security.

Guardians also may come to us in our dreams. One benchmark is the occurrence of the same animal or creature in a dream. This must happen three times—the appearance of the same creature. The appearances must not be spread over months, but must occur within a short period of time.

Once we have bonded with a guardian, we need to put our attention on it:

- Discover its name; ask what it would like to be called
- Research knowledge and facts about this guardian's species
- Collect pictures and objects of your guardian
- Honor your guardian on a daily basis; pray with it, go for a walk with it, spend time with it
- Never kill or eat your guardian's species e.g. shark—do not kill or harm or let others do the same to a shark and do not eat shark meat

Nagual and *Tonal*

There are two general Mesoamerican concepts that refer to Other-worldly guardians and birth guardians—*nagual* and *tonal*. Since these are concepts and words from past oral traditions, we need to see past the linear-ego based meaning that some writers and teachers put on these concepts. In their basic simplicity, nagual implies a guardian, often in the form of an animal that bonds with a person. Many times the Mesoamerican shaman would be viewed as having the jaguar as their *nagual*. In fact, in some parts of the Mesoamerican world, the words for shaman and jaguar are the same.

Tonal on the other hand is the birth guardian, the animal twin of the person. As stated before, this may be termed the guardian angel or known additionally as the higher self or over-soul of a person:

> In contemporary ethnographic literature, the term *tonal* is frequently used in contrast to NAHUAL.[54] Whereas *nahual* generally signifies a form-changer, frequently in the form of an animal, *tonal* is used to refer to a spirit-familiar or soul. Among contemporary Mesoamerican peoples, the tonal is generally synonymous with the concept of the "shadow" spirit of an individual. Among a number of Mesoamerican peoples, the tonal of an individual is discovered soon after BIRTH, frequently by contact with a particular animal. The term *tonal* derives from the Nahuatl *tonalli*, a word bearing such connotations as solar heat, day, day name, destiny, and soul or spirit. According to Sahagún, the *tonalli* soul of an infant was sent from the highest heaven of Omeyocan, the Place of Duality.[55]

Before we limit ourselves to just one Mesoamerican concept of guardian beings, we need to realize that in shamanic cultures, religious belief is not organized according to one set of dogma and doctrine like organized religion, but covers a variety of similar beliefs and practices based on the regional eco-biospherical paradigm. I've studied and done ceremony with Anselmo Perez, a Zinacantec shaman from the highlands of Mexico. In his people's belief:

> Every person's soul has thirteen parts. A fall or an act of witchcraft can cause a person to lose a few parts and become debilitated and sick. Fright can also loosen a person's soul from the body, as the soul is always trying to free itself and return to heaven, from whence it came...

Each person also has a companion animal spirit, which lives in a corral inside the mountains and is fed and protected by the Ancestors. In dreams a person may see or become his animal spirit. The animal often reflects the personality of the individual... A powerful shaman may have more than one animal spirit, including the jaguar, lord of the holy animals; shamans and witchs (sc) have the power to transform themselves into their animal spirits.[56]

Myth or Reality

Do we know if guardians are real or just myth and folk-belief? I can unequivocally state that heavenly and earthly guardians/beings are real and not just myth. This comes not only from my heart but also, most importantly, from my experience. Please see Completion for Now of the Feathered Serpent Chronicles for one of my true stories concerning Heavenly Guardians.

Preparation for *Musha Shugyo*

Just as we pack and plan for any type of journey, our *musha shugyo* is no different. Our spirit pilgrimage will take us back to our past, through the present and into the future as we journey through the Feathered Serpent Medicine wheel. Courage is the keynote when we are asked to look into the mirror of our past, present and future.

Before we gaze into this mirror, we need to set up a sacred area within our home and, if possibly, outside our home in nature. This will be an area where we can do our spiritual work without interruption. Part of this space may also include an altar. This altar may take the form of a simple table or shelf where we place our spiritual items. These items may include an incense bowl, some form of light such as a small lamp or candles, offering bowls of possibly spring water, sea salt and/or rice or corn meal (both symbolic of earth food that sustains our lives), and something representing the greenery of nature.

Whatever items you choose, they need to have a meaning and significance to you, your ancestry and your own personal journey of spirit. As an example, you may want to include a small amount of olive oil on your altar. This would be the case if your ancestry came from the Middle East, or if you feel a connection to the Middle-Eastern cultures and you knew that olive oil symbolized light. Then it would be most important to include olive oil on your altar. If you feel or have a connection with the Hawaiian/Polynesian culture, you could have a *kukui* nut on your altar. The *kukui* also symbolizes light. Or possibly a ti leaf from Hawaii:

- Very spiritual: it is believed that Lono would take the form of the ti plant and watch over the workers in the field and make sure they were safe
- Hula dancers would were ti leaf skirts because the leaves of the plant was the symbol of the goddess Laka
- If you were to plant the trees around your hale Lono would make sure that no evil spirits would enter your house[57]

A sacred outdoor space may be as simple as a large stone or a certain tree that is special to you. At the base of the tree or stone, you can lay a flat stone that you could find in nature or purchase at a garden supply center. On this flat stone, you could place an incense bowl. This would signify the tree or stone as sacred space. Do not worry about doing wrong. As long as you are doing it from your heart and not your ego, there is no wrong.

Initiation

For millennia there has been, and there still is, a formula that lays out the steps to take to achieve spiritual power. This also includes the power of spiritual healing (hands-on-healing). $SP = I + A$. The formula for mastery is $MSP = I + AT$. This trinity of power represents Initiation, Asceticism (shugyo), and Transference. Birth, the journey and death; past, present and future; initiation, asceticism, and transference: each one of these is a reality. Truly the most important one for us, as living, breathing divine human beings, is the middle one of each of the three—the journey of life, the present and asceticism.

There are no shortcuts. Of course, there are systems that fool people by providing a shortcut. You can surely increase your 'ranks' of people by removing the middle requirement of asceticism—hard training. One system that I know of does this—Reiki. It provides people the final part of the formula—transference, which they call attunements. As anyone can see, without the middle part, any beginning and any end are nonexistent and are an illusion. Of course, how many Reiki masters would there be if they had to go through years of ascetic training before their attunements as masters?

Transference is a spiritual transmission of power from master to student. In some rare occurrences, the transmission or enlightenment occurs from the heavens to the student without a master present as in the case of prophets such as the historical Buddha, Kukai, the historical Quetzalcoatl and Jesus. For each of them, the transference occurred with the appearance of the morning star. It was this star that proclaimed their spiritual power and status as messengers.

A few of the old martial art dojos followed this formula—initiation was a blood oath, *keppan*, which was then followed by very severe training and finally, the transference of mastery. But as you can imagine, transference is not the province of this book. However, a form of initiation and the practice of asceticism are both presented within these pages. We begin our *musha shugyo* with a heaven and earth initiation:

Preparation—you will need to purchase two new natural fiber blankets, large enough to wrap around your body, as well as sea salt, alcohol such as sake, tequila or pulque and incense or a burnable plant such as sage or cedar. You will also need a new pair of white sweat pants and sweatshirt and a journal that will record your thoughts and experiences of your *musha shugyo*.

The initiation is done outside in a natural unspoiled area. You will need to pick a site that feels good to you and then visit it a week before your initiation. If possible, choose a space that has an unobstructed view of sunrise. At least 24 hours before your initiation, I would encourage a fast, no food or water.

Initiation—you must be at your initiation space one hour before first light. This is not sunrise but the light that precedes the sun. Before you 'barge' into the site, ask permission with your voice or mind to enter and conduct a sacred ritual of initiation. This is addressed to the earth and the heavens. If you happen to be a martial artist, just as you bow before you enter the dojo, it would be best to bow before you enter this initiation space.

Put one blanket on the ground to sit on. If possible, put it next to a tree so that you can have your back touching the tree trunk. On the blanket lay out your white initiation clothes, incense—such as copal, sea salt or corn meal, possibly a ti leaf or cedar branch (pray and ask permission before taking) and tequila or pulque (fermented agave juice), and your journal. Remove your mundane clothes and sit facing east. Wrap your other sacred blanket around your body.

Light your incense and offer it with prayers to heaven and to the earth. Your prayers are your choice. They could be for strength, courage, health for yourself and loved ones, etc. One part of your prayer must include your intention, as a seeker of the feathered-serpent ideal, to be initiated by heaven and earth—and to grant you 'the heart that sees.'

Next, offer some alcohol such as tequila or pulque to the 'spirits' of the place, pour some on the ground and swallow a small amount yourself connecting yourself to the 'spirits.' Then sit, meditate on your musha shu-gyo and wait for the sunrise. Feel and see the energy of the heavens—the stars. If you are sitting next to a tree, feel the energy of the earth through the tree. Feel the energy coming up through the earth. Become one with this energy of the earth and the heavens.

After you have spent some time feeling this energy, symbolically go into the 'womb' by putting the blanket over your head. Keep feeling the energy. Do not be afraid. If you hear strange sounds or animal sounds, do not be afraid. Stay under the blanket until the sun rises. Then, as the sun rises, stand up, rise up and greet the sun and the dawn of a new day. Breath in the essence, the energy and light of the sun, while letting it circulate throughout your body. Be thankful for life and this experience and accept this initiation of heaven and earth. Put on your white 'spirit' clothes and sit and embrace the sky above you, the earth below you and nature surrounding you. After awhile record in your journal this experience; include any sounds you heard or images that came into your mind while under the blanket.

Completion—Say words of completion and offer the sea salt or corn meal, sprinkle a little on the earth, as a gifting back for this initiation. In addition, leave the cedar branch, ti leaf or any other evergreen as a gifting. Say a final prayer of thank you, take off your 'spirit' clothes and redress in your mundane ones. Please leave the area as you found it. When you return home, keep your two blankets, 'spirit' clothes and journal in your sacred space.

CONTINUATION OF THE FEATHERED SERPENT CHRONICLES

The Wizard of the Four Winds—February
of the year 1988 Common Era

Since I had left the islands of the 'rising sun,' a timelessness of being had permeated my soul. Keko's scream appeared to me like a memory of only yesterday, but four lunar months had turned. It seemed like it was only this morning that Keko had given me a note, pressed into my hands, as I bid her farewell:

> "I always remember your sensitive, strong, sacred spirit. It was a great experience for me, too."

Briefly these thoughts flowed through my mind as I stared at a grand cathedral, a materialistic icon of the organized religion that had invaded these lands so many centuries before. After a long trek through steamy jungles and sun-baked sands, I had finally arrived in the mountainous city of Cusco in the Land of the Candor. It was here where I was to meet the other adventurers in what was considered the 'navel of the world.' At 3350 meters above sea level, my breathing was a little labored, as if with a lover for the first time. But then, why would it not be? I had just traveled from the jungle lowlands where the land met the seas known as the Caribe. Here in this mountainous region, my body was still adjusting to this new and strange, but so familiar, environment.

The indigenous people, known as the 'Children of the Sun,' were busily going about their daily activities. Even the ones who still smiled displayed a broken spirit. And why would they not, considering the grievous destruction of their culture and religion so many centuries before. But if the rumors are true, there are still ones who practice the 'old ways.' And we are gathered here to find them and their lost city.

I was as a stranger, an enigma to many in our group; a band of healers and adventurers drawn from the four winds of the earth. And most appropriately, our leader, a great *Curandero*, was known as the 'Wizard of the Four Winds.' He was a master of the San Pedro, a magical plant that opened a portal to the other worlds—or so I had been told.

It is not necessary to go into the mundane, such as the make-up of the various personalities of our group, for my tale needs to be told with a minimum of words. It was only one night that we stayed in an inn before departing for the little traveled mountainous Royal Road—supposedly, the only way to truly enter and discover the Lost City of the Sun. I had considered downing a few pints of ale in the local tavern before bed. But then, I thought better of it. As always, there is a time and a place for such; but now was neither the time nor the place.

There are many other more traveled and easier paths to the ruins. But then again, you will only discover the remains of a once-great city. To pass through the veil of linear time, one must travel the Royal Road. It is on this path where the trail's guardians—the luminous Warriors of the Sun—will test you. If you are deemed worthy, then you may continue on to Machupicchu—the City of the Sun. If not? Well, the penalty is too awful to mention.

The next day dawned crisp and clear with a sky encased in brilliant blue, dotted with pure white clouds, which seemed to invite us to ascend to heaven. Morning unveiled itself uneventfully and by noon we were at the trail head. My senses were overwhelmed by the beauty of the land and sky. And I wondered why others would not attempt this same passage into the unknown.

In the late afternoon we set up camp on a level stretch of ground only a few hundred yards from the Temple of the Hummingbird. It was here where we would begin our initiatory journey; a quest for spiritual mastery connected with the North Direction of the Inka Medicine Wheel. I had been asked to be a 'spirit guide' for the night ceremony at the temple. It was partly due to this that I discovered my one material intention for this journey—a staff. As I sought for the best path to the temple, I came upon a perfectly formed staff of eucalyptus wood. Why would anyone abandon a perfectly good staff on a mountainous trail such as this?

Meanwhile, just behind the veil of dimensional vibration that separates our world from the Otherworld rested Regulus. But the dragon was not alone. There was another one present, a brighter vibration—an Archangel.

"He has discovered his magical staff," said Regulus with his mind.

"It will be needed by him as he faces his death," replied the Archangel known as Michael. "Only after a human has experienced his/her death in life may death no longer have a hold on him/her. The fear of loss is so great in humans. Every waking moment is in denial of the known truth. Human souls are immortal, but each human's physical body will die. The fear of this loss is the greatest. And this generates in humans many other fears of loss: the loss of relationships, the loss of material things, the loss of power, the list seems endless. Their attachment to loss is so great that they, in reality, lose the most precious thing that they have—the light within their heart and mind and the power of their spirit."

"Thus our brother's message is coming at an appropriate time in the earth's evolution," interjected Regulus.

"That is true my son/daughter. But it is a message that many will not want to hear; a message that will undermine the greedy, materialistic foundation of Capitalism and the evil of organized religion. It is the darkest of the dark periods, but his light will be seen by only a few."

"Will the few be enough to assist him?" asked Regulus.

"He has his family. All are evolved in a way to help him bring his message of oneness. His teachers will have a knowing of his power and uniqueness and they will assist him in awakening further. We can only help so much. It is up to him."

With a twist of his massive head, Regulus replied, "I feel his call—his prayer. I will go to him. He will see me in the night sky lit up by your lightning. And he will know us—in his heart."

As the sun disappeared below the mountainous ridges, darkness quickly descended on the group as they made their way to the temple. Thunder rumbled in the distance. Above them the black-clad night sky, splattered with purplish patches throughout, appeared threatening at times. But then again, it seemed, in a certain unearthly way, magical. Within a short period of time, the group was seated on the ground within the opened-air ruins of the once-great temple. The wizard explained the spiritual purpose of the journey in his own tongue. Berto, the leader of the group, translated the words.

"Quest for the power of the North—the direction of the ancestors," explained Berto as he pointed to the north, emphasizing the wizard's words.

"This is the land of the masters. Seek your mastery without attachment. Still your mind and call on the spirits of the North—the Dragon, the Horse, the Hummingbird…. Call on the ancestors of the Inkas. And they will come—if your heart and mind are pure. You have all been invited on this journey to be initiated in the sacred lagoons. You will be tested by the spirits of the earth and the heavens. Are you worthy?"

At that moment the sky erupted in a clap of thunder and a flash of lightning that startled one and all, including the wizard. This was followed by a few drops of rain and then there was quiet and stillness. Without so much as a pause, the wizard turned and spoke rapidly to Berto.

"This is very out of the ordinary. I feel the presence of San Miguel (Saint Michael) and a great flying serpent."

Like the majority of wizards or *Curanderos*, don Cardo incorporated the conquerors' religious saints into his collection of otherworldly beings, partly to disguise the continuing practice of the traditional spiritual ways. Don Cardo had two mesa (altar) power-objects that were connected with the Archangel—the Sable de San Miguel Arcángel and the Puñal de San Miguel Arcángel. The sable was the saber of the Archangel and a symbol of heavenly justice, while the puñal was the dagger of San Miguel and was used against spirit attacks.

Don Cardo's mesa could be compared to a portable altar that contained his various items of power that would assist him in healings and exorcisms. Physically and mystically, his mesa was constructed according to the 'four winds and the four roads.' His objects would be grouped to the four cardinal directions and be a reflection of their respective meanings: east – rebirth, south – action, west – death and north – power.

"Do not tell the others. I do not want to seed their minds with what might happen tonight. I may have been imagining their presence. Explain to them that we are here to work in the North, the place of mastery, but they must shed their past—the work of the South and face death—the lesson of the West. Tell them that we will now do a meditation to connect them with the energies of the North."

The lightning and thunder had continued, but with a much reduced intensity. Meanwhile, the wind had kicked up and was followed by the rain. It began falling at an ever-increasing rate while Berto translated the wizard's words. Above the assembled seekers, but hidden from their reality, soared Regulus and Michael. Only a hair's breadth separated them from the vibrational reality of Balamcoatl and the others. The moment would soon come when Regulus would pierce the veil and appear in the night sky to Balamcoatl.

After the wizard's opening words had been translated, Balamcoatl had begun praying to the one guardian of the North that he had always felt the closest connection to—the Dragon. Several minutes had passed and Balamcoatl's mind was now focused on merging with the ancestors of the North—his eyes closed in meditation. And then... the wind suddenly erupted into a swirling tempest... and Balamcoatl's eyes flew open... at that moment, Regulus, silhouetted by an intense flash of lightning, manifested in the night sky. Only Balamcoatl could see the immense dragon as Regulus' magic prevented the others, even the wizard, from seeing him.

"You know me... remember... remember...." Regulus' words echoed within Balamcoatl's mind.

"I know you," Balamcoatl thought. And with that, the dragon was gone.

Over the next three days the group of initiates traveled through 'cloud forests' and traversed the 'pass of the eternal woman,' Warmihuanusca, at 13,800 feet. After having crossed the mountainous pass, they soon arrived at one of their early destinations, the ruins of Runkurakay and the beginning of the Inka Royal Path.

The 'sun legends' tell a tale that only the enlightened ones, the children of light, would be able to pass this point and continue on to Machupicchu. It was at this guard-post of Runkurakay that the luminous warriors would scan a traveler's energy-centers. Additionally, these spirit-guardians would observe how the travelers physically moved, if their words matched their actions and the purity of their heart.

If a person was found worthy, he/she would be able to continue on to the Sun City, but at some point, he/she would have to endure the initiation of 'death.' If not found worthy, a seeker would still be able to continue on to the Royal City, but unbeknownst to him/her, without the benefit of awakening to the hidden knowledge of the Children of the Sun.

Of course, the worthy ones who were chosen might not survive the initiation. It was here where Balamcoatl got very sick.

"I'm burning up and it's not from the climb," I thought. "I don't know if I can go on; but I have to...."

At that moment the jungle healer on the journey, a master of the vision-vine, put his hand on my shoulder. Speaking in a broken form of my language, he said, "You do not look so good my friend. Let me help you, if you would like."

I readily agreed as the curandero, from the jungles of the great river—Amazon, led me to the sun temple's circular ruins. Once in the ruins, he took me to the northernmost part of the temple and positioned me standing, facing east. He then proceeded to pray while preparing his pipe with mystical Amazonian herbs and sacred tobacco. I realized that the curandero, known as Agust, was going to conduct a jungle pipe ceremony on me. It is not necessary to go into the details except to say that he blew the sacred smoke on the various energy-centers of my body. And within a short period of time, I felt much better and was able to continue on to Phuyupatamarca—the next sacred site. At 11,800 feet, it was appropriately named the 'town above the clouds.'

As the group continued on, I wondered why don Cardo had not offered to help me. I had recently heard talk that we were not going to the sacred lagoons of Las Huaringas after Machupicchu. I had been asked, as well as the others, to join don Cardo on his own personal pilgrimage to Las Huaringas to claim his right as lineage-holder over the waters of the sacred lagoons. Las Huaringas was a sacred site where shamans for centuries had come to receive their initiation as master shaman. This transmission of authority was to occur within one year of the death of don Cardo's teacher, don Floren, former 'master of the lagoons.' I wonder....

As I walked, I let these thoughts go as I marveled at the landscape that we were traveling through. It was almost like we were stranded on an alien planet whose surface was composed of clouds and not of solid earth. With a clear expanse of blue above us and white feathery clouds soaring below us, my soul and senses were in awe of my surroundings.

As beautiful as it was, I suddenly realized that I was feeling lousy again and my fever had returned. Even though I had been chewing coca leaves (a mild plant stimulant), they were not helping. Chewing the leaves was supposed to alleviate conditions such as fatigue, thirst, and most importantly 'soroche' or altitude sickness.

However, as time passed, each step became more of a burden. If I had not had my staff, I realized that I might not have been able to go on. But the staff seemed to have a life of its own and provided an energizing effect on my fever-wrenched body. After what seemed like an eternity, we finally reached our campsite at Phuyupatamarca. And then I surrendered to whatever my destiny had in store for me and collapsed; but not before the realization that I did not want to die in these mountains and never see my family again.

I drifted in and out of consciousness as the various healers of our group entered my tent to administer their various curative remedies. Nothing seemed to be working as each came and left in a somewhat short period of time; none could stay longer as the inside of the tent was as hot as a sauna—and the cause was my fever. Sometime during the evening I was brought a small bowl of soup made by one of our Inka porters. It was supposed to be an old family recipe that was a remedy for fever. I was very hopeful and thankful even though it just tasted like ordinary carrot soup.

I seemed to be in a bizarre altered state as time wore on. And I wondered what was in that soup, as otherworldly images came and went all serenaded by drumming. The others were participating in a fire ceremony in the ruins of the city. Sick as I was, the vibrations of the drum and the chanting seemed to be healing and comforting. And before long I fell asleep.

"He has survived the initiation," said Regulus as the dragon turned its gaze on the brilliant shimmering form of the archangel.

"Yes he has, hasn't he? And he has an inkling that the wizard is not himself. We both know that don Cardo is off his path; always a common story among humans who get seduced by their own power and persona."

I awoke to the light of dawn and was thankful that I had indeed awoken, blessed by the fact that I felt so much better after what had seemed to be my last day and night on earth. I couldn't remember any dreams except for a brief image of the dragon that I had seen in the night sky.

As I emerged from my tent, I marveled at the beauty of the misty morning and my incredible surroundings. While I breathed in the thin, but invigorating mountain air, I realized how precious life is and how on the other hand, death has such a grip on us as we struggle and deny the truth—that death is a part of living. Intellectually, I knew that our souls are immortal, but still the prospect of dying was terrifying and accepting my death was not an alternative for me. I wanted to live and to be with my family again. Don Agust was standing nearby and when he saw me, he came over extending a hand that he laid on my shoulder.

"You look so much better. May I perform the ceremony on you that I did on the others last night?"

Of course I agreed. His gentle presence had such a healing effect. And when he was finished he leaned over and lightly kissed my neck.

"You will be well and strong for the rest of the journey. Be open and you will see and then you will know. The ancient ones are waiting for you. But first, my friend, let's have some food."

After breakfast, which for me was like manna from heaven, we meditated at the Temple of the Condor before departing on the final leg of our journey into the City of the Sun. After completing the morning meditation and ceremony, Berto asked us to walk in silence and warned us that we might be tested as we approached Machupicchu. My first thought was: what could be worse than almost dying?

The trail from Phuyupatamarca consisted of ancient switchbacks that took us down off of the mountain. I was walking with the drummer of the group while don Agust was a few yards in front of us. The day had dawned misty, but was now bright and clear. After what I had endured, I felt extremely grateful just to be alive. And then....

It was just like a scene out of a low-budget B-grade movie. A swarm of killer bees attacked us. My first hint of something out of the ordinary was the erratic actions of don Agust, who was walking a few yards in front of us. He whipped off his poncho and started running—all the while twirling his poncho over his head. For a split second, I wondered if this was some type of descending ritual. But within a few seconds, it became abundantly clear that it was not ritual, but survival, as we too ripped off our ponchos and followed don Agusts' lead.

If you run away, most bees will normally not follow you over a great distance—but not killer bees. We must have run at least a mile or more before we felt safe enough and far enough away from these vicious mutated human-haters. Even still, I had at least a dozen welts forming on my neck and various other parts of my body.

"Put this mud on your stings. It will help reduce the swelling and draw out the bee's toxin," said don Agust with a slight smile of comfort. "How are you both doing?"

As don Agust asked us this question, my mind immediately flew back to the past, remembering my 12 year-old daughter's final words as I departed from our home:

"I love you Dad. Watch out for the killer bees!"

"Another set of steps to climb," I thought, as I glanced at a weather-worn sign—'Beware of snakes.' Killer bees, now snakes…. As I reached the top of the ridge, my jaw dropped open in astonishment. Even though I was unaccustomed to being surprised, the vision that spread out below me was breathtaking. Suspended in the clouds was the sacred city in all of its glory. Its mythic castle and stone terraces reflected the light of mid-morning. And I realized that I was at the end of the Inka trail. I had survived; I had suffered; I had learned many lessons and finally, I had arrived. It was all worth it as I gazed on the beauty and the spiritual power of the mysterious 'lost city' of Machupicchu.

Time stood still as I paused and silently prayed at the Intipunku—the Gate of the Sun. The gate overlooked the city now shrouded in mist. As each of my fellow adventurers passed by me on their way down to the lost city, they asked how I was doing. The majority called me by the only name that they knew me by—the Inka. And I guess that I looked the part, wearing the same colorful poncho and hat as did our indigenous porters. With a face and body a deep reddish-brown darkened by the intensity of the sun, I could very well have been born in these mountains.

But was there something more below the surface that the others, as well as the porters, were intuitively picking up on? I wondered about my own feelings of connection to this land. Not as strong as the sun-baked jungle lands that I had just left, but still, something was there within the inner core of my soul.

"He is picking up on one of his soul's incarnations." This communicative thought by Regulus was directed to the light-bearing form of the archangel. There were, however, two other bright vibrations present that were intrinsically different from Mikael and Regulus.

"He withstood my awakening energy." This thought came from the bright vibration known on Earth as Fudo Myoo. "But he still needs hard training to remember and to grow. Only then will he be able to bring the message."

The A*kua* named *Tu* communicated next, "He needs to apprentice with the master of the masters, the great elder from the Land of Cedar. And he needs to travel to my land called by the humans—the Big Island. Only then will he have his vision."

"Rest easy, my friends," said Mikael "his life is guided more so than he will ever realize. He has the power, but he is also in human form. He has to face the same temptations as all humans; from these he will learn and grow and be as a beacon for others. In his humanness he will show that awakening and Feathered Serpenthood is possible for all; not just a select few as the corrupt religions that rule Earth preach. All humans need to be awakened to their innate divineness and their intrinsic worth. That is the message that Balamcoatl as the Morning Star will bring."

At long last, I was at a place of rest; an inn that was located just outside the entrance to the 'lost city.' Calling it an inn was a stretch of the imagination, as it had only a few rooms with showers. But then the creature-comfort that I missed most on the trail was taking a long hot shower. At this moment, an inn with showers for me was a golden palace of delight.

Eagerly, I entered my room desiring and wishing for a long-lasting hot shower. I stripped immediately and could already feel the cleansing warmth on my body. Excited beyond words, I stepped into the shower with great relief and anticipation of an ecstatic moment. But instead, I was greeted with an alien-like fungus occupying the majority of the shower stall.

This was the only inn within miles. If I wanted a bed and a shower, I was stuck with sharing the shower with this alien form, seemingly alive and moving. Now mind you, there are of course worse things and I had just been through some of them, but in the moment, I would have liked a clean shower, minus the alien scum, with plenty of hot water. And of course, with the gods and goddesses laughing at my humanness, there was little water and what there was, it was lukewarm.

After my lukewarm cleansing, which still felt awesome, I decided to explore the city before our ceremonial and transformational work later that night. The drummer of our group and a few others joined me.

Machupicchu is a sanctuary of power. Even though it was in ruins and seemingly deserted, the city was still alive with a powerful force. I could feel that the veil was thinly threaded on this sacred mountain top. The veil, as I call it, separates the past and the future from the present. Time is not linear as most people think. The past, the present and the future are all happening now from a perspective of a timeless impermanent pattern of vibrational frequencies. Thus, it is possible to pierce this veil and experience the past.

There are certain sacred places on earth, such as this, where the veil is at its thinnest. There are times such as dawn and dusk, the transitional periods from dark to light and light to dark, that also provide a window of opportunity for a person of power to access knowledge and to experience the mysterious energetic cosmic blood that I called 'the force.'

As we entered the ruins, I offered a silent prayer asking permission to enter the sacred city and to conduct spiritual work. As part of my ritual, I pulled off a few of my chest hairs and scattered them to the four winds as a small sacrifice and gifting to the serpent, the puma and the condor of the 'three worlds' as well as the 'unseen ones.'

Traditionally, you would use three coca leaves held in your palm while praying. Even though I did not have any leaves, it was still necessary to ask permission, to pray and to give a gifting to the ancestors, the 'three worlds' and the spiritual powers of the past, the present and the future. Substitute items such as my hairs instead of the coca leaves were perfectly acceptable as long as I honored and remembered the purpose behind the ritual. A pure, strong heart and mind and an impeccable intent are always the most important aspects of spiritual work.

Two thousand feet below me rumbled the Urubamba River and above me was a cloudless blue sky—surely one would consider this sliver of mountain top a paradise on earth. The whole of the valley below was considered sacred to the Inkas.

Machu Picchu means 'Ancient Mountain' and was considered a *huaca*—a sacred place where the sacred power of the Earth Mother was concentrated. I definitely could feel her power, but I had a feeling that Machu Picchu's true name and purpose had long been lost and forgotten during the passage of time. I had an intuitive sense that the original name would have translated as the 'Mountain where the Sun stands still'—indicating a sacred sanctuary of equality, balance and harmony. Metaphysically, this was a place of initiation where one's soul cast no shadow. Additionally for me, this mountain was a place of wonder and knowledge and an expression of Pachamama's (Mother Earth's) power and love.

If our mind is still and not 'chattering' (mind talk), our senses, including our sixth sense, awaken and strengthen. To look and to listen is to learn. But many people have a problem being in the moment and not talking. And that is one of the reasons I like to explore alone. True to form, the others with me were talking about the past few days and were missing the present moment and the power of this place of cosmic light—the light that is the Sun behind the sun.

Machupicchu was an engineering and architectural wonder. Gigantic stone blocks were fitted so tightly together without the use of mortar so that even a thin knife blade could not slip between the stones. Initially, we spent our time exploring the Sacred Plaza's Principle Temple and the Temple of the Three Windows. The three windows in the open-air temple were unique due to their trapezoidal shape.

The afternoon was slipping away as we made our way up the stairs connecting the sacred plaza to the Intihuatana stone. This sacred carved stone's name could be translated as the 'hitching post of the sun.' We were now at the highest point in Machupicchu. And the stone, with a little imagination, looked like the upper body of a dolphin with its fin being the actual hitching post.

There are many different explanations for the purpose of this ceremonial stone. But conjecture to its purpose was not necessary as I felt the power that was emanating from it. As a moth drawn to flame, I went and sat cross-legged on the stone with my hands in the mudra (hand position) of the Cosmic Sun.

As I closed my eyes, time seemed to stop. I was not aware of the stone seat beneath me or the others by me as surreal images briefly came and then disappeared. I quickly opened my eyes as I felt the immovable sunstone still firmly lodged underneath me. As a picture was taken of me and the others, I had a knowing that I had been here before. But it was a time before the Inkas. Was that possible?

It was early evening as the group was lead into Machupicchu by don Cardo. The gate into the city was normally closed and locked to visitors during the night. The gate's guard, however, was willing to accept a 'gift' and let us enter. Our ceremonial destination was the Pachamama Stone, a bastion of earthly feminine energy. It was here that don Cardo would conduct the 'sacred plant' ceremony using the medicine of the 'magical cactus.'

What an appropriate night it was, as lightning lit up the sky above the Pachamama Stone. As with all excellent tales of wizards and ruined cities, the heavens provided a backdrop that even one's imagination could never conjure up. Rain was falling, thunder was booming as if the Inka's war drums were sounding a call to action. All lit up as if the lightning bolts of the Inka's creator/hero—Viracocha—were being flung through the night sky. Every flash of lightning provided an eerie view of Huayna Picchu, the sister peak next to Machu Picchu.

Vairacocha was considered the creator and destroyer of worlds. Supposedly, we were at the ending cycle of the Fifth Sun or the fifth world. The last world or the Fourth Sun had been destroyed by water. However, the ending of our world would come about through big movement—earthquakes. Before I had learned this knowledge, I had a knowing that we were in the end times; a time critical to the survival of the human race—a race that was destroying itself and the biosphere of the earth. New thoughts and a new view of reality from what was already accepted were urgently needed. A message... but what message...? I seemed to know, but not know....

This night we were going to be working on mastery, again symbolized by the North direction of the medicine wheel. The Inka Medicine Wheel is a mandala, a visual symbolic construct and pathway of transformation and integration. *Mandala*, according to an ancient language, means circle. A circle is power, completion and perfection. The Inka Medicine Wheel is symbolic of the four winds and the teachings and transformations that occur in each of the four directions of the compass.

The journey through the medicine wheel begins in the south direction symbolized by the archetype of the serpent. This is the path of personal healing where we learn to shed the past and erase our personal history. The west direction is 'home' to mother/sister jaguar. This is the path of the Mystic Warrior—the Luminous Warrior. Here we face our deaths and step beyond fear and the uncertainty and doubt that live within us. The north is represented by hummingbird. This is where we learn the way of the Ancient Ones by stepping outside of time with the death of ego. We live in the timeless now, in a state of awakening, unfettered to the past, to fear, or to death. Condor is the archetype of the east. Here we learn to see with our hearts. As the visionary, we see through the illusion of separateness to the reality of oneness. Tonight, we had the opportunity to 'step outside of time.'

As the rain lightly fell, don Cardo set up his mesa in front of the gigantic mother stone and prepared to call in the guardian spirits of the 'four winds.' Don Cardo had placed his various size and shaped power staffs and swords in the ground in front of his mesa cloth—Owl Staff, Serpent Staff, Eagle Staff, Hummingbird Staff, Saber of Saint Michael. There were other staffs as well, such as the Staff of the Maiden—the Virgin. I mention this staff in particular due to the fact that it was presented to me to use in the night ceremony. This was an appropriate staff for me for many reasons, one being that I was born under the sign of the Virgin—a Virgin Birth.

This magical staff, connected with the sacred highland lagoons, was made from black *chonta* wood. It would awaken the nurturing power and feminine energy within me, which I needed to accept. This would balance the strong male energy that I had and would help bring me into a state of inner oneness.

Don Cardo knew that I was also a teacher of the mystical warrior arts as was he. He knew that it was not any of the warrior staffs, but the Staff of the Maiden that would bring me back into balance. He also knew that I needed the sacred power of the great Earth Mother Stone—the Pachamama.

As others received various staffs and went off to different spots to do their work, I was assigned to the Pachamama stone along with one of the females in our group. One at a time, we would come in front of don Cardo to receive our staffs. It was at this moment when I would have my first taste of the otherworldly 'magical cactus.' As I looked into his eyes, he handed me a seashell filled with some type of liquid.

"This is lovingly referred to as 'nose juice,'" Berto said as he assisted don Cardo. "Put the shell to your nose, tilt your head back and let the 'juice' run down the back of your throat. Breathe and if you start choking, stomp your foot."

Breathe, stomp your foot, imbibe a magical elixir through my nose…. I would later learn that it was a mixture of herbs, black tobacco and alcohol that was a powerful stimulant that would open the third eye and affect the various visionary centers of the brain.

It was definitely difficult to swallow and I did stomp my foot, which helped. It was absolutely a rush. As I handed the shell back to don Cardo, I noticed that his eyes were black pools of focused intent.

"This is the visionary cactus juice—the San Pedro," said Berto as don Cardo handed me a small liquid-filled glass.

As soon as I had finished drinking the potion, I 'danced' over to the Pachamama Stone. We were asked to dance after taking the San Pedro, for a reason I was still trying to figure out. But my focus was not on the dance or the reason for it; it was on the anticipated effects of the magical potion.

I waited and waited but nothing happened, other than my normal view of reality. Letting go of any further expectations, I settled in and focused my intent on the staff and my connection with the stone's great feminine energy. Time seemed to be suspended as I closed my eyes and attempted to become one with the Mother Stone.

How long I meditated, I do not know. But when I did open my eyes, the rain had stopped and the stars were shining brightly, and I had an insight. I had never been close to my own mother. In fact, in my mind, I had been raised by my grandmother. I had also always felt that my parents were not my parents.

My insight was that I had just re-established a bond and had become closer to my mother; that is my other mother, the Great Earth Mother—the mother of us all. Would this be an opening to my feminine side? I wonder?

As the night wore on, we did further spiritual work at the main temple where I was a spirit guardian for don Cardo. But it is not necessary to go into the details of the ceremony. Dawn was approaching and our work was complete as we headed back to our rooms for a few hours of much-needed rest. As we approached the entrance to the 'lost city,' I could see that the gate was now closed and appeared to be locked from the other side. We were indeed locked in!

I was standing directly behind Berto and don Cardo as they realized our situation. The only way out was through this gateway, which blocked the path in and out of the 'lost city.' On both sides of the trail were sheer cliffs; one that rose to the upper reaches of the city and the other that was a sheer drop to the distant river below.

It would be dangerous for each person to attempt to scale the gateway. Not only could a person lose their footing and tumble to their death below, but the top of the gateway was fashioned with 'cutting wire'—to discourage trespassers. The irony was not lost on me, as we were attempting to get out of the city, not break in.

Berto turned to me and said, "Don Cardo feels that you could safely scale the gateway. Are you willing?"

The San Pedro had not affected me as it had the others. I felt strong in body, mind and spirit as I nodded in agreement.

"Once you get on the other side of the gate, you must wake up the gatekeeper and get him to let us out," said Berto. "He has been paid his money. He lives in a small home halfway down the mountain. Be careful."

As I prepared to scale the gateway, I wondered if I needed to be careful of the climb or of the gatekeeper.

My tale seems to be getting longer than necessary, for this telling at this time. So I will briefly note that I did find the gate-keeper and everyone got out of the 'lost city' safely. Berto told me the next day that don Cardo had said that I was 'the big cat that flies.' First, the 'Inka,' now the 'big cat that flies' ... but yet again, it was an appropriate name for me.

It does sadden me to relate that we never made it to the sacred lagoons of Las Huaringas. Instead, don Cardo chose to initiate us in the sacred lagoon located on the Markawasi Plateau. It is not necessary, or appropriate, to explain the reasons or the results of don Cardo's decision, or his choice, not to go to Las Huaringas.

There are sometimes ramifications to our choices in life. Life is a mystery. We must always keep in mind that we are each connected in a web of life that extends out to the most distant stars. What actions or inactions that we do or don't do in life will affect us, as well as others.

THE SERPENT PATH
OF THE SOUTH

ARCHETYPE: WOUNDED HEALER
KEY PRINCIPLE: FORGIVENESS
TIME: THE PAST
COLOR: YELLOW

Chapter 3
Shedding the Armor

Dawn breaks, the sun rises on a new day. Philosophically, there is no past and truly no future. The only reality is the present moment. The consciousness of a flower knows only the present. With each energetic beat of its spiritual heart, its heart sees... only the present. But for each human being, the siren's song of the past and the illusionary future wails an incessant spell of saddened madness. It is mad not to live in the present; but so many do not. And if this was not so saddening, what is ever more problematic for the brightness and happiness of our souls is the burden of the past that we carry. This is the metaphoric armor of protection from a past that may repeat and rear its ugly self.

With the dawn of each new day, our hearts and souls trudge through a life of mundane patterns of being that have been encoded in our subconscious by a past that may seem more real than the present moment of our life. Cumulatively, the constant fear of an unknown future results in a non-spiritual, dis-empowered life of crinkled mundane proportions. This is not the life of the feathered-serpent.

The feathered-serpent lives in the present and only 'visits' the past to heal, change dis-empowered patterns of behavior and learn the lessons of wrong turns, missed opportunities, mistaken and possibly wrong behaviors of ourselves and others. The feathered-serpent does not fear the future, but only 'visions' the potentialities of life. To achieve this elevated essence of being is not easy, but it is most assuredly possible. It takes courage, determination and persistence to change and to separate ourselves from the prevailing beliefs of society and the masses. It is much easier to go with societies' flow rather than follow our hearts, common sense and natural law.

Natural law is the ruling aspect of heaven and earth. It is our window into truth. Truth is personal. Each person is ultimately responsible to discover his or her own truth—not society's or religious institution's or another individual's. Truth is _____. Each of us must fill in the blank. Of course, it is easier to follow someone else's truth. But the feathered-serpent path is not the easy path. It is as sharp and diamond-edged as an exquisite sword. This is the sword of truth with which the feathered-serpent must proceed, knowing that at any time she/he may fall and be cut. But the cut will heal and because of it, the feathered-serpent heart becomes brighter, stronger and life is seen not as illusion, but with the diamond clarity of truth.

Erasing Personal History

If our concept of self were based on the past, then the actuality of erasing our personal history would be terrifying. It is one of the reasons why many people stay locked into and remain burdened with the past. The past is their identity. It is familiar terrain. Even though it may be painful, it is still recognizable territory. It is not the unknown.

In contrast to this weakened state of mind and spirit, the feathered-serpent is ever present in the now and is identifiable with the present and not attached to labels of any sort. The feathered-serpent has erased the tracks in the sand and stands erect in the purity of the dawn of every new day. This marks a person of power. The power is internal and immortal. It is not a label or a position of low rank or high rank that designates this spiritual power. It is not the illusionary power of the ego. It is not materialistic power. It is the power of the *Ollin* heart—'the heart that sees.'

Erasing personal history does not mean denying the past; to do this would be foolish. We are the sum total of every moment and every experience of our life. Erasing is the 'letting go' of our attachments to the past. It is not forgetting, but remembrance without the emotional attachments—e.g. anger, guilt, shame, etc. It is not life viewed from the past. It is the present—the prism of our life manifested from the purity of our ever-present diamond heart.

Know Thy Self

This is a basic first step to take in our *musha shugyo*. It is the cornerstone of our feathered-serpent foundation. In addition, it is the key that unlocks the dungeon door to the cells where the unresolved issues of our life hide, and where the behaviors, words and actions that are detrimental to us, and others, lie. As a 'person of power,' we need to unload the burdens that we carry and tear asunder and consume our mask of self-lies. The feathered-serpent wears no armor of the un-resolved past, but stands tall and pure in the sun and moonlight of the present.

We only wear an external mask for transformation and to pierce the barrier between the mundane and the sacred. These are the masks of spirit. The false faces that people present to society are not a part of the feathered-serpent ideal. These faces are the masks that people put on in different circumstances to hide their true identity and purpose. Over time people lose sight of, and a knowing of, their true self. Without a knowing, there is no transformation. The false masks that people wear eventually erode their spirits, leaving a hollow husk of a human.

Society encourages a false face. It is an insidious method of control that forces people to abide by the ruling culture's beliefs—just ask any person who finally 'came out of the closet.' A feathered-serpent must consume these false faces of self. Then and only then will we begin to accept and understand our true self. We begin to uncover our true self by **Consuming the False Face**:

Preparation—Consider the following questions:

- 'Who Am I?' for each self—emotional, physical, mental and spiritual.
- What false face or mask do I wear that blocks me from:

  1. Wellness?
  2. Career Achievement?
  3. Creativity?
  4. Family?
  5. Nature?
  6. Unconditional Love?
  7. Spirituality?

- Pick one of the masks from the above seven categories to consume. Proceed to make your mask by using edible materials. Be creative. If you have never baked a cake before, this is your opportunity. As a suggestion, you could bake a small one-layer cake. The total face (cake) must be consumed; smaller would be better.

- Once your cake is baked, decorate it to represent the false face that you are consuming. Again, be creative in your representation. It would be best to consume your false face the same day that you created it.

Consuming the False Face—As you did for your heaven and earth initiation, be at your sacred space, your inside altar or your outdoor one, at least one hour before first light. Dress in your 'spirit' clothes that you used for your initiation. Do an opening by lighting incense along with saying prayers and blessings from your heart. Sit and meditate on the false face that you will consume and that will no longer be a false projection of your true self. When you consume your false face, bathe in the knowledge that this is a mask that you will never put on again.

As our days turn into months and then into years and decades, we lose sight of our 'tracks in the sand.' We may have established negative patterns and behaviors based on our past without consciously recognizing the source of this 'pain' that we feel in ourselves and that we may cause in others. If we are not aware and have no conscious knowing of the various details of our past, it is very difficult to make the changes needed in the present.

An exercise that will help us remember the various details of our past is called a **Walk through the Jungle/Forest**. This is a mythic map of the past that takes us through the narrow pathways of the dark, shadowy, root-infested jungle/forest of self. Do not be fearful or discouraged as within this jungle/forest lie many sparkling, mossy glens of love, light and truth. We must have courage to enter this jungle/forest of the self. Our mythic map of the past is a creative work of art that each one of us can craft. It is a pictorial story of our life drawn by our own hand. Do not let old 'messages' from the past block you from this exercise. Examples of these self-beliefs that were imposed by others are 'not being creative, artistic or being able to draw and/or paint.'

Determine a beginning age from your childhood for your map, ten years old for example. Then on a separate piece of paper do a timeline of events—positive as well as negative. This timeline would continue on until the present. From this timeline, illustrate your mythic **Walk through the Jungle/Forest**. There may be caves, underground entrances to where 'trolls' live; there might be knights and maidens in your forest, castles and evil wizard's huts, dragons, jaguars and unicorns. It is your choice how you symbolically represent your past journey of life.

At the end of your map, draw a mountain with a path that has begun ascending this mountain. This represents the present day and your *musha shugyo*. As this feathered-serpent journey continues, you may add milestones and events to your map to chronicle your journey. Once you have drawn the map, it is time to write your own personal **Heroic Myth**.

This is the story form of your **Walk through the Jungle/Forest**. Each one of us has a unique tale to tell. Do not doubt this. I would encourage you before you begin writing your myth to read various heroic myths from a mixture of cultures from the East and the West. Our myth is an inward voyage of self-discovery written in the language of supernatural wonder.

Our myth will be a form of a rite of passage that involves the trinity aspects first written about by Joseph Campbell: separation, initiation and return. The theme of separation will occupy the majority of this part of our myth. This is the motif of separation from our true self. We will complete this part of our myth at the point of our heaven and earth initiation in Chapter 2. Our myth will then be a work in progress. From this point forward, we will be adding to our myth as we 'return' to our true self and become the feathered-serpent. As Joseph Campbell points out in *The Hero With A Thousand Faces*:

> The two worlds, the divine and the human, can be pictured only as distinct from each other—different as life and death, as day and night. The hero adventures out of the land we know into darkness; there he accomplishes his adventure, or again is simply lost to us, imprisoned, or in danger; and his return is described as a coming back out of that yonder zone. Nevertheless—and here is a great key to the understanding of myth and symbol—the two kingdoms are actually one. The realm of the gods is a forgotten dimension of the world we know. And the exploration of that dimension, either willingly or unwillingly, is the whole sense of the deed of the hero. The values and distinctions that in normal life seem important disappear with the terrifying assimilation of the self into what formerly was only otherness. As in the stories of the cannibal ogresses, the fearfulness of this loss of personal individuation can be the whole burden of the transcendental experience for unqualified souls. But the hero-soul goes boldly in—and discovers the hags converted into goddesses and the dragons into the watchdogs of the gods.[58]

To help you with your myth, I would suggest taking some 3 by 5 index cards and printing various names of things on them. As an example, you might print the following (one item per card):

- Dragon (Unicorn)
- Owl (Bat)
- Giant (Elf)
- Temple (Church)
- Knight (Samurai)
- Healer (Shaman)
- Sword (Spear)
- Eagle (Hawk)
- Jaguar (Lion)
- Wizard (Warrior-Priest)

In addition to the above items, include your own. Then place the cards face down and draw seven index cards. These seven cards will help you begin your myth by weaving the various items into your tale. In the early 1970's, I studied martial arts at the Philadelphia School of Korean Karate and Kung Fu. The logo of the school included a tiger. A section of my myth might relate this fact in this way:

> As I approached the gates to the Temple of the Tiger, I felt that I was coming home, a return to a familiar place, a place that I had visited many times before—in my dreams and in another lifetime. I had heard the rumors about the master of this temple—Master Sand. Were they true? ...

Forgiveness

From our **Walk through the Jungle/Forest** and our **Heroic Myth**, we will be better able to identify the positive highlights of our past as well as the various incidences and woundings that need to be released. We achieve this cleansing of our past, erasing our personal history, through forgiveness.

Forgiveness is greatly misunderstood. Forgiveness is healing the past in the present and is probably the most important attribute to learn as a 'pattern of being,' as a feathered-serpent. You might find this confusing, or perhaps, intriguing, as I am not talking about typical mundane 'stuff.'

The majority of people would not identify forgiveness as essential to a 'person of power.' On the contrary, forgiveness is one of the cornerstones of the feathered-serpent ideal. Without forgiveness, we are eternally attached to the past. We are attached to others from our past in a dysfunctional manner. We are attached to the past becoming our present and our future. It is most difficult then to achieve a pure unattached mind in the present. One of the secrets to achieving an unattached mind is forgiveness.

Forgiveness is not forgetting the past, but it is letting go of the attachments to the past. Forgiveness does not give license to our behaviors or the behaviors of others from our past. It does provide us with un-attached lessons from the past of the unwanted patterns of conduct of others and ourselves. Forgiveness allows us to learn from the past, and provides us with the strength in the moment to help us not repeat unhealthy patterns of behavior.

Forgiveness is the soothing sun after a bitterly cold night. It helps us let go of our anger, resentment and our guilt and shame. These are the emotions that generate great energy within us. If not released, they may well mutate into the diseases and mental imbalances so prevalent in this early part of the 21st Century. Using your imagination, visualize a swirling mass of energy that is an emotion, such as anger, somewhere within your body, not your mind, but your body. How would this feel? How would this anger affect other parts of your body? How would this anger affect your mind, your heart? Now visualize this anger continuing to swirl, but the mind is no longer focused on it. In other words, it is buried. Now visualize what happens to this energy. Does it change form and harden into a mass? Does it affect nearby cells and organs of the body? If it is still there and not released, it will eventually affect the body adversely.

Metaphorically, this unreleased emotional mass is a 'stone.' This 'stone' and others like it burden us, forming the armor that we carry as a part of our being. These 'stones' symbolically reside in our 'bowl of light.' This is the container of our spirit, our soul—the light that is immortal. These various 'stones' dim or suppress the light of our spirit. In ages past, this container of light has been known as the Holy Grail. The Holy Grail, enigmatic in nature, is a cross-cultural mythic symbology that belongs to all of the races of humankind. It is the jewel of immortality and the cup of abundance that is truly a guiding light for a world divided and confused, such as ours today. Appropriately, the legend of the Holy Grail first appeared at the end of the twelfth century and was borne out of Europe's own 'dark night of the soul.' Is history repeating itself and are we also, in the not-too-distant future, facing our own American 'dark night of the soul?'

In the 1100's, as a result of the Crusades against Islam, there was an increased interaction with, and ultimately interest and awareness in the mysteries of the East. At that time, the East became an open beacon to the West; the refined Islamic culture introduced the mystical Sufis, the knowledge of the Jewish Kabbala and the new ideas of astrology, alchemy and numerology. This cross-cultural spiritual knowledge was just waiting in the wings to light a path to a renaissance of hope and faith in the West. By combining the legends and esoteric knowledge of the East with the ancient Celtic and Christian traditions and legends, the story of the Holy Grail was birthed.

Sacred cups and cauldrons containing the holy liquid of life are woven through the mythology of our lives. One of the earliest writers of the Grail legend, Wolfram von Eschenbach, compared it to a phoenix that is reborn out of ashes. The Celtic god *Cernunnos* is reborn when he is boiled in the Cauldron of Rebirth.

It is essential to understand that the Holy Grail is not an external 'thing.' It is not to be sought after outside of us. We must seek it within ourselves. It is the most precious thing that we possess. It is our *Ollin* heart. We have the ability and opportunity to re-claim what has been lost—the purity of our hearts and minds.

Bowl of Light

According to native Hawaiians, and I agree with them, each of us at birth has a 'bowl of light.' We are born in purity, not in sin. This 'bowl of light' is our *Ollin* heart—our deified heart:

> Each child born has at birth, a Bowl of perfect Light. If he tends his Light it will grow in strength and he can do all things— swim with the shark, fly with the birds, know and understand all things. If, however, he becomes envious or jealous he drops a stone into his Bowl of Light and some of the Light goes out. Light and the stone cannot hold the same space. If he continues to put stones in the Bowl of Light, the Light will go out and he will become a stone. A stone does not grow, nor does it move. If at any time he tires of being a stone, all he needs to do is turn the bowl upside down and the stones will fall away and the Light will grow once more.[59]

To awaken our *Ollin* heart as well as lighten our burden of armor, we need to 'drop stones.'

Dropping the Stone

We have already identified the various 'stones' within our 'bowl of light.' A few of these stones may indeed be boulders. To begin shedding our armor, we need to choose a more recent 'wounding;' one that is not too large. We want to begin with a small stone, not a large boulder from our distant past. The boulders are only finally released after years of feathered-serpent work. This is the reasoning behind the need for patience and persistence in our *musha shugyo.*

A feathered-serpent does not deny emotions. If we deny emotions, we deny our humanness. Each 'stone,' as you may have guessed, is linked to one or more emotions. The sooner we drop our 'stones' and release the emotional entanglements connected with these woundings, the closer we are to achieving a feathered-serpent ideal. Before we drop a 'stone,' we need to identify the various emotions that may be connected with it such as:

Anger—it is one of our greatest enemies. When anger arises it separates and blinds us to our inner source of love and then binds our heart with a coldness of discord. Unresolved anger will separate family and friends and result in a conditional love where words of truth are unspoken and hearts lie broken.

Everyone gets angry and everyone has been hurt. But to keep this hurt and anger alive and fresh is to live a life of bitterness and pain. Anger, unreleased, will lead to resentment. Resentments keep us in the painful past, day after day after day. Over time, this can affect our emotional, as well as our physical and spiritual, well being.

Resentments also keep us from self-responsibility, by allowing us to blame others for our own unhappy and unfulfilled lives. We might even hold on to our anger to make others feel guilty. But negative practices such as these only increase our own guilt and emptiness.

Guilt—it is a rocky road of an unreleased past that hardens us with each passing day. It haunts us with each step that we take in life. It wears on our spirit, our body and our mind. If you have committed a wrong and/or acted dishonorably and you feel guilty, then forgiveness is needed. Guilt arises, not only from the actions taken, but also from the actions not taken. If you turned your back on the wrong actions of others, you need to forgive yourself and then have the courage to speak up and right the wrong. If not, as time goes on and the results of your non-action become vividly apparent, the guilt that was a small pebble within your 'bowl of light' will grow into a boulder that hardens not only your mind, but also your body.

Sometimes we feel guilty for things in the past that are not worthy of our guilt. Our mind may have exaggerated what really happened based on our own guilt-filled belief of who we are. Always remember, no one is perfect or does not make mistakes. Open your eyes and do not dwell on the past and the actions taken or not taken, be compassionate to yourself, let go of the past, learn from your mistakes, speak up to the wrongs and injustices of life, forgive yourself and others and finally walk straight and tall in a new life of love and courage, not of fear and guilt.

Now that we have identified the wounding and the emotional connection, it is finally time to 'drop the stone.' Our experiential exercise is conducted in the following manner:

- Focus your intent on the forgiveness and the wounding (issue/emotion) you want to release.
- Find a stone in nature and ask permission with your mind to use it. Then take the stone and sit with it alone (preferably in nature) and talk your feelings and emotions—cry/shout/yell, whatever it takes, into this stone. You may only spend a few minutes doing this; then put the stone away in a special place or you may even carry it with you.
- When you are ready to say more words of healing to the stone, repeat as often as necessary. This process may take hours, days, weeks, or months (depending on the 'size of the stone'). But when you feel ready to release, visit a stream/lake/ocean. It can be at any time of the day, but dawn or dusk is the best symbolically.
- Sit by the water's edge and relax. More words may need to be said and more tears shed; when you are ready: Let Go, Forgive, and Release—drop (or toss) the stone into the stream/lake/ocean…as you let go of the stone—you are letting go of the stone, the wounding within, in your bowl of light. If you are unable to open your fingers and release the stone, it just means that you have more work to do on this wounding. Keep this stone and take it back home again. Repeat talking to your stone. When you feel

you are ready again, re-visit the stream/lake/ocean and release. When you have forgiven and let go of this past wounding, sit by the water's edge and feel the lightness within you. Bless the experience... the place, give thanks, and leave an offering before you depart. Bless, thank, and love yourself for having the courage, wisdom, and love to forgive and let go.

Chapter 4
The Wisdom of the Serpent

It is truly amazing to me the number of people who give lip service to nature and the animal kingdom, seemly choose not to have an intimate relationship with either. There is no relationship with nature when we lock ourselves away within the confines of our home or business. If you happen to be a martial artist or a want-to-be shaman, you're still isolated within the comfortable confines of the dojo/studio. I do mean comfortable. Any stress that is usually encountered in most modern dojos is ego-based discomfort rooted in winning/losing, performing correctly, and striving to achieve the next belt level. Of course, if you are a master, who would expect you to perform? I may be wrong, but I always thought of the martial arts as being a tool to 'crush the ego.' Isn't the ego-consciousness the barrier that must be torn down to achieve any type of true martial power? The same is true for the person who has participated in a few classroom sessions and all of the sudden is a 'shaman' retrieving souls and healing the 'masses.'

On the contrary, if nature is our dojo/our training ground, there are no corners for our ego to lurk in. There are no scorecards to hide behind. Rank and title have no meaning to Mother Nature and her children. They are not impressed with the color around our waist or any titles of 'master or shaman.' Nature sees within our hearts, and responds accordingly. Nature sees our degree of purity and has little tolerance for human ego. In fact, ego will kill you in nature's wildness; your ego as well as your teacher's.

Please do not misunderstand the point that I am raising. I am not referring to traditional or 'old school' *koryu* dojos or the ones that have paid their dues through shamanic ascetic training. But the martial (merchant) art dojos that are operated not by martial artists, but by 'merchant' artists, even though they may call themselves martial art masters. However, even *koryu* dojos may become complacent and neglect nature training. Even indigenous shamans-curanderos may lose their way as I've witnessed several times. When it's happened out in nature, someone's gotten hurt, physically as well as spiritually. Be aware of your teacher's degree of purity when you train, because training under the sun and moon is necessary and essential for a martial and/or spiritual student's growth and development.

By far, this is not a new concept. Since the earliest recorded history of humanity, people have sought guidance from nature and have demonstrated a reverence and respect for natural forces. The wisest ones saw the divine in nature and nature in the divine and sought for themselves to be in harmony with both, not separate. The knowledge and wisdom was there for the learning, if one had a heart that saw through the fear that nature and its forces may provoke.

For these first 'people of power' the serpent represented wisdom. It was the knower of all earthly mysteries and its brother the feathered-serpent—the dragon, was the keeper of the heavenly secrets. The serpent is ever watchful—vigilant—with its lidless eyes. By observing the movements of the serpent, we discover one of the prime patterns of existence. The wavy passage of the serpent is the flow of life in its undulating immortal dance of life everlasting.

The serpent is the intermediary, the messenger, between us and the Earth mother. It suggests the regenerative power of water as well as the cyclical changes of life. The coiled serpent symbolic of the micro-DNA and the macro-spiral of creation's truth is a guide to self-discovery. It is the supreme master teacher. It holds for us the secrets of immortality. It teaches us to 'shed the skins' of our existence, to be ever in a state of renewal. And it represents the central life-force that is ever creative and destructive—two fold but then, the higher aspect where two becomes one. The light and dark that are seemingly separate; but yet again are one.

To begin achieving this serpent power of constant renewal, work on consistently performing the following ritual:

Preparation—Daily contemplate this question: What small stones or woundings are forming or have formed in my bowl of light from the events of today? In addition, please keep the following metaphor in mind: 'as the sun sets, I release, I let go, I forgive, all of the negative actions and words of the day. As the sun dies, I die; I shed the skin of this day and accept renewal.'

Renewal Ritual—It would be best to perform this ritual outdoors while standing facing the west—the direction of the setting sun. Begin by doing slow deep breathing. This will put you in the present moment and will help you relax and clear your mind. Become mindful of all of your senses. Identify what you hear, smell, see, taste and feel. Recognize the love and power in yourself and in all of Creation, even in those who may have hurt you today. As the Sun metaphorically dies, let die this day by saying your words of forgiveness—shed the skin of this day. Now, say the words of renewal; these are your words of power in all that was right with this day as well as the lessons learned. Bless yourself, this day and all the things/people that have crossed your path.

Nature as School

Like the masters of old, we need to seek our knowledge and power in nature. This is the best way to begin to develop a feathered-serpent ideal. The workings of heaven and earth have always provided an enduring source of spiritual wisdom and knowledge. Immersing one's self in nature under the sun, the clouds and the stars will reveal insights and knowledge that is unattainable within the human-made walls of a school. With their hearts firmly entrenched in nature, many masters of the past have felt that the mountains, streams and waterfalls were the location of their true schools and their true selves. It was here that they were inspired as well as tested in the immovability of their hearts and minds.

Training in nature far away from the irritations and distractions of modern life will help you uncover the body-mind that is so important in your feathered-serpent training. This is not the body or mind, nor the body and mind, of dualistic thinking, but the actual experience and being of the *oneness* of life. With the heavens overhead and the earth beneath your feet, you may experience what the masters of old felt—nature as school; but remember that nature and the earth are unforgiving of one's ego and stupidity. Common sense as well as preparation are indispensable in nature's wildness. Many people lack directional sense, and even if you do have a good sense of direction, a compass, map and the knowledge of how to use them are essential. If you choose to go alone into a wilderness area, it is best to let someone know where you are going and your expected time of return. Water, a knife, matches (I prefer a Bic lighter) and a day pack with a change of clothes, extra socks, and some fruit and trail mix are a good idea if you are planning on spending the day out in nature; in addition, be informed of the local weather conditions.

Once you are in nature, there are many methods that will help you develop and strengthen your spirit and wisdom. I will suggest a few basic exercises that I have used with my students:

- A meditative walk using all of your senses except your eyes, which can switch back and forth from half closed to fully closed to fully open. Our eyes happen to be one of the prime gateways for spiritual afflictions or attachments to occur in our mind. The majority of people's eyes normally see, and what they see they attach to, thus arresting the mind and allowing desires, judgments, fears and the many other mind afflictions to arise.

  Our goal as a Feathered Serpent is to see with our heart as well as with our metaphoric third eye or intuitive eye, which is above our physical eyes and centered in our forehead and connects us with the pituitary and pineal glands in the brain. The Buddhist deity *Senju Kannon*, of the one thousand hands and one thousand eyes, teaches us that even with a thousand hands or a thousand eyes, if even just one hand or eye attaches—the rest are useless.

  We have only explored our eyes, but each of our senses may be deemed the source of our desire. Think about this and then develop an experiential exercise based on this knowledge to help you develop your feathered-serpent knowledge and energy.

- Training and moving on the earth in your bare feet is also very beneficial, especially on a forest floor. Not attaching to the discomfort or the possible pain of such barefoot training will strengthen your spirit and develop your immovable heart-mind-body. Breathing the mountain or forest air will invigorate your body as well as your spirit. It is optimal for spirit development to practice next to a fast moving stream, waterfall, the ocean or mountaintop, if possible.

- A mini vision quest would be another tool to help you in discovering self-knowledge. This involves nothing more than just sitting, or a little harder, standing in one spot for one to two hours. This means just being with yourself, with the sky and the earth without moving or doing anything. Sitting against the base of a tree would be very enlightening as the tree has its roots in the earth and its branches reaching towards heaven, symbolic of the unity of and connection between heaven and earth.

- Finally, be respectful of all things: i.e. do not litter and give thanks when you leave for your safety and all that you have learned and experienced.

Dr. Husfelt questing for power - Mexico, 2005

Questing for power, truth and enlightenment through the rigors presented by nature's elements, and by taking one's body and mind from the known (the familiar and accustomed life) into the unknown world of nature's wildness, will provide you with the building blocks for a feathered-serpent ideal.

Cosmic Tree

Nature is glorious. Even in its most furious expression, it is ever-renewing. Heaven in its own time will set the forest on fire. And in its charred remains resides new life—death, but then, renewal. Volcanoes release their fire and ash and in the aftermath, the land is transformed and 'baby earth' is born. Buzzing a spring song of creation, bees pollinate, assuring us of a renewal of life and sweetness on earth. As a symbolic and true cycle of life, bears emerge from the darkness of their dens of sleep to once again ascend into the light of life.

Truth is before us, but our human ego separates us from this truth. However, our heart, if we let it, sees the truth in nature's wonders. Whether it is the spiritual cedar, the magnificent *ceiba* (Maya tree of light) or the lordly oak, every tree is rooted within the earth. Their branches reach towards the heavens while their trunk connects heaven and earth. This is truth and one of the reasons for the metaphor of the Cosmic or World Tree. This is the mythological symbolic tree that connects heaven and earth. It is the medium between the natural and the supernatural. It is the *axis mundi* of creation as well as the central pillar of humanity—the primordial narrow passageway to other realities, knowledge and wisdom. Sometimes viewed as being centered on the summit of the World Mountain, the Cosmic Tree is the unparalleled creative imagery that allows our imagination to bridge the gulf between heaven and earth, spirit and matter.

Depending on the spiritual/religious tradition, the Cosmic Tree has many different expressions. It is the Tree of Fertility connected ever so intimately with the Great Earth Goddess. This goddess is the Earth Mother that embodies the regenerative powers of the earth and its waters. To our ancestors, nature's cyclical drama of death and re-birth was a Mystery Play that was brought to life through their own ritual and ceremony. The modern Maypole celebrations are vestiges of this ritualistic ancient fertility tree worship. The pole, as you may have imagined, represents the Cosmic Tree of Life.

The Cosmic Tree, in addition to its aspect as the Fertility Tree, is the Tree of Sacrifice. This is not death for death's sake, a scapegoat for other's sins, but a surrender of ego. It is a cleansing of the mind and a polishing of the heart. It is a tree whose fruits we must partake of in our quest for healing, power and love. It is our tree of tears where we may dampen our rigid and parched mind. It is the tree that pierces our soul. It is our 'sun-dance' tree and our 'seat of vision.' We follow in the symbolic footsteps of the ones who have passed before.

As a manner of honor and sacrifice, some Native American tribes honored the Cosmic Tree by ceremonially conducting the sun dance:

> In an elaborate ritual a sacred cottonwood tree is felled and brought ceremonially into camp. The tree becomes the centre pole for the sacred sun dance lodge.... 'We are really making the universe in a likeness,' says Black Elk, 'for each of the posts around the lodge represents some particular object of creation, so that the whole circle is the entire creation, and the one tree at the centre upon which the twenty-eight poles rest is Wakan-Tanka – the Great Spirit, who is the centre of everything.'

After the construction of this cosmic house, eight of the bravest warriors are chosen and painted with sacred symbols: the circle, the cross, the sun and moon and morning star. They then put on rabbit skins to make them docile and to help them accept their sufferings in a spirit of humility – 'a quality we must all possess when we go to the centre of the world'....

The breast of each dancer is then pierced in two places by wooden pegs, which are attached to a leather thong, which is tied to the upper part of the centre pole. When the dance begins, each warrior in turn leans back upon the thongs, which represent 'rays of light from Wakan-Tanka,' and dances around the pole until the pegs break loose from his flesh. The ritual ends with each of the dancers placing a piece of his severed flesh at the base of the tree, while the following prayer is addressed to the Great Spirit. 'These eight people have offered their bodies and souls to you; in suffering they have sent their voices to you; they have even offered to you a piece of their flesh, which is now at the foot of this sacred tree. The favour that they ask of you is that their people may walk in holy path of life and that they may increase in sacred manner.'[60]

Siddhartha Gautama, the historical Buddha, was a wanderer, a seeker of the pearl of wisdom. After many years of sacrifice searching and seeking for the truth of existence, he was finally spiritually open for a vision—the time must be right—all in heaven's time and earth's time. While sitting under a *Pippala* tree, the sacred fig tree that was later to be known as the *Bodhi* tree, he stayed detached to all the things that occurred in his mind that tempted him. He stayed immovable vowing not to get up until his vision came. Then, in the pre-dawn light, he had his vision as he saw the star of enlightenment, the star of the prophets, the messenger star—the morning star. At that moment, he was one with the morning star. At this moment, he realized that its bright light was not only within him but was also within all other things of the earth and the heavens. He awoke to the truth and became a Buddha—a Sanskrit word meaning 'one who is fully awake.' He was not a god, but a human being who perceived the true nature of reality—the spark or divine in all things.

Gautama sat under the *Pippala* tree, also known as the *'Tree of Ambrosia'* **or** *'Tree of Perfection'* and sacrificed illusion to achieve oneness. This sacrifice would reveal the truth that he was seeking. This 'immovable seat,' *fudoza*, this concept of non-attachment is a beacon and a guide to all who would strive to achieve spiritual enlightenment.

With many historical spiritual prophets or messengers, the words and actions are recorded at the bare minimum—second hand. Gautama, as well as Jesus, never wrote down their teachings or beliefs. Even the Buddha's awakening date, when he observed the morning star, is in doubt. One account has it occurring in December and one in May. We then must ask; how much of what is taught and practiced in the modern era is accurate? Faith becomes dogma and truth flies out the window. I would suspect that these messengers would like the record to be corrected with the truth of their teachings and beliefs. Since this seems impossible, our only alternative, outside of having blind faith, is to 'see' all things with a clear heart and common sense, as well as to have faith in ourselves, our divine self as well as our intrinsic human self.

Tree of Knowledge/Tree of Life

Associated with the Cosmic Tree is the Tree of Knowledge. So-called in its mundane form, while in its sacred form, it is referred to as the Tree of Life. The knowledge that this symbolic tree portrays is the illusionary aspect of duality—such as the knowledge of light and dark, male and female, all dualistic expressions of life. In its transformation into the Tree of Life, the illusion dissipates and the truth of the oneness, the non-dual interpenetration of all life, is revealed.

In truth this tree of knowledge and life is not external from us but lies within our very bodies even in their unperfected state. This very body of ours contains the Cosmic Tree. And this tree of knowledge, that contains the sacred 'life' of oneness, is none other than our spinal column.

Throughout the length of our tree (spinal column) from the base to the top lie vortexes, 'wheels' or 'circles' of energy. From the Hindu spiritual tradition, these energy centers were and are still called 'chakras.'

Chakras

The original esoteric name meant 'discus,' as in the lethal throwing weapon, with the meaning of destroying the passions that hinder a person's journey towards enlightenment. This meaning opens up a totally different view of what is most commonly known about chakras as just being 'wheels' of energy. This meaning implies the esoteric importance of our body's energy centers or chakras.

Traditionally there are seven major chakras beginning at the thighs, the roots of our tree of knowledge, and completing at the crown or just above the crown of our head. In one esoteric system there are five instead of seven. However, most commonly known are the seven beginning with the root chakra; next is the hara chakra, followed by the solar plexus chakra, the heart chakra, the throat chakra, the third-eye chakra and the crown chakra.

It is believed that chakras are depositories of memory. Our emotional woundings and the past issues connected with those woundings may be locked away within the various chakras. These blockages will definitely affect and inhibit the energy flow throughout our body. Over time this disharmony will affect the body's various health systems such as the organs and glands and will ultimately result in a state of unhappiness and disease. Following this pathway of the Feathered Serpent will help us heal the issues that may be affecting our chakras. (Please see Appendix 3 for chakra awakening meditation.) Below is a brief description of the seven primary chakras:

- The 1st chakra is the Root Chakra. It is located at the base of the spine and deals with issues of security, basic needs, basic human survival, profane and inappropriate sexual activity and one's connection to the earth. The color symbolism is red.
- The 2nd chakra is the Sacral Chakra. It is located in the *hara* region, right below the navel. It deals with issues of internal power and sacred sexuality. The color associated with the 2nd chakra is orange.
- The 3rd chakra is the Solar Plexus Chakra. It is located in the area of the solar plexus. It is the seat of our external power—our 'voice in the world.' This is the Earth's Gateway to the Heart. The color is yellow.
- The 4th chakra is the Heart Chakra. It is the lotus of the cardiac region. The issue of the heart chakra is love, and one's connection and relationship to all of humanity and nature. Love is centered here; a state of oneness we experience in relationship, in a harmonious and peaceful way, with all other things in the world of existence. This means every human, animal, bird, tree, rock, etc. The associated color is emerald green.
- The 5th chakra is the Throat Chakra. It is located at the base of the throat and deals with truth, manifestation, the expression of 'who we are' and communication. This is the Heaven's Gateway to the Heart. Its color is blue.

- The 6th chakra is the instruction and command lotus. It is situated approximately behind the forehead between the eyebrows and is often referred to as the 'third eye.' It is the emerald jewel in the center of Lucifer's crown that fell to the earth due to pride and separation. It is the intuitive power center, associated with the pituitary gland and connects us with the ability to 'see' beyond, to awaken from our earthly sleep and witness the sacred marriage. The color of the sixth chakra is violet.
- The 7th chakra is the Crown Chakra, the Thousand-petal Lotus. It is located on the top of the head. It is our connection to the Heavens, the Divine World and Oneness. This is our spiritual power center. The pineal gland belongs to this chakra as well as the command chakra. Its color is white.

The five chakra mentioned earlier are from an esoteric Buddhist system corresponding to the elements that form a *stupa* within the body. A stupa is a physical geomantic representation of the five elements, esoterically the Great Six Elements, and has various symbolic meanings ranging from the World Mountain or Cosmic Axis to its original purpose as an East Indian reliquary shrine. The geomantic forms of the five elements are: the cube of Earth, sphere of Water, pyramid of Fire, hemisphere of Air and the jewel-form of Heaven or Space. The five chakras are: the thighs chakra—Earth, the navel chakra—Water, heart chakra—Fire, face chakra—Air, and the head chakra—Space.

The Sixth Great Element, which interpenetrates the other five, is Consciousness. This belief opens up worlds of opportunity, knowledge and the wisdom that form is inseparable from mind and the mind is inseparable from form—a non-duality or oneness. And we realize that we are never alone or out of touch. Everything has a consciousness that is all connected in a web of life extending out and back to the furthest star in the most distant galaxy.

2012

Just as the serpent represents nature's micro-regenerative force, the Cosmic Tree reflects the undying regenerative center of creation—the macro-immortal truth of life everlasting. Imagination is nothing more than a seed of reality. To the Mayas, the imaginative Cosmic Tree was not some implausible religious belief, but it was reality—it was the Milky Way. Additionally, the Milky Way was also considered the Cosmic Mother:

> The Mesoamericans mythologized the Milky Way as a cosmic tree, a cosmic mountain or volcano... a Great Mother, a snake or crocodile monster, a white road, and a river....
>
> The Black Road, the crook in the calabash tree, the cosmic birthplace, the crossroads, the jaguar's mouth, the Sacred Tree, *Xibalba be*—all of these mytho-astronomical concepts point to the same location: the dark-rift in the Milky Way. In its deepest meanings, the dark-rift is a place of connection between life and death, the Earth and the Underworld—a place where Creation occurs. It is the portal to the Otherworld and a birth-death nexus. The dark-rift is a central player in the Maya myth of cosmogenesis, as well as in the precession-caused astronomical alignment that culminates in A.D. 2012....
>
> On 13.0.0.0.0, December 21, 2012, the December solstice sun is dead center in the *Xibalba be*, right at the crossing point of Creation in Sagittarius. The December solstice sun is First Father and the Milky Way is Cosmic Mother. Mythologically speaking, on this date First Father and Cosmic Mother are joined. Actually, it might be more accurate to say that Cosmic Mother rebirths Cosmic Father, our star, the sun. Here we see a reflection of a very ancient cosmogonic Creation myth, attributable to a substratum of history prior to patriarchal overlay: The Cosmic Mother is the head-point of a trinity involving the birth of a male deity who is also her mate. This Trinity principle involves the dynamic between mother, father, and child, and shares with many Old World traditions the idea that the Great Mother, as the first principle of Creation, must give birth to her mate, First Father, and only then can engender the multiplicity of created beings. On the cosmic level, the astronomical trinity is Galactic Center, solstice sun, and humanity....
>
> For the ancient Izapans[61] and the early Maya, and in the earliest version of the Long Count-Popol Vuh Creation myth, Creation occurs on 13.0.0.0.0, December 21, 2012, when First Father and first Mother join forces to engender a new World Age.[62]

To fully appreciate the preceding, we need to understand a few facts about the earth; its relationship to the sky and our own galaxy—the Milky Way:

- The ecliptic is the path traveled by the sun, moon, and planets through the sky. Twelve constellations lie along the ecliptic, and the sun passes through all twelve during the course of one year. The ecliptic crosses over the Milky Way at a 60° angle near the constellation Sagittarius. As such, it forms a cross with the Milky Way, and this cosmic cross was called the Sacred Tree by the ancient Maya. (The cross form was also known as the "crossroads.") Amazingly, the center of this cosmic cross, that is, right where the ecliptic crosses over the Milky Way, *is exactly where the December solstice sun will be in A.D. 2012.* This alignment occurs only once every 25,800 years.

- The Milky Way is observed as a bright, wide band of stars arching through the sky. In the clear skies of ancient Mesoamerica, many dark, blotchy areas could be observed along the Milky Way's length. These are "dark-cloud" formations caused by interstellar dust. The most prominent of these is called the "dark-rift" or the "Great Cleft" of the Milky Way. It looks like a dark road running along the Milky Way, and it points right at the cosmic crossing point, the center of the Maya Sacred Tree, right where the sun will be in 2012! The Maya called this dark-rift the Black Road, or the Road to the Underworld. They seem to have imagined it as a portal to another world, and the December solstice sun can enter it only in A.D. 2012.

- The area of the sky where all of these symbols and celestial objects converge is the center of our Milky Way Galaxy.... The part of the Milky Way that the December solstice sun will conjunct is also where the center of our Galaxy (the Galactic Center) is located. It is the cosmic womb from which new stars are born, and from which everything in our Galaxy, including humans, came.[63]

2012 is a time of ending and a time of beginning, a moment of death and a moment of birth, the birth of a New Age—the Sixth Sun. There is a transitional period of time between the ending of an Age and the beginning of another just as we experience transitional periods of time every day—dusk and dawn. These are daily times when the veil between our world and the Otherworld is at its thinnest. Dusk and dawn are magical moments just as all transitional times seem to be. But what about the transition from the end of an Age to the beginning of another? If Cosmic Mother is re-birthing Cosmic Father—our sun, what will the birthing time be like? What will our dream be?

Dreaming

Life is but a dream; however the dream, which I call our earthly dream, is real and one of our own making. Each one of us dreams or, if you will, observes and by the pure act of observing, sees life based on a collection of thoughts (i.e. assumptions, beliefs, and expectations). For example, if, based on our thinking, we 'see' rain as a wondrous occurrence that brings growth and life to our planet, then for us, the reality of a rainy day — our 'dream' of that day — is positive and beautiful. If our mind is not in the present, but in the future worrying about something, then our reality will be based on this 'dream' of the future, not the 'dream' of the present. Consider your beliefs, assumptions and expectations and see how they form your sense of reality. Then reason if you would like to change your mode of thinking. The focus and thoughts of your mind determine your reality; simple, but also profound!

Our earthly dream is also a part of the heaven's dream and involves our soul's destiny and purpose. Heaven's dream for us is locked away within our heart. To fulfill this dream we must listen to our hearts and walk our path on earth in harmony and with purpose. This is our *Ollin* heart.

The one purpose that we each share together is to evolve our soul in love's light. However, each of us has a different destiny in which our purpose is fulfilled. It is this destiny that we need to discover. Our soul knows; we just need to listen.

Night Dreaming

Dreaming is a universal aspect of Creation. It connects us to the Oneness of all things. Because of this, our dreams during sleep may be a doorway, a gate, to increased knowledge and power. Many cultures believe in this power of the dream:

> In dreams, we had ways of telling ourselves simple truths. These were things we needed to tend to but had put aside or forgotten. Dreams were the spiritual self speaking to the body. Messages were often simple and to the point....
> Dreams were useful as ways to learn lessons begun in the day,

and a problem taken to bed could be solved when you awoke in the morning. Forgotten facts could be brought to mind, chants and songs learned. It was very useful.

Dreams of flying were spiritual dreams. These were dreams beyond the earth state. They were of an eternal nature and of many lifetimes. It was a returning to the condition and place (state) where we were between lifetimes. We were with our spirit family.[64]

As we can see, night dreaming is one of the ways that our soul speaks to us. Ironically enough, how many people have a problem falling asleep and/or do not sleep well throughout the night? Sleep problems equal soul problems. The stresses of modern society have caused many of us not to sleep well and to lose our connection to the dreamtime.[65] In order to dream, we need sound, natural sleep. Nighttime, during darkness, is a time when our spirits return to heaven in a sense, shall we say, to be recharged.

One of the reasons that sleep is such a problem is that we consistently bring our worries with us into the evening and the night, instead of letting them go at the end of the day. And in our ego-arrogant world, many work late into the night sacrificing family and home for materialistic goods.

The end of the day when the sun metaphorically dies is the time for our daily forgiveness and for learning the lessons of the day. Then we are able to enjoy the evening interacting with ourselves, our friends, our family and other loved ones. When we spend our evenings in peace and harmony, we sleep soundly and arise refreshed and excited as we enter a new day.

The following are a few guidelines that will help empower your night dreaming:

1. Buy or make a 'dream journal.' Keep it right next to your bed to record your dreams as soon as you wake up. Share your dreams regularly with someone you trust.
2. Reduce stress in your life and/or practice relaxation exercises. Make sure your eating patterns include plenty of B-vitamins, which help to both relieve stress and assist in dreaming.
3. When you wake up and can't recall a dream, move back into the body position you were in while you were dreaming, to help reenter the dream.

Conscious Dreaming

Night dreaming is not the only dream tool available to us. We have the grand ability to consciously dream. Conscious dreaming is accomplished through a 'journey of spirit.' To dream this way, though, we have to recover something that has possibly been lost and belittled in society today —the imagination. Too many of us have lost the bliss of our imagination — that wondrous ability to imagine what may seem impossible, and then make the impossible happen through our belief, love and power. People have lost the ageless knowledge and their song (their voice in the world), because they've lost the ability to imagine the great dreams.

We dream using our imagination. Remember that reality is a dream! But it's a "real" dream, because we each manifest the dream through our beliefs, assumptions and expectations. To achieve the ideal state as a Feathered Serpent, it is very important for us to see the possibilities in life and then to learn the skills of dreaming. There was an ancient shamanic belief that in this world, there are the ones who are being dreamed, and then there are the dreamers. We must be the dreamers. Like the spiritual leaders of the past, the lords of the imaginary realms—the shaman-priests, we must learn to dream the impossible and then make it a reality.

Creative Imagination—Mind/Body Link

As a Feathered Serpent, we need to work with the power of the mind to become a 'person of power.' A 'strong mind' is essential to our journey through the medicine wheel. Our spiritual quest is directly linked to the strength of our mind and its relationship to our body. Taking the images in the mind and manifesting them in physical reality is the key to exercising the creative power of imagination. This can only be accomplished by maintaining a harmonious interplay between mind and body as well as body and mind. The body has been identified as the 'temple' of our spirit. In other words, the health and well-being of our body directly affects the health and well-being of our mind. The mind and the body are linked together and are the sources of our power.

A 'strong mind' utilizes creative imagination. To the shamans of the past, a 'strong mind' was the key to their journeys of spirit to the worlds beyond this world of matter. These 'imaginary worlds' are usually connected by the World Tree, the mythical *axis mundi* that is at the center of all things and connects three primary worlds—the Upper, Middle and Lower. These worlds are as real to a 'person of power' as this world is to all others. The 'magical flight' to these worlds is only limited by the parameters of the shaman's imagination.

Reality is a product of our mind. Our sub-conscious mind does not distinguish between what is tangible in our reality and what is imagined in our minds. Because all our perceptions are filtered through the sub-conscious, 'imagination' and 'reality' are indistinguishable. Whatever images are in our mind is a reality to our sub-conscious and directly affects our body. This is the interaction and healing power of the mind and the body. To the sub-conscious all is reality.

How our mind affects our body is illustrated by the following exercise:

- Sitting in a comfortable position, slowly close your eyes, focus your attention on your breathing and take long slow breaths from your stomach. After a few seconds focus your attention on the following image in your mind: butterflies flying and landing on bushes and flowers in a beautiful garden overlooking a crystal clear blue-green sea with a brilliant blue sky with white clouds slowly moving through the air. Let this image expand in your own way. After a few minutes, open your eyes and feel how relaxed and at peace your body feels - This is the positive power of imagination!

- Next, stand up and close your eyes. Now imagine in your mind an argument with your partner or your closest friend; see shouting, critical words, etc. Let this image expand, as you like. After a few minutes, open your eyes and feel the tension in your body. This is the negative power of imagination!

- Now, to put you back in a positive state, re-imagine the first scene.

To experience how our body affects our mind, try these two exercises:

- Over-eat a very high fat meal and then sit and do nothing. How do you feel? – (Like an average American!)

- Eat a very light meal (a salad and very little dressing) and then go for a walk. How do you feel?

Journey of Spirit

Conscious dreaming, or what I call a 'journey of spirit,' utilizes the imagination. Please be sure to let go of any of your old, negative messages about imagination. Some people fear that they can't or won't be successful journeying with their mind, imagining, or visualizing. This is not so. Everyone can do conscious dreaming. The following exercises will help you to understand this:

> First, be assured that you can imagine, meditate, dream, and journey. Right now, close your eyes and see your car, or a friend's car. Use all of your senses. What color is it? What type of car is it? What does it sound like? What does it feel like? What does it smell like? When was the last time you were in it? See yourself now in this car using all of your senses. This is what a journey of spirit is all about — it is as simple as imagining this car!

To help guide you in conscious dreaming, I have included a foundation journey of spirit in Appendix 4. When you feel ready, please do this journey.

First Attention/Second Attention

If our basic patterns of life are based on our 'first attention,' what then is 'first attention?' You may have heard of the expression, 'energy flows where attention goes.' Repetitive energy flow, a constant focus of our mind and our thoughts will establish a belief about life—about the earth, nature, others, and ourselves. It will erect core beliefs about all kinds of things including life, death and religion. From these core beliefs, our rules of life, assumptions and attitudes will be formed.

Each of us is more of a product of our past than we even realize. Troubling behaviors become ignored or unconscious in our stress-filled hectic materialistic lives. In addition, these behaviors are connected to our basic rules of life or belief system. All are a result of our 'first attention.' This is where our patterns of life were formed growing-up.

However, our 'first attention' is not solely restricted to our early life or adolescence, but can occur as an adult as we buy into the 'dream' of society and turn our attention to its message, which is, in today's world: work, consume, waste, and quantity over quality. Is it any wonder that we have an epidemic of obesity in children?

There are positive aspects of our 'first attention' that may provide power and love to us later on as adults. The soft-nurturing touch of a grandparent can manifest later on in life as a compassionate awareness of other people's struggles through life. But the sexually inappropriate touch of a parent is wounding and potentially leaves a legacy of betrayal and fear as 'first attention;' this pattern of being will be destructive to the child, even as an adult, and can affect others connected with him or her. The number of 'first attentions' that are potentially destructive to us as adults may be just a few, but on the other hand, there may be many.

All of our reality comes from our mind. By transforming our 'first attention' to a 'second attention', we will change our patterns, our rules of life and our beliefs, which will eventually transform us into a Feathered Serpent. As we see more of life from a 'second attention,' we begin to develop a 'second sight.' You could call this 'shamanic sight.' And one of the signs of it is the 'vibrant coloration' of nature. Things will begin to seem more alive, more colorful; the world takes on a different vibrancy and sheen. And you'll begin to see things in a symbolic instead of a literal way. It is awesome to be so connected to all things.

To begin achieving this 'second sight' and to consciously change our 'first attention,' we must have an awareness of who we are, what our beliefs are and what are our rules of life. Usually the greatest 'first attention' that we accept is fear. The opposite emotion from fear is the emotion of love.

In our quest to become a person of power, our 'second attention' will not be on fear, but on love, a fearless spirit and being *pono*, a state of being where fear has no place to reside.

Pono

The Hawaiian concept of *pono* refers to a balanced state of mind and heart—harmony. *Pono* also means being in harmony with others, nature and the spirit world. Illness comes from losing our natural state of *pono*. Restoring harmony restores health. Speaking, thinking and acting properly are the keys to wellness and maintaining *pono*.

Keeping ourselves and our relations (all other things) in harmony is essential for us in our journey of awakening and becoming a Feathered Serpent. Harmony, however, seemingly is a foreign concept in our out-of-balance world of work, work, and more work. Fear of lose, fear of terrorism and just, fear of being, keeps the masses of humanity out-of-balance and at a moons-length distance from being *pono*.

Terrorist acts are not under our control. What is within our power is how we think and respond to things that upset our balance and harmony. Worrying about terrorism is an act in futility and only keeps us out of harmony with ourselves and all others. What we do need to focus on (second attention) is speaking, thinking and acting properly so that we may re-establish *pono* with ourselves and other divine human beings:

> Perhaps the importance of harmony in relationships can best be summed up by the attributes of the word *aloha*. This often-used Hawaiian word expresses love and also is a greeting and a farewell. More subtly, it suggests the highly valued character traits of generosity, friendliness, patience, and productivity. The spirit of *aloha* carries with it an understanding that the ability to soothe and prevent conflicts, shame, and other disruptive occurrences is important, and that if the harmony has been disrupted, one should have the courage to ask for and give forgiveness.[66]

As demonstrated above, I feel that the Hawaiians developed one of the best practices for preventing as well as resolving conflict and thus restoring *pono* called *ho'oponopono*:

> A rich body of knowledge about the physical, emotional, and spiritual well-being of an individual in relationship to family, community, and environment has existed in the Hawaiian culture for centuries. One of the specific practices is a complex system for maintaining harmonious relationships and resolving conflict within the extended family; this system is called *ho'oponopono* (pronounced, hō'ō pōnō pōnō), which means "setting to right."[67]

Please see Appendix 5 on how to conduct *ho'oponopono*. Restoring harmony within ourselves allows us to express a fearless spirit in our quest to become a Feathered Serpent.

CONTINUATION OF THE FEATHERED SERPENT CHRONICLES

The Vision—October of the Year 1993 Common Era

It has been five solar years since Balamcoatl was initiated by don Cardo on the mysterious plateau of Markawasi. After leaving the Land of the Condor, Balamcoatl had sought out various wizards and reclusive elders in many different lands and islands, such as the Northwest Coast of the Cedar and Salmon people, the lands of the Bat people, the jungle lands of Jaguar Magic and the islands of 'Tahiti Na'—the tranquil Land of Dawn.

It was to 'Tahiti Na' that Balamcoatl came to in the fall of 1993 as leader of a group of spiritual seekers. 'Tahiti Na,' a grouping of eight islands, was known for their mystical magic-users and healers called *Tahuna*, meaning 'guardian of the secret.' It was rumored that the *Tahuna* were some of the most powerful wizards known throughout the lands of the four winds. Their healing and magical arts were known to be able to mend broken bones as well as influence the actions of sea creatures, the wind and the waves. But there was also a deep and dark side to some of these wizards; many were feared.

It was for these reasons that Balamcoatl had first voyaged to these islands so many years past, only to return again and again, ever seeking more knowledge and power. Even though he had apprenticed with the most powerful medicine doctor known alive, a master shaman-priest of the Cedar and Salmon people, Balamcoatl still had a restless and adventurous nature. This drove him to seek out and to explore the power and the knowledge of the other cultures' healing wizards, a trait others would view as ridiculous. They would want to only study one culture's magic. But not Balamcoatl; he felt the need to discover the 'first knowledge' or the ancient root knowledge that had been forgotten, or even worse, that had been suppressed, manipulated and/or changed.

As I breathed deeply of the salt air, I was overly ecstatic that I had returned to the islands of 'Tahiti Na,' especially to the isle of the volcano goddess. The previous year I had been drawn to this island of fire and water after having spent much time in the past on the rainbow isle and the valley isle. Each island of 'Tahiti Na' is different, energetically and emotionally. Some say that each isle is linked to a chakra—a name used for an energy vortex.

I had felt a connection with the Land of the Condor; but these islands felt as if they were part of my essence: fire, water and wind, all elements that made my heart smile. It was a land that I loved; a paradise permeated throughout with beauty, mystery and power.

Sometimes the mysteries of life seem unfathomable as I was supposed to have been leading a group of seekers to the Island of the Rising Sun, not to 'Tahiti Na.' But at the last moment, the person whom I was working with there cancelled in a most mysterious way. For whatever reason, I was destined to be here and not there.

On this journey, I was being assisted by my wife and our two adult children. Family, the *ohana*, was very important to these islanders as it was to me. It stood for unity, love and always loyalty. The *ohana* referred to an extended family ideal, which included not only the immediate family of mother, father, children and grandparents but also all things of the land, the sea and the sky. The *ohana* also included the ancestor spirits—the *'aumākua*.

I had arrived on the volcanic isle ahead of the group and my family to be able to spend some time alone with my friend *Kuamoo*, a *tahuna* and 'keeper of the sacred healing pools.' We had experienced many adventures together the year before. That year, my wife, *Kuamoo* and I had taken a group of seekers to witness the volcano goddess giving birth. It was a moment in time that words could never really describe. To be able to witness the power of the creation of new earth, which I deemed 'baby earth,' as it merged with the sea is a memory that will stay with us and impact us for the totality of our existence. This was only one of many such adventures that we shared together that year.

Shortly after I had arrived, I conducted what these islanders call *ho-okupu*. This is a ritual of gifting and honoring. I included prayers honoring the land, the people, the *'aumākua* and the *akua* as well as asking for permission to do my spirit work, guidance and protection for myself, my family, the seekers and *Kuamoo*. My gifting was a flower. *Ho-okupu* means 'to cause growth' as well as 'ceremonial gift-giving.' It could be a flower (something organic) or as simple as a prayer with the intent of giving something unconditionally back to the land and to the unseen and seen sacred ones.

As I finished my 'gift giving,' I turned around and saw *Kuamoo* approaching. As usual, he was a few hours late.

All the while, just behind the thinnest of veils that separated the natural from the supernatural, soared Regulus; as always keeping watch over Balamcoatl. Once again Regulus was not alone. Next to him/her was a form as brilliant as an archangel; a guardian of these isles—*Tu*.

"The time has come," said Regulus, speaking through his/her mind to *Tu*. "He is ready to learn who he is. His message will also become much clearer to him.

"When it is right, I will send one of my ancestors to *Kuamoo* with a message for Balamcoatl," replied *Tu*.

"You realize that there are ones locked on these islands in spirit form," said Regulus.

"You mean the spirits who still linger around the ruins. The ones who haunt the sacrificial temples, the *heiau*," Said *Tu*.

"Yes."

"*Aloha*, my brother," *Kuamoo* said as he embraced and hugged me.

"*Aloha, Kuamoo*," I replied as I felt his breath and the warmth and loving spirit emanating off of him.

Aloha means that I acknowledge the creator within you as you acknowledge the creator within me. *Alo* means 'in the presence of' and *Ha* is 'the breath of life/creation.' *Aloha* spirit is the spirit of oneness and the love that is the breath of the soul. It is a loving state of mind where hate has no resting place. To these islanders *aloha* represented love. All of life was founded on this love, the love of the sea, the love of the sky and the love of the land, and all its inhabitants. And to these beautiful people, the greatest earthly expression of this love was the love of family, the *ohana*.

"*Howzit,*[68] *brah*[69]? Sorry I was late. Have you been waiting long?"

Time has a different meaning to these islanders. They are not slaves to the human paradigm of 'being on time.' They are so closely connected to the rhythms of nature that society's human imposed time constraints do not matter to them. What matters is the present moment; not being a 'time-slave' that is so soul-destroying and destructive to one's sense of balance or being *pono*.

"I'm back on the islands so mainland time doesn't really matter, does it?" I replied.

"Right on, *brah*. Man, it's good to see you again… you been *pono, brah*?"

Pono is a balanced state of mind and heart—harmony. It also means being in harmony with others, nature and the spirit world. Illness comes from losing our natural state of *pono*. Restoring harmony restores health. Speaking, thinking and acting properly are the keys to wellness and maintaining *pono*.

"Most of the time *Kuamoo*, but as you know, being *pono* with nature and the spirit world is easy. Staying *pono* with humans is not so easy."

"You telling me… wife especially. And kids."

"How's your family?"

"All good... they're on the other side of the island. We're going to be staying at my place on this side. You and I got some work to do before your group comes. I feel this journey could be big experience."

For the next two days, *Kuamoo* and I traded stories and teachings while spending the majority of our time at the place known as the Refuge. Its formal name is *Pu'uhonua o Honaunau*. As a refuge it provided a place where a person would be given a second-chance at life. This place of forgiveness was located on the ocean and contained the healing pools that were part of *Kuamoo's* medicine. The ocean and its salt water are a continuous source of healing medicine for these islanders.

After my son arrived, the three of us began an adventure that preceded the arrival of our group. Our first destination was the 'white sand beach' before we headed to an ancient, and no longer populated, fishing village.

"People from mainland are so up-tight, *brah*," *Kuamoo* said as we walked quickly over the white hot sand. "This sand would help them heal. Let them experience what is to be relaxed... to be loose, *brah*... like 'hang loose.' I'm going to show you both old-time healing methods using this sand... then we're off to the fishing village."

It was one of those beautiful days that lovingly vibrate to the depths of one's soul. We spent time looking, listening and mimicking *Kuamoo's* actions and knowledge. This is one of the key philosophies of the *tahuna*— *Nānā ka maka, ho'olohe, pa'a ka waha, ho'opili*: observe, listen, keep mouth shut, mimic, mimic and mimic. After a few hours, including time in the surf, we headed for the fishing village.

Calling it a fishing village does not reveal its true identity. Yes, the village sustained itself through fishing, but the primary purpose of the village was as a gathering place for practitioners, students and teachers of the healing arts. It dated back some 600 years when magic was a way of life. The village was deserted when we arrived and only the sound of the wind and the surf broke the silence that surrounded us. Ever present *Tane*, the sun, warmed us with its hot embrace. *Tane* of the west was one of the four major deities of these islands. The others were: *Rono*—lord of the east, *Tu*—lord of north and *Tanaroa*—lord of the south and the deep seas.

"*Haku, Honu* much *mana*[70] here," *Kuamoo* said to us as he waved his hand in a sweeping motion from the sea to the snow-covered peak in the distance.

He insisted on calling me and my son by different names from our mainland ones. It was not much of a stretch for me having a different name. I already had been known by other names such as the Inka, the 'big cat that flies,' and even the 'puma that smiles,' which was a name given to me by a grandmaster of the mystical warrior arts from the Island of the Rising Sun.

But I did wonder why *Kuamoo* always called me *Haku*. My son did not have to wonder about his name. He liked being called *Honu*, which meant sea turtle. He loved the sea and he loved turtles. It was a good name for him.

As we walked the pathways that crisscrossed the ancient village, I replied to *Kuamoo*, "I also feel the power. Man, what a sacred place this is to learn and to heal."

Soon we arrived at a ledge that overlooked Grandmother Ocean. "Here *brah*, good spot to meditate, to pray," *Kuamoo* said as we each took a seat on the rocky ledge.

Time passed; images came and went in my mind as the veil between the worlds became thinner and thinner. After a period of time, I was back in the present hearing the surf and feeling the hot breath of *Tane* on the side of my face. As my eyes slowly opened, adjusting themselves to the light and to this reality, peace and happiness settled on me as if a mantle of *lehua* blossoms were a part of my soul.

"Pretty awesome, eh," said *Kuamoo* who was sitting on my right a few feet away.

"It sure is," said *Honu* who was sitting on my left. "I could live here with no problem."

"Right on, *brah*, I could too," replied *Kuamoo*.

A few minutes passed in silence. And then I turned to *Kuamoo* and said, "There is something I need to ask you."

"*Kay den,*[71] *brah.*"

"There is a ceremony that I would like to perform for these islands and your ancestors. It's called a 'burning.' It's an honoring and blessing to the land, the sea and your people. It's also called 'feeding the spirits'—the ancestors, the ones that have passed-over, the unknown-forgotten ones. "

"You do this for my people?"

"Of course I would. I'd be privileged to," I replied. "However, there is one condition."

"A condition?"

"Yes, once the day of the burning is determined, it can not be changed, no matter what happens—earthquakes, eruptions—the burning must be done."

"No problem, *Haku*," replied *Kuamoo*.

A few seconds flew by before I replied to *Kuamoo*. But before that could happen, a bat came out of nowhere flying towards us, circled us, and left!

"Did you see that? That's a great sign, *brah*. Bats don't come out during the day; *Tane* is too bright. Bat only likes *Hina's*[72] light," said *Kuamoo*. "This one came to show us that this journey is a blessed one—nothing will stand in our way. We'll be able to flow around any obstacles, physical or otherwise just like this bat… that uses that thing…."

"You mean radar," I said.

"Yea, *brah*; that's it. This journey is special."

I spent the next few minutes explaining to *Kuamoo* the burning ceremony. He was touched to the core of his soul that we would be willing to do this type of sacred blessing for his people. He explained that this ceremonial way was a part of the island spiritual tradition centuries past, but was a lost art and seldom practiced today. We both decided that the perfect site to conduct the "burning" was the City of Refuge.

"The Refuge it is," said *Kuamoo*. "We'll ask my cousin that works there permission to do the burning."

"I don't know… might be best not to ask and just do it."

"No worries, *brah*… I'll take care of it."

Our last stop of the day was to be at one of the sacrificial temples of these isles—*Mo'okini Heiau*. It was situated not too far from the fishing village, and it as well, over-looked the ocean. Even though it had been built as a temple honoring *Io*, the creator god of these islands, it had been changed into one that worshipped *Tu*, the war god. It was here where human sacrifice was practiced.

The temple had long been deserted, but that did not mean that it was uninhabited. Stones hold memories and destructive spirits may still linger in the inner recesses of such temple ruins. Caution, respect and common sense are important when approaching a *heiau*. And the proper prayers and offerings are not only necessary, but essential. Stones are never to be taken from a temple; not only out of respect, but also because they may carry memories that could adversely affect a human.

It was late afternoon when we arrived at the heiau; a time to be extra-cautious as it is the time when the spirits would begin awakening.

"I wanted to bring you here last year, *Haku*. You saw a dead *pueo*, owl, lying on the side of the road in the Puna district of this island. You and wife had me turn my car around to get it," said *Kuamoo*.

"*Pueo* are special to me," I replied.

"I know *brah*. The *pueo* is also special, *'aumakua*, to the *tahuna* that cares for this *heiau*. You may be connected to this temple. But we need to be careful."

As we approached the *heiau*, I knew that *Kuamoo* was doing prayers. No words were spoken as the three of us entered the ruins of the temple. Time suspended. And I had an un-easy feeling about this sacred area that at one time had witnessed the sacrifice of humans to 'feed' the war god. As we left the inner ruins, *Kuamoo* threw a stone into one of the open enclosures. All the while I felt that we were being watched by unseen eyes and followed. On the way back to our vehicle, I kept looking over my shoulder, expecting to see something at any time.

"One of the spirits stalks *Haku*," said *Tu*. "It senses his power and is curious."

"Yes it does," replied Regulus.

"Dad, that was intense," said *Honu*.

"*Brah*! Did you see my *'ōkala-chicken-skin*[73]...?" said *Kuamoo*.

"Mine too," I said. But I had a feeling that it was not the end of it.

"Getting late; we've got to get to the other side of the island."

"*Kuamoo*," I said. "Is there a place close by to get something to eat? We haven't had anything to eat since early morning and now its late afternoon."

"*Shoots*,[74] *brah*... not much around at this end of the island. There is a small village not far from here. We can try there."

Indeed, it was a very small village and only one small inn where a traveler might find some limited food and drink. And limited it was... we each settled on, really the only choice, some sort of meat patty squeezed between two slabs of bread. The whole time that we were waiting for our, I believe the innkeeper called it—meatloaf, I still had an unsettling feeling that we were not alone.

I was seated in the back of the vehicle while *Kuamoo* was driving and *Honu* was seated in the front next to him. *Honu* had the slabs of bread with the meat in-between in front with him. As *Kuamoo* took off, *Honu* started to pass the meatloaf bread back to me but instead, it flew out of his hand and landed on the seat next to me....

"*Ho brah*... you see that...," shouted *Kuamoo* as he slammed the vehicle to a sudden stop. "Something not right... that thing flew through the air...."

"Dad, it just jumped out of my hand… I'm sorry…."

"No need to be sorry, *Honu*. It wasn't your fault," I said as I picked up the meatloaf and put it back between the slabs of bread.

Kuamoo took off again. We were headed for his home on the east side of the island. As the time passed, no words were spoken. I had just finished eating half of my meatloaf bread, when *Kuamoo* slowed down the vehicle, pulled off the path that we had been following and said, "I want to stop and show you a beautiful view… of the sea and of *Waipi'o* Valley—a very sacred valley to my people. This is good lookout place."

I could see that indeed this was an awesome place to stop and feel the spirit and love of *'āina*—nature. *Kuamoo* and *Honu* were first out and were walking towards the edge of the cliff. I got out still clutching my meatloaf bread and was walking toward them when they both turned in my direction, as if to say something to me… when, all of a sudden, the meatloaf bread flew out of my hand and landed on the ground….

"*Ho brah…!*" exclaimed *Kuamoo* again.

"Dad, this is too weird…."

"Man… leave it on the ground… I thought that an *'uhane*[75] had followed us from the *heiau*… time to go…."

Two days passed and many other adventures unfolded on the other side, the east side, of the island… but those need to be told at another time. We were back on the west side and *Kuamoo* was determined to ask his cousin at *Pu'uhonua o Honaunau,* the Refuge, about conducting the burning. I still felt that it was seldom wise to cause a ripple in a clear and calm sea. The city is walled but the land outside of the walls is still considered part of the Refuge and sacred. It was here by the ocean that I had planned on conducting the ceremony, not within the confines of the walls.

Pu'uhonua o Honaunau, a place of sanctuary, peace and beauty, was situated on the volcanic coast south of the village called *Kailua-Kona*. This sanctuary was originally a sacred place that provided people with a second chance—a true place of forgiveness. It was here that people, who broke a *kapu* or sacred law, would flee for refuge. If they could reach the sanctuary, their life would be spared and all forgiven. This was and still is sacred ground where life can begin anew; a perfect place to honor and feed the ancestors and the spirits.

I'm no stranger to this most sacred of sites. The city, the lands and the ocean surrounding it speak to me of a time long lost in memory. Standing on this volcanic shore with the beauty of the ocean before me, I can tap into the awesome power of the elements in their virgin nature. It's a feeling that words cannot properly portray; only through the experience can you ever hope to pierce the veil that encompasses the mysteries of heaven and earth.

This land also holds the thoughts, the memories and the spirits of the island's ancestors, such a perfect place for the burning. I was sitting outside the Refuge under a coconut tree playing my *'Ohe Hano Ihu* – Nose Flute waiting for *Kuamoo* to return from asking the 'rangers' permission. This land and the Refuge were now protected by the mainland authorities and were designated as an historical park.

After I finished playing my flute, my mind traveled back to the time when a *tahuna* had been my teacher in making the nose flute. There were three things that I had to agree to before he would let me begin the making/teaching process:

1. I had to be able to make music on it before I left with it; if not he would burn the bamboo flute.
2. I had to vow to never put it away and play it regularly.
3. And last, I had to promise that I would share the music with others.

Soon as I finished these thoughts, I felt *Kuamoo* approaching. I stood to see what the answer was of the ranger.

"No can, *Haku*... you were right... my cousin said that all fires must be contained and also you need to apply for some permit."

"Did you tell him that it is a religious ceremony?"

"Yea, *brah*, but make no difference; have to follow rules of National Park Service."

"Well, heaven's rules out-trump park service rules. We still need to do the burning on Saturday afternoon... so we'll just go further down the beach."

"*Eh, geev 'um,*[76] *brah*... still be on sacred land and Park Service land... let's do-it."

My wife and daughter came ashore the next day along with our students. Anticipation was high as they all had heard me talk about *Kuamoo* and how powerful a healer he was. It was so good to see my wife and daughter.

After everyone was settled in to their own *hale*,[77] the four of us had some private time together without the presence of *Kuamoo* or our students.

"How was your time with *Kuamoo*?" asked *La'a Pua*. That was the name that *Kuamoo* called my wife. So it was the name that she used whenever she was on the islands and even sometimes on the mainland. It was a beautiful name; it meant sacred flower. And our daughter was called *Keiki Meli* or Baby Bee.

"You know him. It's always an experience; and did we have some experiences, right *Honu*?"

"Unbelievable Mom; bats during the day, flying food and spirits following us...."

"Come on, *Honu*," said *Keiki Meli*.

"It's all true, isn't it Dad?"

"All true and much more; but we'll share those stories later on. Now we need to go over the teachings and the burning that we're going to be doing tomorrow."

A burning or 'feeding the spirits' is a timeless ceremony that actually involves cooking food and then burning the food so that the substance and energy of it is taken into the Otherworld. This was human beings' original ceremony that honored, blessed and 'fed' the ancestors and the gods and goddesses of heaven and earth. However, over time this sacred pure ceremony had been corrupted. During certain past ages and in various cultures around the world this ceremonial rite had been perverted, resulting in humans becoming the sacrificial food for the 'gods.'

The day of the burning was spent collecting and preparing the food and offerings. It was important that we feed the proper food to the spirits. There were certain foods that were *kapu* or in mainland language, taboo.

It was late afternoon when we finally arrived at the Refuge. As a group we walked down the coastline until I felt that we were at the proper place to conduct the ceremony. It was still on the Refuge land but out of sight of the walled enclosure of the city. *La'a Pua* agreed that this was the right place for the burning.

As we began preparing the wood for the fire and the food offerings, a light rain began falling on us.

"*Haku, La'a Pua*, this is a very good sign," said *Kuamoo*. To these islanders, a light rain was a sign of blessing. "*Brah*, the ancestors are happy, they honoring us."

"I know, *Kuamoo*. I can feel them gathering. They have been waiting a long time for this ceremony."

Time became meaningless as I prepared to open the gateway to the Otherworld. Becoming one with all things of heaven and earth, I began the ceremony by calling in the ancestral spirits. It is not necessary or proper to describe the actual burning or feeding the ancestors. It is not to be known by a tale such as this, but must be experienced in person.

As I completed and ended the ceremony, a ranger from the Refuge appeared.

"*Brah*, he giving us s*tink eye*[78]... Let me go talk to him," said *Kuamoo*.

As *Kuamoo* approached the official, I could see that the ranger was eyeing the remains of the fire. And he didn't seem to be too happy about it. The energy ebbed and flowed between *Kuamoo* and the park ranger.

Kuamoo does have a temper and I was wondering if I needed to intercede like I did once before many years past. At that time, we had just finished *ho-okupu* for Madame *Pele*, the volcano goddess of these islands. Another park ranger had approached us and demanded payment for being on the land of the volcano. Of course, this didn't set right with *Kuamoo* as we were doing a religious ceremony. They almost came to blows before the ranger agreed that the rules were unjust.

Just as I completed these thoughts, *Kuamoo* and the ranger hugged and then parted. *Kuamoo* turned and walked towards us, all the while smiling.

"Amazing, we flowing—that bat *brah*... my cousin was much 'ripped' that we went ahead and did the fire without a permit and without it being enclosed. Then I told him what we did... this type of ceremony 'feeding and honoring' our ancestors. He was happy but couldn't believe that a *haole*[79] did this... but the most amazing thing is that he's going to try and get the rules changed so that this can be done again...."

After we had completed the burning and scattered the ashes of the fire around the base of one of the palm trees, we all returned to where we were staying to shower and then to share a meal together as an *ohana*.

We all retired early to our beds anticipating our journey the next day. We were going back to the white sand beach and the fishing village that *Kuamoo*, *Honu* and I had visited only days earlier.

Pre-Dawn the next morning... Am I asleep or awake? I sit up in bed, am I sitting or still lying; is this a dream or am I awake? The night sky before me.... that star, why is it shining brighter than any other? A Heavenly Voice—This Star is you; you are this Star! The great purification is of the people! All are one....

Am I asleep? I lie back down….

As I awoke Sunday morning, I was in awe with my pre-dawn experience. I was not sure if I dreamed it or if I was awake. The star was shining ever so brightly in the East. But what star was it? Who am I? What does this mean?

I briefly shared my experience with *La'a Pua*. We only had a short time before we needed to gather our *ohana* together and depart for the white sand beach. She suggested that I share the vision, as she called it, with *Kuamoo* and get his feedback. I agreed that I needed to ask him his opinion.

Kuamoo and I were both standing in the surf of the white sand beach facing the ocean. There's one hard and fast rule on these islands—never turn your back to Grandmother—the ocean. It was one of those most beautiful late mornings on the islands. The sky was a brilliant blue touched throughout with white fluffy clouds.

A short distance away our students were relaxing and swimming. *Kuamoo* had taught them the same healing techniques that he had shown *Honu* and me a few days before. We had a few minutes to talk before we needed to continue on to the fishing village.

"*Kuamoo*," I said.

"*Brah*, I got something big to tell you," answered *Kuamoo*.

Before I could reply, he began explaining what he meant.

"That burning… it was powerful, *brah*… more than I thought it would be. After you had called in the spirits one of my ancestors came to me… dressed in full warrior regalia—*'Ahu'ula*[80] and *Mahiole*.[81] This is big, *brah*. Mostly, ancestors don't come to us like this…."

He paused, staring out to sea before he continued.

"My ancestor brought me a message… but it's for you… *brah*, my ancestor said that you are a *tahuna po'o*[82]… *Haku*, you a prophet bringing back 'first knowledge'—the lost knowledge and sacred teachings that have been mis-understood, forgotten and corrupted… you have a message, path and way to share with this world… do not identify it as being from these islands or other lands… that separates people—knowledge all the same… don't get discouraged… it's your destiny… you the one, *brah*."

I was amazed, but in my heart, I had always known the truth of what *Kuamoo* was saying. It's sometimes difficult to determine if it is your own truth from your heart or your ego speaking. To have it verified by another, as well as by the spirit world, was always important.

"My heart's touched *Kuamoo*. I also have something to tell you. Last night, really it was early this morning right before dawn, I had a vision as *La'a Pua* calls it." I then proceeded to tell him about the voice and what it said.

"*Brah*, you got big *mana*… that was a vision… but what star…?"

"I don't know, *Kuamoo*," I said.

"In the East, brighter than the other stars… must be *Iao*![83] You know brah… *Haku* means master."

Now that you have heard a bit of my tale, let me relate to you, my dear friend, the teaching chronicles of Lord Regulus.

The Teaching Chronicles of the Feathered Serpent (Dragon) Lord Regulus as told to the Morning Star:

"It was a time after the Bright Vibration, what your world calls the Word, or the Big Bang, that we were birthed. But your word of birth does not really do justice to acts of creation. But alas I must impart these thoughts to you in a form that you may barely comprehend. I do not boast nor belittle your world and the race of humans, but you are still infants in the evolution of your souls' vibrations. You may refer to us as the Lords or as some of your world have called us—Feathered Serpents (Dragons). We are your 'wayshowers' and your protectors. You may only see us if your mind is not filled with fear or thundering with useless thoughts. And only then will we appear in the mist or at the breaking of dark or light. Look to the ones who know us—sadly there are only a few. They are our children, guiding where we may not guide. And they are the grandchildren of the Archangels, as you call them. The Archangels are our parents and they also look over and protect this world.

There is much wrong with your race as well as there is much right. Your minds hide behind the veil of fear and darkness, refusing the light, and shunning the ones who bring the light. You forget that you are stars, what you would call divine. And you think you are only human and the lone ones in all of Creation. Many of you follow the dogma and doctrines of others that keep you locked in fear and separate from your divinity, separate from humanity and separate from the wonders and beings of Creation. In the darkness, which is not only an illusion but reality, you see hundreds of specks of light. You are only witnessing a grain of sand out of all of the sand on your world.

You must tame your darkness. There is nothing that will harm you except your fear. The star that is you is within your heart. This is the key. We are waiting for you. We have your wings of light. But alas, it is up to you and if not...."

"Morning Star, please take this knowledge and share it with your world. Your race tends to hide behind a veil of darkness, separating themselves from their starlight and from each other and from their relatives: the trees, the rocks, the animals, the fishes, the birds and even the bees that bring the sweetness of life. This keeps them blind to the light of truth. All on your world and all worlds are conscious and are a part of the starlight that is also within you. When your people lovingly remove their veils, they will see once again and remember that your world is one family working towards a commonly shared destiny of light evolution. And when the veil is removed they will have a knowing of the timelessness of time. Time is always now; eternity is now; past and future are now. The ones who would keep you in fear teach that time is linear with a beginning and an ending. But there is no beginning, no ending, only now. The cycles of nature are windows to truth that we use as a teaching. But there are truly no cycle's, only spirals. Remove your veil for just an instant and you will see the illusion of linear and cyclical time. Each cycle is not a cycle but a spherical spiral of infinite proportions."

"Morning Star, your world is not the youngest of the entire ones that we guide and protect, but it is still young. Your world is not alone, just isolated. When you analyze your spiritual beliefs, you will understand that your race is not alone, only spiritually young. This is the beginning point of spiritual growth. It is the realization that you are a part of the One, but only a part of the whole not the whole. Only when you build your kingdom from this cornerstone will you know. You will see through the blind deception of what you call organized religion. Let your minds be free of this bondage.

Human minds are a source of freedom. But alas, many minds are imprisoned racing and thundering with their own illusion of 'self—the I.' Others on your world only see the 'We.' 'I' and 'We' are never separate. When your mind understands this that the 'I' is in the 'We' and the 'We' is in the 'I' then the illusions dispel, as does the fog in dawn's early light.

Your world is purified in creation's blink of an eye; but in your human time, only after many ages have passed. This purification has occurred numerous times in the life of your world. The last one was of water. Because it is the End of a Great Age, the next purification is of earth, water, fire and wind. Your race calls these elemental forces: earthquakes, tsunamis, volcanoes and hurricanes. As you are aware, the purification has already begun.

Because of greed and materialism, only thinking of the 'I,' your race has damaged your great Mother's skin. And now your great Mother and Father are purifying your world. But all do not have to suffer and die. Transform your ways and let go of the greed and materialism. Embrace the starlight that is within you and let your voice be heard. It will make a difference."

"Morning Star, you are bringing to your world a message of the divine spark that resides in all things—in all hearts. You call this divine humanity or as an honor to us, feathered-serpent.

Let your race know that the time for the next star evolution of your world is beginning now. Your race will call it the Sixth Sun, but we call it the time of the Awakening. Your race must awaken to this message by shedding their veils of darkness and accepting the mantle of light. It is your world's destiny. But the ones that are attached to greed, materialism and power will suffer. There are no chosen ones; all are equal. It is up to each human to choose his or her path. But again some are destined to choose the wrong path; it is in their soul's evolution to do so. This may not make sense. But it is the working ways of the Mystery.

Some will be in fear and doubt in accepting their divinity, not wanting the responsibility of what it means. The present religions of your world encourage fear and doubt for their own self-serving control. They do not teach self-responsibility or self-authority, desiring only the finite power inherent within the illusionary materialism of earthly structure and form.

Fear is the greatest motivator of your race. Fear is separation. Fear comes from your humanness. But light, what your race calls unconditional love, unites. This is not the light of your dualistic minds dark, but the light of love of creation 'that' is an oneness of being. It is pure consciousness. Divine unconditional love comes from your divinity. It is the opposite of fear."

"Words are empty and hollow without the manifestation intrinsic within their vibration. Talking truth is a seldom-used quality of your race. And your hearts are where your truth is stored. Many speak words out of fear and/or control. When your words match your heart, the starlight within you vibrates quicker and shines brighter. To see this starlight look within each other's eyes and when words are spoken, look to the eyes and you will see.

This is what we call the quickening, the surge of fire and ice. The old wise ones of your race referred to this as the heating. It is all the same. But the ones that use words that are cut off from their hearts and vibrate shadow-actions, will never reach the quickening. It is up to each one to speak, to see and to act in a right way with every breath of every moment.

Few who clothe themselves in the outer illusion of the world ever reach the quickening, caring too much for the power and control of their illusion. Do not be deceived with this illusion. The divinity, the starlight is within you.

Do not also be fooled by the ones that clothe themselves in the garments of God. They do not speak for God nor does a Book. You speak to God directly with each thought. You do not need to go through another human being or a finite institution acting as a gatekeeper between you and God. At any time you may directly drink of the waters of creation and know truth."

"Few have the courage or trust to know the fire and ice. The quickening is bliss but it only comes to those that speak pure and have a quiet mind. A mind that thunders will never discover the quickening or the peace that surrounds it. Why do so many hang on to the past, Morning Star? It is to be learned from and then, if need be, forgiven. It is not to be re-lived day after day, which only erodes the youthfulness of your soul's experience. There is no moment of Creation that is ever the same; yes, all are spirals and spheres but no spiral or sphere is eternally the same. Let your people ponder this.

Where is your mind at this moment? Is it in the present or in the past feeling guilt or anger? Or is it in the future with worry and fear? Where is your mind? Morning Star, help your people with what has been called by the wise ones an immovable mind. This is a mind that is totally aware but quiet and non-attached by the healthy ego. This is the opposite of the mind that thunders and attaches in servitude to the illusionary ego. That is enough...."

"One of the beauties of being on earth as a human being is your human emotion. It is the source of earthy love and joy. And it is the happiness and peace that comes from seeing nature in all of its wonder and beauty. But, unfortunately, there are also the other emotions; the ones that separate and cause conflict and strife. These only harden your soul to never seeing the earthly paradise. Morning Star, tell your people to never deny their emotions only to reduce the harmful ones and to increase the helpful ones.

The vibrations of your emotions allow you to experience the depths of humanness and the appreciation of divineness. But many of your race shut off their emotions hoping to protect themselves from the pain of the past; and the possible pain of the future. They seem to have forgotten the oneness of earthly existence. Without pain, there is no pleasure. The idea is not to resist the moment of emotional vibration; experience it and let it flow through you. If you resist, your body, mind and spirit sicken.

Your world refers to this resistance as stress. And your world is full of stress. Stress breaks down your natural harmony within and leads to the suffering that so many of you experience today.

Your body affects your mind and your mind affects your body. Every moment of your life is etched within your body and may or may not dream the dream of that moment. This is an opening to the afflictions that plague your race. Your eyes are the gateways to the mind but there are not just two, there are three. Only when the two are as pure as a baby's eyes and the third activated, will the body and mind lighten. And then, once again, there will be the original one eye that sees and knows all. This is first teaching, please contemplate this...."

"There is a consciousness in heaven. You may call it your heaven's mind. It is the awareness without the presence of ego and emotion, which you may call your earth's mind. Your people must trust this. It cannot be proven while on earth, but the greatest freedom that you have as divine human beings is the ability to believe in whatever you choose to believe. This is also a great power of the mind. But your mind my either free you or keep you chained to your greatest enemy, fear, the illusion that separates and causes misery. You must learn to trust. Due to human behavior, many of your race have had their trust broken many times. This directly affects your hearts. And your hearts are your lotus flowers. As they open, they remain un-soiled in your mud-filled world of corruption and destruction. You each may remain un-touched...."

"Stop looking externally for the causes of the heart problems that you term heart disease. Look within. You must first begin the process of mending your hearts through forgiveness, not only of others but also of yourself. You must let go of the emotional chains that are breaking your heart, and you must learn to trust once again. This provides faith in the workings of life, in whatever life may bring you. With trust and faith restored, you will begin to see yourself and the world through different eyes, confident eyes. This is the confidence of the heart not of the ego. As you forgive and lighten your heart, it will begin to blossom. Your heart, which is like a flower, will open, bringing beauty and love to all that you encounter.

As your heart opens and you begin to trust once again, you must face the fear of having your heart and trust broken once again. This is why courage is paramount and is of the heart not of the mind. Courage allows you to do away with boundaries. Boundaries and walls, figurative, imaginative or real, only separate and keep one's heart cold and barren. Your race loves boundaries. No part of the earth belongs to any one person or to any one nation. It is a materialistic illusion encouraged by the 'haves.'

With wisdom you will know that your race does not need boundaries due to the truth that your race has the capacity for enormous amounts of sharing, compassion and un-conditional love. But sadly it does not realize it. And that is why a few take advantage of the many.

Your religions separate even further; saying this section of the earth is holy but merely for us. This is about the 'I'—the ego and the great disease of your race—greed. All of the earth is holy and may be looked to for ceremony and guidance. Morning Star, anything that separates causes sickness and un-happiness and results in diseases of greed and materialism. This results in massive amounts of pain and suffering. Help your people become one—to become equal. They will then understand their purpose—healing the separation from God."

"Morning Star, I will attempt to tell you in human mythic terms how divinity became a part of everything in creation. This may help your race understand that not only is every human being a divine human with the light of God within them but all trees are divine trees, all animals are divine animals, the earth is divine earth; everything is divine as well as having its unique intrinsic expression:

A time long, long ago—a time when there was no time, even before the bright vibration, our Creator, God, the Great Mystery of all, was vexed in what was to come about. The expression of creation would be immense in relative terms to the created. It was to be and always to be that. But how to love and light, and hear the delicate vibration of the slightest but grandest created? How to equally care and watch over the vastness that was to be birthed? God, with the greatest divine love/light, would not create the uncreated, the un-pure. How to be that? And then... 'I am one and all shall be one. A part of me shall be within all created and each created may then know me forever and ever. But each will also be a unique, conscious, intrinsic created expression from the dimmest to the brightest vibration. All created will have my love/light within them. My created will speak to me directly with each vibration of their consciousness and my/their love/light may increase with their will and their choice. Their createdness will be separate but not; all one and always connected. They will know but not know. All a part of all; my love/light forever and ever.' And that is how it was, is and will be."

"There is a magic about being on earth. And that magic is what your race refers to as nature. All of nature has its own intrinsic divine light within, which as divine humans you may tap into and partake of for healing, joy, peace and oneness. Mother Nature is the greatest Magus of your world and may present to you her magic at any time. Ones who destroy nature destroy the magic and the protection that the magic provides. The skin of Mother Nature has been worn down by a few of your race in their beliefs and their greedy quest for earthly power and control. Many of your race put their trust and belief in scientific investigation that supposedly discovers truth through observation, analysis and reason. This has wrongly displaced the magic of nature and the magic trinity of contemplation, intuition and vision. Additionally, in their pursuit of earthly control, organized religion in an act of spiritual tyranny banished nature while science, in effect separates humanity even further from its roots, expelled God. No wonder the past millenniums of your world will be seen from the not so distant future as the 'Ages of Darkness.'

A world devoid of nature in partnership is one deeply embedded in spiritual ignorance and darkness. The dawn of each day is the awakening of love and light and presents the opportunity for humanity to evolve and involve themselves in the gifts of nature. Morning Star, the transition phases from dark to light and light to dark are the most powerful times for the knowing and the seeing of the Otherworlds. It is a time of spiritual power or natural power for the personal transformation of self. It is the magic time.

Nature in its yearly cycles portrays earthly existence. What you call spring is the birthing time for all, a new beginning on your world. This is followed by a period of growth and then a harvesting of that growth, and then at the dark of the year, an ending but also another beginning. The longest dark, what you call the winter solstice, teaches a most important spiritual lesson that in the darkest of dark, the light is always there and will always return. It is a time of celebration, a time of the letting go of the dark and returning to the light. It is a most important time. Many on your world celebrate it as the birth of their lightbringers, the sons or daughters of light. This is most appropriate, but teach your people, Morning Star that many times the true birth, the heavenly lineage, of the lightbringers occurs during the harvest under the sign of the virgin. However, the conception, the earthly lineage, happens sometime around the longest dark.

Many of your human race have separated themselves from nature in the so-called name of progress. This destroys the spirit within and leads to unresolved conflict within and without and eats away at the natural harmonizing aspect called the immune system. Many of your race are sick not only of body but of mind. To harm nature is to harm your race. To destroy nature is to destroy your race, as you know it. One of the greatest lessons to learn on earth is partnership... of yourself, of others and of nature—every tree, blade of grass, every animal of the earth, every bird of the skies, every fish and, yes, every insect and every stone that sits."

"Morning Star, your earth has many places that provide enormous amounts of spiritual power and energy. These are the areas that have a higher geomagnetic vibration. The mystery of one is coded within the two, the attraction of opposites and the repulsion of ones alike. This is a key to star travel but your race will never discover the gateway until they heal themselves and see their race as one as well as divine and human.

Your earth, your Mother, provides everything that is needed for your race's prosperity, health, well-being and evolution. But in the name of progress and power, you have chosen to look elsewhere. The geomagnetic vibration of nature can provide you, not only with healing but also with spiritual power and abilities previously unheard of. Look to the three pyramids to discover the navel of the earth. This is the connection to the past, present and future occurring now.

In its separation from nature, your race has gradually become sicker and sicker not only in body and mind but also in spirit. Your electro-magnetic noise is destroying your innate spiritual potentials and the proper functioning of your brains. Ones that do not heed this warning will lose memory and any semblance of intuition and vision.

Your quest in earthly life as divine humans is to lighten your heart and to birth the white stone. Morning Star, you have spoken before in dream of the white stone and the hidden manna. The potential of the white stone is within each person. It is referred to as the pineal gland. The fusing or the oneness of the quartz crystals that it is composed of births the white stone. And the hidden name is divine.

The spiritual seat of the soul is the heart while the spiritual gateway is the pineal gland. The serpent-fires fuse and open the gateway but your race has never learned and has been led astray from this internal fire of fires and thus only seeks the illusions of life."

"Morning Star, your race, as human, has a great gift of joy and grief. But alas in your race's quest for material external illusionary power, seldom do they know true joy or true grief. They fear and usually deny each emotion, never truly knowing either of them. These two emotions are the essence of human existence and provide the light to help each person understand the workings of life on earth. To feel the joy of life allows one to also feel and understand the grief of human existence. In joy there is the silent grief that the moment will never be again. But Morning Star in grief there is also the silent joy that the moment will never be again. To truly understand joy and grief is to know with one's heart and mind that life is everlasting and infinite. Our soul's essence is a spiraled journey, eternal in existence never an isolated moment in time.

Do not be lost in the so-called chaos of life; the stresses that wear and tear at your soul's brilliance. Embrace the joy of living, the joy of partnership, friendship and love and the joy that is the garden paradise called earth. Know joy, then when life happens, the mysteries of the why, let yourself know grief.

Morning Star, guide your race in understanding that when one is passing over, or as so many of you say—dying, this may also be a time to experience joy with each other, the joy of each other's presence, the simple joy of holding each other's hands, the joy of gazing into each other's eyes and the joy of each moment as a precious moment of eternity. And then when the loved one passes over, the grief can then be embraced, experienced, honored and released; in a way of love and power not in anger, guilt or resentment."

"A thought, a heartbeat; another thought, another heartbeat. What is reality? Is reality the thought, the heartbeat or is it the space between the thought, the heartbeat? The thought is created; the heartbeat is created but the space, Morning Star, ah that is the core of creation, the essence of potentiality, the moment of truth and light, the merging of the creator and the created. Your science looks to the thought, the heartbeat but not to the space. This is where the miracles occur. It is time but no time, a way to see beyond and know beyond and to go beyond. The space between is also the land of freedom, the opportunity to change a thought or to change a reality of fear and ugliness to one of beauty and love. As divine, you are the space between but as human, you are the thought, the heartbeat. Ask your race what they choose to do with the space between. It is their choice not ours."

"The double sight or second sight is the transcended knowledge of reality with 'baby eyes' being the transformational knowledge of oneness. Ignorance encourages the first sight or the illusionary reality of life where fear, anger, guilt, shame, doubt, greed, and all the earthly "isms" reign supreme. Human eyes judge and separate into boxes of illusionary filtered safety based on an imprinted past that controls a deluded present. Divine human eyes or 'baby eyes,' on the other hand, sees your world through the clarity of truth where there is only one race, human that is divine, in partnership with its self, the earth and all its creatures.

It is essential for your people to lovingly open their eyes and mind of God. Your eyes may 'eat' light or darkness, love or fear, the mind follows and absorbs this food of life or death, the body responds accordingly and finally your hands and month manifest either a hollow profane life or one that is spiritually fulfilled. As goes your mind, goes your heart and too many people's hearts are cold, broken and wrapped in a thread-less blanket of materialistic reality."

Under the eyes of heaven and earth, it is done! For now.
The Feathered Serpent (Dragon) Lord Regulus

THE JAGUAR PATH
OF THE WEST

ARCHETYPE: LUMINOUS WARRIOR
KEY PRINCIPLE: LOVE
TIME: THE PRESENT
COLOR: BLACK

Chapter 5
Mountains, Jungles and Valleys

As I have stated, *musha shugyo* is essential to us in becoming a person of power—a Feathered Serpent. Entering into the mountains, jungles and valleys, we become detached from the limitations of ordinary life. We step into the extraordinary, and it is in this space that we develop and grow our ideal and the 'heart that sees.' We have already begun to 'shed our armor' and to release our past, no longer seeing ourselves as who we have been, but who we are becoming. We now work in the present by facing our fears and releasing the doubts and uncertainties that we all harbor.

The present moment is lost to so many people that it has become a void filled with endless fear. The fear is hidden by an ego focused on the future and the supposed power and security associated with materialistic accumulation. The security of money and material things is illusionary, but a useful illusion to the ones in power. Manipulation of the ones in fear is a strategy of the ones in power that directs the attention of the fearful ones to a deceptive utopian goal of safety, security and salvation. The fears of the people also make possible an ongoing 'war on terror' and its ongoing erosion of personal liberty, all in the name of 'security.' The freedom of the present moment is blurred by a promise of a secure future.

If the present moment is at all times real and life-giving, and if the future always contains the specter of death, why then do so many people seem to focus on the future and not the present? The present is the only actuality of time that is real. However, time to most people is an interface between the past and the future—linear time. The present is not as important as the past or the future. But to a person of power, time is circular with the present moment being the center of the circle and thus the most powerful. The linear past and future are not as important or as real as the present moment. In our belief, the present moment also contains the past and future all occurring in the now; but do not be led in a false direction. This belief and concept is not as simple as it seems when we realize that each moment is never permanent—never to be exactly repeated.

Philosophical musings notwithstanding, as a person of power, we need to live in the present, only visiting the linear past to heal our woundings and to learn from our past mistakes. A person of power never 'lives' in the past, as so many people do, nor do we 'live' in the future, but only visit the potential future of who we are becoming. When we live our lives in the present moment, we release our souls from being ever haunted by the past or ever fearful of the unknown future. This is the power that we have within our grasp. Do not squander it.

More importantly, the present moment is a place of love and happiness. It is the magical moment that fills all of our senses with the smell of flowers and the sight of loved ones. It is beholding the awesomeness of a sunrise or a sunset and the beauty that surrounds us. It is the essence of life that so many miss in their stressed-out whirlwind of materialistic seeking. So many miss the present due to their 'chattering' mind—a mind that is constantly talking to itself. The awareness of the present is nowhere to be found. To be present is to be aware.

Awareness

Our minds are clouded with our chatter—a smoky mirror that is smudged with the unresolved past and the unknown, fearful future. At work our senses are dulled within an unnatural environment of glass and steel. Many leave for work in the dark and return as such, never to experience or feel for any length of time the healing presence of nature. The sun never shines on so many; it is no wonder that they are stressed-out and sick in heart, body and mind. People's hearts and minds are so filled with materialistic desires and details that they miss the wholeness and wonder of life. Rushing to and fro, the natural awareness found in childhood is but a memory long lost to consciousness.

But it is never too late. In our journey to become a Feathered Serpent, we must reclaim the power of the present moment and our natural, but hidden awareness. To accomplish this, however, requires us to be outside in nature without the interference of human pollution. We need to spend time in the mountains, jungles and valleys of the world as a part of nature, not separate from it. Extreme sports do not count, nor do activities that involve a recreational mindset where you walk, bike, hike, climb, etc over nature in a separate ego-based, conquering frame of mind. We need to be one with nature, not separate from it in an attempt to win, triumph over or over-come.

The awareness of the present moment comes through our senses. If our senses are dull, we experience little of the paradise and the banquet that is set before us. We need to 'look, listen and learn.' This is the key to power at all times. If, on the contrary, our mind is chattering, we will not truly see or truly hear. And if we are constantly talking, most damagingly on a cell-phone, our eyes become clouded and deluded while our mind becomes blocked to all sensory input. We miss life; we miss the paradise; we suffer needlessly.

Do not continue down the same path of life. In our journey to become a Feathered Serpent, being out in nature and being aware are essential to our growth, power and love. We need to sit and smell the ground beneath us. We must stand and gaze at the tree in its totality and then see the shape of the leaves, the texture of the bark and the bend of the limbs. We must crawl as a child on our Mother Earth while feeling, hearing and seeing with our hearts the crawling ones invisible and meaningless to most ego-warped people, but meaningful, visible and consequential to us. We must listen for the passage of the serpent and the buzzing of the bees. The more we use our senses, the more we will stay in the present; it is up to you. The choice is yours.

Safety and Security

Fear is a great motivator that many times precipitates an ego-based need for safety and security. If it is a present moment external stimuli such as a knife-wielding assailant, our basic survival response may be called into action or frozen into a fear-gutting inaction. But it is a reality of the moment. Fear for our safety or security, however, is usually not based on the present, but on the unknown future, which in many cases may be a construct of the past—our personal past or others. It could even be a past cultural paradigm or past societal event, such as the terrorist attack on New York City on 9/11/2001.

Safety, security and survival are all first chakra issues. The second chakra is based on our sense of inner power—our power within, while our third chakra deals with issues of external power—our power and place in the world. The awakening of our chakras, or the ascension of our serpent energy up our spine to merge with our divine energy and thus become a

Feathered Serpent, is done one step at a time. And the first step is dealing with the first chakra and its issues of safety, security and survival.

If we are still locked away within this base chakra then fear will rule our lives as well as lead us to develop various dysfunctional behaviors that are triggered by our core earthly survival/safety issues. These are all based on the separateness of our ego state. Everything is seen from the perspective of the 'I' without any regard to the 'We' of life—our connection to others and the creatures of the earth as well as the earth itself. This may give you some insight into the complex problems plaguing our earth as first chakra issues are not limited to survival, but also extend out to all of our basic needs, which may in fact give rise to the rampant materialism and greed running amok all over the world.

In the aftermath of traumatic events such as 9/11, people who are still burdened by a 'darkened' first chakra react not from their heart, but from their ego-mind. Revenge—getting even—is a first priority. This leads to a swirling cyclone of fear masked by anger and hate for the ones who are not like us or do not believe as we do. As a person of power, we have taken that first step of working with our first chakra issues and are ascending our energy out of the serpent's/dragon's cave of materialistic safety and security upward towards our hearts. The power is within us to achieve our own world of peace and harmony—we have the power to achieve what others only fantasize about.

Awareness for Survival and Renewal

2012—what does it have in store for us? It may be an unknown, but do not let it breed fear within you. Seasons come and go and so do the Ages of Humanity. This will be a time of cleansing, but in addition, it will be a time of righting the injustices and inequalities of the world. As a reader of this book, you may very well be one of the luminous warriors who will help locally or globally in this transition of Ages. Awareness is the key to survival and renewal.

There are knowledgeable legends that refer to a catastrophic earthly event, which has occurred at various pre-historic times, called a 'Pole Shift.' This is when the magnetic North and South Poles switch their polarity. From humanity's perspective, the sun would now rise in the West and set in the East. When the magnetic poles shift, it will affect many things including computers and our own bodies. But the greatest effect will be on the iron-rich magna within the earth. Sudden shifts of magna trigger earthquakes.

And as I mentioned before, according to the Maya prophecies, the Fifth Sun, our current age, will come to an end in 2012. It is prophesied that 'movement' will be the cause of the end of the Age. The prophecies tell that it will be a time of great earthquakes that will literally 'shake-up' the world as we know it. There will be a cleansing; but then, an awakening and a new earth—a new Age.

To be aware and knowledgeable is the first step in survival and the resultant renewal; to be otherwise is to be blinded by one's ego and to be stupid. Stupidity along with arrogance and fear are three of the soul's enemies. Usually stupidity is the cause of arrogance and fear. A sleeping spiritual state is a haven for stupidity. Look around and see how many people are in such a state of spiritual ignorance and poverty. As a person of power we are aware and knowledgeable and follow our deified heart, not our destructive ego.

The symbol for this Age of the Fifth Sun, as you know, is called *Ollin*, which means movement. Symbolically, *Ollin* refers to the 'movement' of our heart—a deified heart, a divine heart:

> The ordinary word for heart was *yollotl*, a word derived from *ollin*, movement. Thus the ordinary human heart is the moving, pumping organ that keeps us alive; but the heart that can be made by special efforts in life is called *Yoltéotl*, or deified. The phrase used to describe the face that we must make if we are to be truly men is *ixtli in yollotl*, which signifies a process whereby heart and face must combine. The heart must shine through the face before our features become reliable reflections of ourselves.
>
> Thus heart-making and face-making, the growth of spiritual strength, were two aspects of a single process which was the aim of life and which consisted in creating some firm and enduring centre from which it would be possible to operate as human beings....[84]

The Fifth Sun is viewed as the Fifth Direction—the symbolic center of the four winds of the Mesoamericans. Individually, our heart/our spiritual sun is at our center and it is the core of our being. Could this all mean that the key to our survival and renewal at the end of this Age is predicated on us achieving a 'heart that sees' and becoming a Feathered Serpent? I believe it is!

Stupidity

I am ever amazed at the number of people who seemingly do not consciously know their core beliefs and rules of life. People exhibit behaviors that are connected with these rules and beliefs without thinking about the results and legacy of their actions. Stupidity renders people blind to the foundation of their beliefs and severs the connection to their heart. Ignorance is bliss as the masses blindly follow the Shepard over the cliff of war, all in the name of security and prosperity.

Ignorance means the absence of heart-light or enlightenment. It is a lack of knowledge and wisdom that allows a person to practice ego-based beliefs that may ultimately cause pain and suffering to others. Stupidity is a mental dullness that separates the heart from the mind. Look around and see how many people go through life not only with a dullness of mind, but also a dullness of spirit. Additionally, stupidity creates incompetence and a lack of understanding about the true nature of things.

Our culture bombards people with information. This is the digital information age, is it not? But information without knowledge and wisdom dulls our mind and leads us to accept the information being fed to us without questioning the truth of the things that we are being told.

There is another insidious aspect of stupidity. It generates fear and arrogance. Just look around at the arrogance of so many Americans. Arrogant on the surface, but just gaze beneath their egotistical faces and you'll see fear.

Fear

What can be said? Fear is a reality of human existence. In a few instances it may help us in life by waking us out of a complacent stupor. On the other hand, our 'fight and/or flight' mechanism helps us deal effectively with fear that is connected with any life and death situation. But there is another category of fear. This fear by far is the most damaging to us. It is our worst enemy. It is insidious. Daily, it steals a part of our soul. It is the fear that separates—the fear of the unknown.

The fear of the unknown is the fear of death as well as a fear of life, which creates a sense of powerlessness within us. This may lead to dysfunctional behaviors that give rise to an illusionary impression of power. Fear-based belief systems thrive in such a cultural environment as ours. Terrorism is ever present in people's minds, and this fear drives people to accept the erosion of their freedoms, and to accept an unjust religious and greed-based war. This type of fear enlarges people's egos, as their minds need a secure sense of power. Have you noticed that people have even more 'attitude' today, as if they are the only ones who count, especially with people who they deem different from themselves? The rise of 'talk-radio' and cable-news has only fed the flames of separatism and elitism in America. The religious right is marching to its apocalyptic beat, sowing in its wake the seeds of fear, while spewing venom to those of different religious beliefs.

Fear is the opposite of divine love. It will keep us from our bliss and our *ollin* heart. It sees the world as a dangerous place, recognizing not the earthly paradise that is truly laid before us. Fear, in its innermost recesses, generates greed and the desire for materialistic accumulation. It is the breeding ground for external power and the abuses that go with that power. It is the curse, but then again, the salvation of humanity, as it has the potential to wake us out of the illusionary sleep of separation. When we let go of fear, we let go of separation; the veil is lifted and we see and know oneness of self and others. Our light has evolved.

In a culture and society ruled by fear, as a person of power, we must access the inner core of our strength—our heart, which will help us bring our fears out of the darkness and into the light. This transformational power, which we all have within us, fosters the courage for us to face fear. Confronting our fears, we are then able to let go of some, transform others, and finally make peace with the fears that we can't let go of or transform. It's normal and human to have fear, just never let it inhibit your life, keep you separate or keep you from your bliss. To conquer fear is to triumph over death. So what fears do you still harbor?

The Dark – The Underworld

The dark—symbolic of the unknown is an unsettling territory containing many people's fears. But without the dark, there would be no light. This is difficult for many to accept. They see life as a separation between the symbolic light and dark and never realize that they are both components of one reality. When we deny the dark, we leave the light in a vulnerable position in its so-called sole existence of truth. Seeking wholeness, the so-called light takes on the role of the dark through behaviors that are dysfunctional and abusive. Just witness the amount of sexual abuse within the Catholic Church. Denying the dark seemingly opens the gateway to abusive behaviors. But why is this?

Dualism encourages and supports a battle between the dark and the light—good and evil, Satan and God—while validating fear-based religious belief systems such as Christianity. If you believe in this nonsense, then there is no other option than to deny the dark as part of your own make-up. To do otherwise would acknowledge that Satan is at work within you. Of course, blaming your actions on Satan is a good and easy excuse and allows you to not take responsibility for your actions. Confession and absolution by the church are all that is needed.

Duality, on the other hand, recognizes the complementary interaction of the light and the dark—spirit and matter—as forces that make up the whole of existence that is held together and surrounded with another force, the force of creation or the love/light of God. There is no irreconcilable opposition at work here, only the spiraling creative unfolding or flowering of creation. And each one of us is a part of this flowering of 'who we are becoming.'

However, 'dark/destructive' behaviors do stand in the way of our flowering and accepting our place in the garden of paradise. These are not necessarily the things of nightmares, but are more commonly the emotional hindrances of fear, separation and the behaviors that result from them. Fear strangles love and generates patterns and behaviors within us that are often destructive to others and ourselves. These need to be recognized and released and/or transformed into the dark of creation—the fertile ground, the cave of potentiality—that exists within each of us.

This is the Underworld that may harbor our fears, but it is also the place of our potentiality and the birthing place of our heavenly, creative self. Have you ever wondered about the 'dark' behaviors of so many past and present creative people? The 'dark swallows many' who never realize or acknowledge that it is the source of their creative essence, but think that there is something different and/or wrong with them—thus the suicide, drug/alcohol abuse and other abusive patterns. And how about the many unknown others who give up their creative side, thinking that it is the only option to stop their 'dark' destructive behaviors?

In our journey to become a Feathered Serpent, we must have fierce courage to create, but not 'cave in' to the 'destructive dark' of our Underworld. We must all journey within the Underworld. It is not a place to shun as in the 'hell' of Christianity, but a place of creation, resurrection and salvation as we leave the dark to be re-born in the light. All cultural heroes at one time or another must pass through the Underworld. A hero/heroine cannot be birthed without this 'rite of passage!'

Rites of Passage

A portal of initiation, a moment of transformation, a death and a re-birth and a time of knowing immortality while still being mortal, these transcendent aspects only go so far as words can ever go in describing 'rites of passage.' Rites of passage are essential to the growth, development and spiritual evolution for every single divine human being. But such passages of courage are not given the spiritual importance that they deserve. For example, marriage is a loving and powerful rite of passage, but few in our fearful, quick-fix society see it as such and therefore honor the external more than the internal betrothal of two souls.

We began our journey of power with our passage into the unknown identified by the term *musha shugyo*. This is a journey that takes us into the mountains, jungles and valleys of the world that are outside of us as well as inside of us—the outer and the inner.

As we continue in our quest to become a Feathered Serpent, we need to battle the dragon of materialism and greed. At this point in our quest, this is a quintessential rite of passage for us. When we slay this earth-bound flightless dragon, our sleeping serpent of creativity and potentiality awakens and emerges out of the cave of darkness into the light. It may now grow its wings and ascend upwards to eventually become the Feathered Serpent.

The Qualities of a Feathered Serpent

Slaying the materialistic dragon opens the gateway for us to develop the personality of a Feathered Serpent with the following ideal qualities:

- Intelligence based on knowledge
- Wisdom based on the experience of knowledge
- Harmony as defined by the Hawaiian concept of *pono*
- Extraordinary courage
- Creativity
- Compassion
- Spirited swift thinking
- Passion for life
- Sense of humor
- Receptive listener

In our becoming and flowering as a Feathered Serpent, we will express these qualities above by 'seeing with the eyes of a baby,' 'talking our truth' and opening, to the world and to ourselves, our 'heart as a flower.' To achieve these ideal qualities, there is one attribute that we need to strive for: the fearlessness of the Jaguar.

Chapter 6
Fearlessness of the Jaguar

Mother Sister Jaguar, we ask of you, come and bring us your gifts and your
knowledge of death, of re-birth, of releasing fear, uncertainty and doubt…
Mother Sister Jaguar show us the power of the mid-night sun…
let us stare into your golden eyes to discover fearlessness…
show us the power of your voice, claws and teeth so that we
may learn this power; teach us to be the luminous warrior
Mother Sister Jaguar, please grant us the gentleness
and love that comes from having no fear…
bless and thank you, Mother Sister Jaguar.[85]

The above prayer summarizes the challenges facing us as we journey
to and through the West direction of the Feathered Serpent Medicine

Wheel. Fear and death are our constant companions as we strive to over-come these two enemies of our soul. Here we transform the body of death into the resurrected body of light, as we become a luminous warrior.

The mystical jaguar is our guide and mentor to assist us in facing these issues of the West. To the people of Mesoamerica and beyond, the jaguar was revered for its power, bravery and its ability to cross the boundaries of earth, water and sky. As a supreme predator, capable of crushing the skull of a caiman, the jaguar was symbolic of strength, power and the awesome and destructive force of nature. Weighing between 200 and 250 lbs., the jaguar moves, climbs and swims with flawless movement and assured con-fidence, with humans as their only threat. Golden-reddish in appearance, jaguars are uniquely identifiable through their markings of dark rosettes, each enclosing one or two smaller spots. Black jaguars are also common and if the light is right, you can see the rosette markings very lightly etched on their bluish-black coat.

The jaguar, as well as the historical shaman, is recognizable as being a 'boundary crosser:'

> In order to accomplish his difficult and dangerous duties the shaman must, in effect, become what is called a 'Master of Thresh-olds.' He must be able to integrate different planes of existence and experience: he must be able to understand the nature of, and traverse the boundaries between, body and spirit, individual and village, natural and supernatural phenomena, and times present and past....
>
> Becoming a Master of Thresholds means achieving and main-taining a spiritual balance both within himself and within the spirit and earthly worlds....
>
> ... Equally at home... in water, on land and up trees, the jag-uar is the hunter *par excellence*, impressive, beautiful, and above all resourceful. The natural behaviour of the jaguar parallels the supernatural behaviour of the shaman who is seen as a boundary crosser, able to travel in magical flight through the air, across the land and over water.[86]

Boundary crossing is a skill that we need in our quest to become a Feathered Serpent. The power to cross the barriers between our false self and our true heart and the boundaries that separate nature, time and space is essential. In addition, we need to maintain a state of spiritual balance—a balance between spirit and matter. However, none of this is possible until we slay the Dragon of Materialism.

Slaying the Materialist Dragon

As is told in the many heroic mythic tales of dragon slaying, it takes first and foremost the abandonment of the mundane sleeping state of being—the common scourge of the masses. This allows the hero to begin a quest of heart. Early on in the quest, there are many temptations put forth to lure the hero back to his/her former state of sleeping ignorance. It takes much courage to continue on seeking that which many others do not see or care to see.

On a daily basis the majority of the ones who we interact with at work or in public are sheltering and feeding their own materialistic dragons with a steely dedication based on personal fear, doubt, possibly religious dogmatic zeal and most importantly, ignorance. The more that you feed this dragon, the greater that it breathes the fires of arrogance and want—the desire for more and more things and the so-called power they bring. Often this is the reason that the hero is identifiable as the 'fool' at the beginning of his/her quest. Surely only a 'fool' would swim against the tide of culturally accepted life and willingly face the unknown.

But I must ask you: is life about accumulating things or is it about increasing one's own soul brilliance? If you answered soul brilliance, then it is time to slay your Dragon.

Entering the Mountain and Befriending the Trees

In reality, the slaying is not an actual killing per se, but it is a transmutation of the energy. The wingless dragon or serpent that is comfortably coiled around our first charka is released from its bondage to personal safety, survival and earthly treasures and allowed to begin to unfurl its heavenly wings of spirit and light and ascend skyward. In our mind, it is the releasing of fear, uncertainty and doubt and accepting a new paradigm of life: a balance of matter and spirit. We are not born in original sin, but are born pure and divine. There is no separation, an illusion, to life—only equality and a consciousness and oneness to all living things—the 'I' in the 'we' and the 'we' in the 'I.'

This paradigm shift must occur not only in our heart and mind but most importantly, it must happen through our body's participation. We must actually put ourselves out in nature—what I call 'entering the mountain and befriending the trees.' (See Appendix 6)

One of the greatest acts of stupidity that humanity has gleefully embraced is its willful separation from nature. To make matters even worse, in its arrogant superiority, humanity has been led to believe by the all-prevailing science, technology and religion that nature is in service to, beneath and lesser than—a garden to be raped by—the 'all-knowing' humans.

On the other hand, nature can respond and send a message that is loud and clear. The deep-toned belch of the Earth Mother, the 9.0 deep-sea Indonesian earthquake and the resulting tsunami of December 26, 2004, showed us just how inferior the whole of humanity is to the cyclic evolution of the earth and to the wrath of nature. Only the animals and the indigenous people, who were still living the 'old ways,' close to and in partnership with nature, survived. In our journey of survival and renewal, what lesson is there then for each of us to learn from this sad catastrophe?

The lesson is simple. I believe that we need to become closer to nature and be in partnership with the earth by stepping into its stream of evolutionary changes. To do this, we must 'enter the mountain and befriend the trees' and work with the power of the elements.

The elemental makeup of life is often overlooked and taken for granted. When was the last time that the sun hit your face and you realized that the sun represents the element fire and corresponds to your spirit? The wind picks up, the sun disappears behind storm clouds and the rains fall. Wind represents the air element and our mind, while rain represents the element of water and emotions. And as we run seeking shelter, our footsteps take us over the earth—symbolic of our body. Our journey through life can be chronicled by our repetitive patterns of elemental behavior. For instance, how much time do we spend on mental activities as opposed to spiritual activities? How about our body and physical actions? And how do our emotions rule our life? Balance is always the key.

Mountain Practice

Entering the mountain provides us with the opportunity to experience the elements in their most natural state of being. Earth, water, air and fire are known as the basic elements. These four, however, are isolated and incomplete without the addition of a fifth element just as our four fingers are imperfect without the fifth—our thumb. Five is the symbolic number representation of humanity and as such is essential to the understanding of life as it is experienced here on earth.

As we discovered under charkas, the fifth is the space/heavenly element with the addition of consciousness as the sixth element. Both the heavenly element and consciousness bind all things together in a oneness of creation. This knowledge of the sixth element is very important in our journey. What this means is that everything is alive, has a consciousness and is responsive to other consciousness. This needs to be one of our primary beliefs of life. With this belief and the absence of doubt, conscious or hidden, we will truly be able to 'talk to animals' and to understand the 'language of birds.'

But there is another way to view the elements and their interaction, which is referred to as the Chinese Five Element theory. This system of knowledge and power recognizes that the five elements are water, fire, metal, tree (wood) and earth. As this system is a study within itself, we will only briefly describe its theory of the generation and regulation of the elements. In the generative process one element creates another:

- Water generates wood as the rains feed the trees.
- Wood generates fire as the wood feeds the fire.
- Fire generates earth through the production of ash.
- Earth generates metal as metal is mined from the earth.
- Metal generates water through condensation.

In the process of regulation one element conquers another. This is one of the reasons that it is used in esoteric work to achieve victory by inscribing a pentagram in the air while voicing a mantra. Each point of the pentagram represents an element. The victory process is as follows:

- Water puts out fire.
- Fire melts metal.
- Metal chops down trees.
- Trees break up the earth.
- Earth dams water.

Following the 'old school' of teaching, the victory mudra (using the hands) and mantra that is used must be orally transmitted, not written. You may feel that there is still something missing. The missing part is what I refer to as the 'force.'

The Force

The mysterious intangible power that energetically connects and permeates all things is known by many names, for example: *mana* in Hawaiian, *ki* in Japanese and *chi* in Chinese. It is probably best represented by the magical and spiritual qualities of the 'force,' the term that George Lucas utilized as the 'glue of the universe' in *Star Wars*. It recognizes that there is an all-powerful force, which is the primary source of creation.

This force, the mysterious energetic cosmic blood, is a divine mystery and with all such mysteries it is hard to explain and sometimes even harder to comprehend. Seemingly the only way to really pierce the veil of such a mystery is to experience it. In today's world, the Hawaiian elders and other cultures' indigenous elders, who have not lost the 'old ways,' accomplish this. Spending time with these wise ones will help reveal the truth of this integral, divine and most important facet of life, the source of our existence.

To the Hawaiian elders, *mana* is power. Not the external power of wealth and position, but the internal power of our soul's vibration. There is spiritual *mana* as well as personal *mana* and they go hand-in-hand. There are many in this world who have external power, but are devoid of *mana*. However, as long as we are not enslaved by the external power and wealth—as illustrated in the Lord of the Rings trilogy—we may still achieve it.

Mana allows us to accomplish amazing feats and to express the spiritual gifts that are sometimes hidden deep within us. This first source of creation is always with us only waiting to present us with its power. But few see what is in front of them: with their minds and lips chattering, they miss the beauty of a flower, the sun on their faces or the light cascading off of the ocean at dawn, and thus they never accept the gifts of life that very well may change their lives.

In certain ways the Eastern *ki* and *chi* follow the same philosophical methodology as *mana*. *Mana* is the term that refers to the 'primary source' of existence that surrounds and permeates all things—an all-powerful force (cosmic blood). Everything has an intrinsic unique *mana* such as the *mana* of a tree or the *mana* of a stone. There is great *mana* as well as *ki* in words as witnessed in the mystical power of a *kāhuna* (Hawaiian shaman/ healer/priest) chant or the martial power of a sensei's (martial arts teacher) *kiaijutsu*. To heal or to harm through the *mana/ki* power of the voice depends on the personal power, the heart/mind power, of the individual. The greater the connection, unity and oneness that we have with the 'primary source,' the greater then will be our *mana* (*ki, chi*):

> *Mana* is life force, the power that enables us to live…. The gift of *mana* is all of ours, and we can command this *mana*. You generate mana through prayer, through deep breathing and through meditation.[87]

Maya *Ch'ulel*

To the Maya the Force is known as *ch'ulel*. It is believed to be the single, dynamic sacred force or energy that is the unifying totality of all things—a universal life-force. It's in constant movement eternally self-generating and self-regenerating while encompassing and interpenetrating the whole cosmos. It is immanent and at the same time, transcendent:

> *Ch'ulel* is the word for the inner soul or holiness that resides in all living things, in powerful objects, in sacred places, and in the many energy-laden objects in the Maya world.[88]

The Maya believed that *ch'ulel* resided in blood. Therefore, we may see the reasons for and the emphasize put on the bloodletting rituals of the Maya:

> For the ancient Maya, human beings released *ch'ulel* from their bodies when they let their blood…. Through bloodletting, they 'conjured" (*tzak*) the *way* and the *ch'u*, the "companion spirits and the gods." …
> When the ancient Maya let blood, they were feeding the gods their *ch'ulel* and giving of their souls.[89]

Along with the Maya concept of *ch'ulel* is their belief in a cosmic substance called *itz*:

> *Itz* is the magic stuff brought forth in ritual and as secretions from all sorts of things….
> … *itz* refers to special liquids and essences that include morning dew, the holy water sprinkled by ritualists with an aspergillum, and semen. *Itz* can also refer to the nectar of flowers…. On the altar, the dripping wax of the votive candles, also food for the gods and spirits, is *yiitz kab*, "wax," and this represents the flowing liquid of heaven.[90]

Fire, Water and the Sword

For the purposes of our journey of the Feathered Serpent, we need to learn how to tap into the cosmic power of the 'force.' This 'first source' both surrounds us and is inside of us. The key to unlocking its magic and power is through our heart and mind. The purification and cleansing of both are essential. In this way we will achieve a bright heart and a strong mind, which are the attributes of a Feathered Serpent.

The elements that we will utilize in our purification are fire and water. Traditionally known as the purifying elements of heaven and earth, the power and mystery of fire and water have awed humans since the dawn of time and provided us with a means of purification, spiritually as well as physically. Both may be utilized for transformational work. Water has traditionally been the source for various initiatory experiences as well as being the means to experience death in life—ritualistic submersion symbolizing death and re-birth. Fire may also be used for initiatory rites witnessed in the practice of fire walking.

Both hold the mysteries of creation, death and life and in many of us conjure up feelings of fear. But the awe of their power is limitless. I remember one time being on the Big Island of Hawaii with my wife, a Hawaiian healer friend and students of ours, witnessing the magical birthing power of fire. It was dawn and we had driven over storm swept roads to observe the Fire Goddess, Madam Pele (Kilauea), giving 'birth.' Feelings of reverence were overwhelming as I bent down to touch the newly-formed and still-warm earth. I spoke to it, calling it 'baby earth,' as I welcomed it into being. At that moment, I remembered that our own fire—of spirit and will—may also create a life path of our choosing. One that is of our heart; and one that we need to follow.

The elemental forces of fire and water will help us to slay and transform our Dragon of Materialism. This pure act of power opens the gateway to our re-birth as a Warrior of Light. In addition to fire and water, we also need the mythical symbolic power of the Sword. The sword is the warrior's soul. Exoterically, it may be seen as a weapon of war and destruction. Esoterically, it is a symbol of Knowledge and the cutting away of ignorance and illusion. Double bladed, the sword signifies the Double Wisdom that sees only the Oneness of existence. The sword in the scabbard symbolizes the unity of the male and the female principle and denotes a state of peace and wondrous unity.

The doubled-bladed sword and the twin-pointed vajra are related esoterically as tools of 'heavenly thundering clarity.' The vajra is an esoteric scepter-like ritualistic tool with multiple meanings such as 'diamond,' 'thunderbolt' and 'clearness.' As a scepter, the vajra represents the *axis mundi* and may be viewed as our spine—our inner 'tree of life.' It is the diamond-thunderbolt that crushes, and in a sense, vaporizes illusion.

The double-bladed Sword of Wisdom, of the great Esoteric Buddhist Light King—Fudo Myoo, cuts away the impediments to life caused by passion and false knowledge. In our Feathered Serpent journey, it is essential for us to cut away all false knowledge. This will enable us to 'see' our truth.

False knowledge is an impediment to being a person of power—a Feathered Serpent. We must see through the 'spin doctors' of society's patriarchal organizations, secular as well as religious. We must not believe the materialistic message of accumulation (things and wealth), which detracts us from our heart—the center of our being—and leads to the unbridled destruction of the earth and all of her resources.

It is time to slay our Dragon of Materialism—an awakening and transformation of our true energy. As our serpent/dragon releases its illusionary hold on our base instincts of security and survival, it begins its ascension to the higher states of being where love and peace reign. (Please see Appendix 7)

Warrior of Light

What does it mean to be a 'warrior of light—a luminous warrior?' In today's consumer-oriented world, the term 'warrior' is blathered about without any type of discernment. Many use the term without an inkling of its true essence. Many view a warrior as being one-dimensional; i.e. one who is skilled and successful in battle. But an authentic warrior has many different shades of being.

A warrior must have a basic physical constitution. You do not have to be able to run marathons or even in fact, 10 kilometers (6.2 miles). But a warrior must be able to walk distances without becoming winded and to have a body weight that does not interfere with physical or mental functioning at a level that is higher that most people's standards. So it is not a question of being overweight or underweight, but it is the ability to feel good and clear—inside and out.

Perseverance

In addition, a warrior faces adversity with a clear and strong heart. In our journey of power, we must persevere and endure where others would only find fear and would make excuses to turn away from their heart by quitting the quest. At all times we must have a patient spirit as we go through the highs and lows of life. We must always 'keep going.' We must never let our doubts or the doubts of others keep us from our task of spiritual evolution.

As a warrior we must always endure through the uncertainties of life. With a gentle heart, we must endure through the hardships of life, always realizing that such hardships are but temporary. We must persevere and not let our fears, uncertainties and doubts keep us from our destiny as a Feathered Serpent. At all times we must have an unshakable spirit as exemplified by the esoteric Light King—Fudo Myoo.

Personal silence is a key to a persevering spirit. Keeping silent and not talking is difficult for many people. Not talking and not having one's mind chatter (mind talk) is very difficult for most people. A warrior looks, listens and learns. He/She values silence, exhibits stoicism in the face of suffering and speaks truth from his/her heart.

Fearlessness

Fearlessness is not the absence or suppression of fear. Only a fool's ego or drug/alcohol-induced bravado would shout 'I am fearless' in certain life-and-death situations. Fear is sometimes necessary. Without fear, there would be a flat line of emotion in the presence of the unknown. When we suppress fear, it will come back to haunt us at a later time.

Fearlessness comes down to two things: the amount of fear and the attachment to it. The less the unknown (by having more experiences of life) the less the fear, although fear is still present. Part of my spiritual/shamanic training involved bathing and submersion in ice-covered streams at pre-dawn. Driving all alone in the dark to the stream would take close to an hour. Even after years of this type of practice, there were still always a few grains of fear on my drive to the stream. Once there, the fear was shed in the same way that I dropped my clothes to enter the stream. I detached from any apprehension or fear of the excessive cold, the ice-covered swiftly flowing waters or the dark.

Fearlessness, a total regeneration of our being, comes from *detachment*—pure and simple. Detachment is the key element not only in achieving a fearless spirit, but in addition, attaining great spiritual and healing power. Fearlessness may then be looked at as achieving a state of mental tranquility. Our mind is not attached. It is not chattering with issues of the past, present and/or future that are upsetting our state of 'mind-*pono.*' This state of detachment and mental tranquility is referred to by indigenous elders and shamans as having a 'strong-mind.'

Extraordinary Courage

In our journey of seeking the light and the purification of our heart and mind, the most courageous thing that we may do is to embody unconditional love—divine love. It takes a fearless spirit without doubt or uncertainty to be able to live in a way where all of our actions and reactions are courageous and a reflection of this heavenly love. Our intent is always one of courage—a courageous will. Our actions in life are routinely based on bravery with the result that our heart and mind always express divine love.

This extraordinary courage of heart strengthens us to take risks in life. It enables us to persevere in the face of difficulties that would stop others dead in their tracks. We must have this level of courage to embrace life to its fullest; to be able to express a compassionate attitude to all that we come in contact with, no matter whether they be friend or foe. This extraordinary courage is the foundation of our heart and our connecting source to all living things.

It takes extraordinary courage to acknowledge and believe that there are no limits in life. Of course, there are self-imposed ones. But in reality, there are only unlimited possibilities. The reason that so many people limit themselves is due to one simple thing—fear.

Fear keeps us from being balanced. This limits our possibilities. If you always say yes but seldom say no, your possibilities in life are limited and you are out-of-balance. Many people who find themselves in abusive relationships will have a difficult time saying no out of the fear of further abuse and the abandonment into the unknown. Abuse is a known factor, but standing up to the abuse is a fear-ridden unknown. In these types of circumstances it takes extraordinary courage to say no. Many times life is not easy, but all of us have the power within to survive even the most difficult of times. We have the power to laugh and to cry, to say yes and to say no, and our heart still keeps beating.

So far we have been discussing the various attributes of a warrior, but still, we have not answered the question—what is a 'luminous warrior?'

The Pearl of Light

Have you ever wondered about the meaning of 'halos' or the 'rings of fire' visually depicted around saints, Buddhist deities and other heavenly figures? These are not just the whimsical musings of artists. There is a deep spiritual meaning to these symbolic representations of light and heavenly power. There is a biological and physiological truth to these artistic renderings. That truth is called the epiphysis, more commonly known as the pineal gland. I refer to it as the pearl of light.

It is not well understood by the medical/scientific community. But why would it be understood? It is the gateway to heaven and to earth—a passageway of light that science, in its separation from spirit, and medicine, in its separation from the healing spirit, will never comprehend.

The pineal is small (8mm), about the size of a pea; a pine cone of light that is a physical manifestation within our body of cosmic reflected light— our pearl of enlightenment. It is our moon circle of perfection/imperfection regulating the ebb and flow of our ocean of being. It may be our serene pond of compassion and love or our angry ocean of self-destruction.

In Shingon (true word) esoteric Japanese Buddhism, Dainichi Nyo-rai—the Great Sun is the Cosmic Buddha—the Great Mystery. On the other hand, it is the Known Mystery that surrounds us and that is inside each one of us. This is the universal Light that transcends all limitations.

In Shingon the lotus flower with 8 petals is the artistic representation of the physical heart with its 4 arteries and four veins. The lotus flower also represents the concept of Principle and the total cosmos—the Body (all things/forms of the total universe) of Dainichi Nyorai.

The artistic renderings of moon circles in Shingon symbolism represent Knowledge and the mind. Knowledge is the Mind (all consciousness of the total universe) of Dainichi Nyorai. The moon reflects the light of the sun. The moon circle symbolically reflects the light of Knowledge emanating from the Great Sun—Dainichi Nyorai. In Shingon belief, Knowledge and Principle/Principle and Knowledge are non-dual and interpenetrate each other. Body and Mind (macrocosmic) and mind and body (microcosmic) interpenetrate and are non-dual and perfect/imperfect.

Another approach to this is to accept that the solar sun symbolizes our hearts and the lunar moon our minds. The moon has no intrinsic light of its own but relies on the sun for its illumination and most importantly, its re-flection. It is an accepted fact that light is a common symbol for knowledge; solar light (the heart) represents direct knowledge, which may be termed 'heart knowledge' while lunar light (the mind) corresponds to reflective knowledge. Our hearts know intuitively divine truth while our minds can only find reason through discursive knowledge and cannot function prop-erly except through the guidance of the higher intellect of our hearts. Our heart and our mind must work together to determine truth.

Taking this knowledge one step further, the halo of light or the rings of fire may be thought of as the artistic renderings of our pineal gland, which is at the center of our brain. The pineal gland is egg-shaped; spherical at one end and conical at the other, and is ultra-sensitive to light. Our heart also demonstrates these shapes and may be postulated as being the container of cosmic light within our bodies—a small sun.

The pineal gland secretes melatonin, which is responsible for proper sleep. In addition, melatonin levels directly influence the function of various brain centers that control appetite, the hypothalamus and the pituitary gland. The proper functioning of our hypothalamus is important for our longevity. Along with the pituitary gland, it is the coordinator of our entire endocrine system.

The pituitary may be referred to as the master gland. However, it depends on the hypothalamus to secrete specific chemicals to its frontal lobe. The frontal lobe will then produce one of six different hormones, which sequentially will stimulate the thyroid, adrenal and reproductive glands. Fascinatingly enough, these hormones also stimulate breast milk production. This is interesting knowledge that brings us to our concept of the luminous warrior.

Luminous Warriors have felt the first awakening or 'quickening' of the divine spark within themselves. This began them on a journey of self-discovery. Through ascetic training, the erasing of their personal history, the strengthening of their heart and mind, they have reached a point where they are able to remove the obstacles of time—the three worlds of past, present and future—and conquer the three poisons of greed, anger and ignorance. Fear and the unknown no longer have a grip on them. From this comes the opening of the heart, which crushes the delusion of dualism and separation.

The luminous warrior now realizes that there is no death, only transformation. This awakens the mind (pineal gland) from the 'sleeping state' of ignorance to the truth of unity and light. The mundane person (the illusionary self) dies and the luminous warrior (the authentic self) is re-born.

Our *Musha Shugyo* has brought us to this point in our quest to become a Feathered Serpent. It is now time for us to die, and to be re-born as a warrior of light—a Luminous Warrior.

Death and Re-birth

Our symbolic death is the death of our old self and the transmutation of the fear-based serpent energy—the materialistic wingless dragon. Our symbolic death results in a re-birth and the awakening of our Feathered Serpent energy. Everything that has been accomplished in the South and the West of the Medicine Wheel has hastened and brought us to the place where we may experience the death of the old self and then the birth of our new self as the Luminous Warrior. (Please see Appendix 8)

And it is now with our symbolic death that we are able to begin to develop a resurrection body. We must face the teeth and the claws of Mother Sister Jaguar in the Otherworld and willingly be torn asunder. This is one of the oldest patterns of shamanic initiation—to be ripped apart and then to be put back together again; a new heart and a new mind—a resurrected/regenerated spiritual body, the awakening of the divine within. This is sacrifice/suffering, death and re-birth; a primal theme that has been corrupted by the church.[91] When we put our resurrection into the hands of another, as the Christian Church preaches, we achieve easy and illusionary salvation using the language of Christianity. When we are not responsible for our own resurrection of self, we are prevented from becoming an authentic divine human being.

The resurrection/regeneration body is a Mesoamerican theme emphasizing the concept of life coming from death, highlighted by the Maya creation story, the *Popol Vuh*, of the Hero Twins' journey to Xibalba (Underworld). It is not the physical resurrection of our body after physical death. In addition, it is not the salvation of Christianity. If we have 'eyes to see,' nature teaches us the lesson of immortality. It's all around us but specifically to the religion of the Maya, it was the rattlesnake that taught us to be 'born again.' It symbolized a material and spiritual regeneration through its tearing off of its worn-out skin to emerge as a brilliant new serpent with an added rattle.

To the Mesoamericans, there was no original sin so there was no need for the concept of grace[92] or salvation[93]. On the contrary, theirs was a belief in sanctification[94], not the Christian's view of salvation. We can clearly see, with the arrival of the Europeans and the Roman Church, the clashing of cultures and religious belief—sanctification vs. salvation. This led to the unbridled destruction of a people and their culture; all in the name of God.

To a believer in salvation, ecstatic dancing while scantily clothed (an expression of the regeneration/resurrection body) would, heaven forbid, be deemed the work of the 'devil.' There is no need to become sacred in body and mind for salvation. It has already been done for you. All you need is faith and the acceptance of Jesus as your personal savior.

Interestingly enough, what is known about the historical Jesus would lend one to believe that Jesus' teachings and spiritual practices were truly the teachings and practices of sanctification not salvation. And I doubt that grace would have been in his belief system, as we shall see.

Bathing vs. Baptism

Baptism is one of the major sacraments of Christianity. It is a Christian initiation—a granting of grace, entrance into the holy arms of the Church and thus one's salvation. This ritualistic practice has nothing to do with sanctification.

However, if you are to believe the church, this was one of the major teachings of Jesus; thus the justification, so-called truth and the reason that it is a major sacrament of Christianity. But is it the truth? Is it fact? Everything that is known, which is not too much (second, third and sometimes forth person or more accounts), leads us to believe that a one time ticket to heaven, granted by an institution, was not his spiritual philosophy. On the contrary, he taught, practiced and believed in practices of sanctification. One of these purification rites that he taught and practiced was called bathing.

According to Jewish religious law, if a person was polluted by childbirth, sexual activity or various other sources of contamination, such as contact with the dead, they needed ritualistic cleansing through immersion in water—*mikveh*:

> To the ancient Jews, both Essene and non-Essene, the mikveh was a process of spiritual purification and cleansing, especially in relation to the various types of Turmah or ritual defilement when the Temple was in use. We learn from the Clementine Homilees that Peter practiced daily pre-dawn Mikveh immersion. We may infer from this that all Nasorenes, including Yeshu and Maria,[95] also practiced daily purifications.[96]

If you were wealthy enough, you could afford a 'bathing pool' within your own home. But for the majority of people, it meant a trip to the local temple to bathe. Of course, a fee was charged every time that you bathed within the confines of the temple or on its holy grounds.

Jesus would have been outraged at these bathing policies, which favored the rich over the poor, and demonstrated the materialistic-greed of the Jewish temple and its priests. Why would any Jew need to pay to be purified; just as why would you need to pay someone else to grant you forgiveness? It was not necessary; in fact, it was corrupt and wrong in the eyes of God.

Jesus must have sought out a means to counter this corruption of the priests and the inequality that it demonstrated between the rich and the poor. He needed to find a way for everyone to purify themselves without having to be rich or to pay money to an earthly human-constructed institution. He discovered his alternative on the banks of the Jordan River in the person of John the Baptist, whose immersion rite "was a silent protest against the urban cadres that controlled Judaism in Jerusalem, as well as a genuinely devoted practice."[97]

John took Jesus on as a student, and after a period of time, initiated him into the esoteric teachings and inner wisdom of bathing as well as the *Chariot* or *Throne of God* meditation, and many other equally mystical practices. During the act of bathing, John would tell the ones in the water, prior to immersion, to repent and thus release their sins:

> For John, and in ancient Judaism generally, repentance meant a 'return' (*shuv* in Hebrew, *tuv* in Aramaic) to God. By repenting, one acknowledged being headed in the wrong direction; by changing course, one was realigned with the divine. Repentance did not emphasize sin or depravity; the notion of original sin as a hopeless condition was a later motif in Christianity, developed by Augustine of Hippo during the fifth century C.E. John, far from preaching hopelessness, offered in repentance a pragmatic alternative to being estranged from God. In both Hebrew and Greek 'to sin' (*chata, hamartano*) originally meant to miss the mark, as in archery. A rabbi's teaching showed how one could go right again, and only implied where one had gone wrong.[98]

Jesus was treated no differently than the others who came to John. He embraced the teachings and practices of John while strengthening his spirit and releasing his own anger, guilt and resentment:

> John demanded repentance from all those who came to be immersed by him, so that Jesus stood on the same ground as everyone else. The hurt inflicted during his childhood, the sense that he was an outcast, in the wrong through no fault of his own, was healed through his repeated immersions. The Jordan's waters washed away his feeling of estrangement. He repented of the anger he had felt, of his resentment against his own people in Nazareth. He knew he was released from sin in John's baptism. And, in turn, he was prepared to release the grudges he felt against others. His reward was a place in a group dedicated to a respected religious practice.[99]

Jesus watched and listened to John and eventually learned to conduct the sacred rites of immersion himself. During this period of time a spiritual philosophy developed within him that would stay with him throughout the rest of his life:

> John's insistence on the dynamic relationship between repentance and release from sin was the source of Jesus' emphasis on the same relationship throughout his own ministry. This release from sin, which is translated into English as 'forgiveness,' referred to the actual loosing or freeing (*aphiemi* in Greek, *shebaq* in Aramaic and Hebrew) of a person from the consequences of his own action by God. Jesus' conviction that release from sin makes every Israelite pure—and thus acceptable in God's eyes—is perhaps his most enduring legacy, and it was derived directly from his experience with John the Baptist.[100]

It seems that Jesus was not only a fast learner but also a dedicated student of John's. His intense spiritual practice of immersion and *Chariot* visualizations brought the world of spirit closer and closer to Jesus. The *Chariot*, as the moving *Throne of God*, was one of the primary esoteric visualizations within Jewish mysticism. With its wheels of fire rolling through the heavens, accompanied by the sound of mighty waters, the *Chariot* meditation brought the divineness of creation intimately alive within the body, mind and soul of Jesus.

As a devoted student, he bathed and bathed in the Jordan's 'living waters,' that roared with the same sound as the heavenly Chariot. Steadily, he increased his spiritual powers; until one morning while standing waist deep in the chilly stream with the morning star in the East and the first light of dawn breaking through the darkness of the night, he had his vision. As recorded in the Bible, it was the vision of a 'dove.' In esoteric teachings the dove not only symbolized the holy spirit of divine love but it also represented Venus, the morning star. The dove or the star descended into him, and for Jesus, this symbolized the divine spirit or the light of divinity within all things. Keep in mind that Jesus, as a student of the original Kabbalah, believed in the sacred knowledge that we all have the 'holy spark' of God within.

The vision of the morning star was the moment of awakening and enlightenment for Jesus, just as it was for Gautama, the historical Buddha. This awakening and enlightenment for both was not the completion of a path but the beginning of a 'way'—bringing a message of light to a darkened world.

Jesus still progressed on his path, continuing his own ascetic spiritual training and development to the point where he became known as a *Chasid*—a Jewish shaman, faith healer and sorcerer. During this 'strengthening of spirit' period, Jesus came to view John's bathing philosophy of cleanness differently.

Directly related to his vision and repeated pre-dawn immersion practice as well as his own visionary and prophetic gifts, Jesus came to know, first-hand, within his heart and mind, that all people were already clean or pure with the divine spirit within them:

> Jesus had been brought by John to see that every Israelite had the means of purity at his disposal, and he came to insist that every Israelite was in fact already pure, embraced by divine Spirit, as he had been.[101]

To Jesus, purity became one of the most important issues in his spiritual mission. But it was not the outward purity that mattered. What was necessary in the eyes of God was one's inner purity. To Jesus, the brightness and the lightness of a person's heart were more important than money and one's social and economic status. Ritual immersions to cleanse away one's outward pollutions were not only ridiculous but were unnecessary. However, bathing to cleanse one of the inner pollutions of fear, anger and guilt was not only necessary but was also one of the ways to increase God's Spirit within—a resurrection in life. And, increasing the divinity within each person—could change the world.

Jesus was not the only spiritual teacher to bring this knowledge of purification, light and resurrection to his people. Quetzalcoatl also taught his people the importance of symbolic death and re-birth through ritualistic water immersions—a resurrection of spirit. In addition, like Jesus, he brought the knowledge of the 'light body.'

Every day the light of dawn precedes the rising of the sun. It is the light that comes out of the dark of the night. The lightbringers of humanity, past and present, are that light. It has been prophesized that Quetzalcoatl, like Jesus, is destined to return when the world is at its darkest. Are we in the darkest of times?

Bathing

Ritualistic immersion in running water (stream/river) or the ocean is the oldest form of symbolic death and re-birth. It is an essential step in becoming a Feathered Serpent. It is frightening but necessary. We need to physically symbolically 'die' to the old to be 'born again'—our second birth. It is not membership into an earthly or religious institution. It is the beginning of an awakening to the truth—of the world and one's authentic self.

Few in the world still practice, teach and conduct this form of purification. Outside of the *Mandeans* of the Middle East, the greatest concentration of 'dawn bathers' are to be found within the indigenous communities that still practice and adhere to the old ways. But even here, there are few still alive that can 'initiate' and put people into the 'living waters' of the earth.

I am blessed to be one of those who still practices and 'initiates' people into bathing.[102] This 'initiation' is not one of membership, but one of 'death and re-birth.' After I put a person into the stream, they are free to revisit any stream and repeat the ritualistic immersion. Going bathing will help a person release the stress and hurt that comes from living in today's chaotic and fear-filled world.

After the initial 'initiation,' there are multiple reasons for a person to revisit a stream and bathe. Bathings will increase a person's spiritual power/mana and their inner heat; the stream will also help release anger, guilt, resentment, fear and uncertainty as well as the other emotional baggage that we seem to carry and seemingly refuse to release. In addition, I use it as a method of healing others.

Each bathing tradition is slightly different. The way that I was taught was four immersions while other traditions such as Hawaiians would do five and in the Middle East three immersions:

> The term mikveh in Hebrew literally means any gathering of waters, but is specifically used in Jewish law for the waters or bath for the ritual immersion. Ancient sages teach that the word mikveh has the same letters as Ko(v)Meh, the Hebrew word for "rising" or "standing tall," therefore we see the idea of being baptized "straightway."
>
> The Essenes were anciently known as regular practicioners (sc) of daily immersion. In the Talmud these daily Mikveh practicioners (sc) are called *tovelei shaharit* or "dawn bathers." Not only Nasaraens, but several other Jewish groups observed ritual immersion every day to assure readiness for the coming of the Messiah. Epiphanius mentioned one of these groups called Hemerobaptists which means "daily bathers" in Greek. The *Clementine Homilees, or **Recognitions of Clement**,* tell us that Peter always washed, often in the sea, before dawn which was no doubt a custom of all

Nazarenes of his time....

Ancient dawn bathing Nasaraens used at least three forms of Baptism, or mikveh purifications. We know this because the surviving remnants of these Nasaraens, the Nasorai sect (Mandeans), still preserve these forms of this ancient Nasarene purification rite once practiced and promoted by Yeshu (Jesus) and His messianic Spouse Maria. They are the daily *Rishama* Mikveh immersion, performed before dawn. The *Tamasha* immersion, and the *Masbuta* immersion. The surviving Mandean versions of these are:

- RISHAMA BAPTISM: The first of the *miqvah* purifications performed is the *rishama* (signing), the priests presence is not required, such that each man or woman is his or her own priest or priestess. This should be performed daily, and with covered head, just before sunrise after the evacuation of the bowels and before all religious ceremonies.

- TAMASHA BAPTISM: The second, the *tamasha*, is a simple triple immersion in the river ... this is performed without the aid of the priest or priestess....

- MASBUTA BAPTISM: The third ablution, or 'full baptism', encompasses all aspects of baptism and must be performed by a priest or priestess....

The Jewish baptism candidates were often immersed three times. The idea of total immersion comes from the Scripture in Leviticus 15:16 when it says, "he shall wash all his flesh in the water." One reason it was customary to immerse three times was because the word mikveh occurs three times in the Torah. We know this to have been an early Nazarene practice under Yeshu-Maria.[103]

One of the things that Vince taught me was to watch how people came up out of the water from their squatting immersion. They were to come straight up. For thousands of years true bathing has apparently been done similarly:

In ancient times immersion was to be performed in the presence of witnesses (Yebam. 47b).... The individual stood straight up with the feet spread and the hands held out in front. The candidate would totally immerse themselves by squatting in the water with a witness or baptizer doing the officiating. Note the New Testament points out the fact that Jesus came up straightway out of the water (Matthew 3:16).[104]

You have to wonder about the baptismal rites of some Christian sects, not only the sprinkling of some water on the head of a baby but also the 'born-again rites.' In the 'born-again,' they lie a person during the light of day[105] down into the water (not squatting) and then pull them back up to an upright position.

This type of corruption of the original teachings and practices of Jesus is reprehensible. I've yet to hear of any Pope immersing himself in a stream or ocean; much less any other Bishop, priest or clergy man. If the Church changed and corrupted this most basic teaching and practice of Jesus, we must ask ourselves: what else have they changed and corrupted?

Bathing is an awesome experience, but I can not realistically physically initiate all who read this book. However, if you are interested in studying with us, please contact us.

Heart as a Flower—Divine Love

Our journey has taken us through the caverns of self-doubt—our dark underworlds—slaying our fears and uncertainties of life. This has brought us out into the light of our true hearts and souls. Basking in this light of our true selves, we are able to express divine love and open to the world our 'lotus of selves'—our 'flower hearts.'

As a warrior of light we must walk the path of *Ollin*—the heart that sees. We must keep ourselves well-balanced and live authentic lives of beauty expressing our hearts as a flower. A 'flower heart' is one of the three pillars of light that we must always keep in the forefront of our conscious:

1. Baby Eyes. These are eyes that are non-judgmental and tolerant, that view the world with awe and excitement and recognize the oneness of the light and the dark of existence.

2. True Talk. This is listening more often than talking, and when talking, speaking truth from the heart. It is to hear, understand and perceive.
3. Flower Heart. This is always expressing love from the heart and letting others, as well as ourselves, view the beauty and the divine perfection that is the true essence of our hearts. This is the 'heart that sees'—the *Ollin* Heart.

A Luminous Warrior is impeccable in speech and action. To maintain this impeccability, we need to make a spiritual pact/contract/vow to ourselves; not to some patriarchal hierarchy, but to our own hearts covering the following five aspects:

1. Maintain constant awareness of our actions, the actions of others (which are not to be taken personally), and the actions of the earth and the heavens. This is the vow of Baby Eyes. This is the vow of Humanity.
2. Recognize, honor and respect the power of speech by being impeccable with our words. Listen more often than talking. Hear, perceive and understand. This is the vow of True Talk. This is the vow of Humanity.
3. Commit to act our best in life, bringing beauty to ourselves and others while expressing our heart as a flower. This is the vow of Flower Heart. This is the vow of Humanity.
4. Agree to shift our attention from fear (our first attention—human up-bringing) to love, a fearless spirit and being *pono* (our second attention—divine essence). Energy flows where our attention goes. This is the vow of Divinity.
5. Maintain constant awareness and the belief that all things of creation have consciousness. And remember that all things are alive and responsive to our thoughts, words and actions. This is the vow of a Feathered Serpent.

We have explored the work of the South and West of the Feathered Serpent Medicine Wheel. The knowledge of the Hummingbird and the North of the Medicine wheel will await you for later on in your journey, because working with the knowledge and wisdom of the South and West requires years of practice and focus. But do not despair; the results are worth their weight in gold. Be patient, the journey is what is most important, not the destination.

During the journey, there is an important role to play in the lives of others. As luminous warriors, we need to take the light of our heart energies to the ones in darkness to awaken them to their divine selves. As Holy Knights on a holy quest of spirit, we need to take our light out into the world; to be beacons for others who are trapped in their darkness of fear and bound to unresolved past issues and the people that have caused them pain and suffering.

It is up to you. I leave you with a quote from Margaret Mead, "Never doubt that a small group of thoughtful, committed citizens can change the world. Indeed, it's the only thing that ever has."

COMPLETION FOR
NOW OF THE CHRONICLES

Text.

The Visitation—August 1997 Common Era

Four years have passed since Balamcoatl's vision. Realizing the depth and difficulty of bringing his message to a world ruled by money and the power-worshipping elite, Balamcoatl persisted step by step in an effort to bring his message to a wider audience. He still traveled the seven seas talking to all who would listen and ever seeking more knowledge and wisdom. During this time he and his wife had attracted a few new students, while others who had been with them pursued other paths.

As new ones discovered the spiritual lineages and knowledge that Balamcoatl and his wife, Kolilkab, held in trust, requests were made for them to share these teachings—working towards a mastery of the 'first knowledge.' This teaching 'canoe' was simply called the 'Masters Program.' Balamcoatl used the term 'canoe' for the meaning and symbology of what it takes to sail an outrigger canoe across the oceans of the world—paddling and sailing from one land to another.

It is the symbolic bridge between lands that are separated by the seas, just as the rainbow is the bridge between heaven and earth. The canoe also taught that all must work together as one to keep the canoe on course. Working together as one, the canoe will never capsize and the destination will eventually be reached.

Voyaging across the seas replicates our journey through life—at times the seas may be calm and sailing smooth, but then the sea may instantly change into a tempest and all must pull harder on our paddles to make it through. All the while, we must keep our eyes trained on the stars overhead—our guides to our destination.

Little though did Balamcoatl realize the monumental spiritual phenomenon that this year would bring.

"If you so choose, please take your shoes and socks off, do not put on a jacket and join me outside," said Balamcoatl with a smile on his face. "I know it is winter with snow on the ground and very dark outside, but this is a good teaching environment to help you learn how to increase your inner heat."

Not all chose to participate but the few who did were gifted for their courage with a great sign traveling through the heavens—a comet that had not visited the earth for an untold time. Balamcoatl put the moment to good use.

"Keep your eyes focused on the great fiery light traveling across the sky. That light and fire is really within you; there is no separation between it and you; you both are connected; feel that fire. What would it feel like; what would you look like—to have that fire and light within you?"

The next morning was the completion of the spiritual training that Balamcoatl was providing for a group of community food providers. They didn't farm the food but only distributed it throughout the greater communities spread out over this part of the mainland called 'Land of the Dawn.' This land felt the warmth of the sun before the rest of the mainland did.

"I would like to thank you all for being open and willing to listen and to learn," said Balamcoatl.

Before he could continue, Balamcoatl felt something out of the ordinary. He turned and saw at least a dozen eagles soaring overhead; a bird seldom seen within these parts! As all in the group who also saw the eagles rushed outside to get a better view, they were met with an empty sky. Balamcoatl could see that many had been pushed to the limits of their beliefs and this was just too strange for some. As everyone returned inside, Balamcoatl lingered outside to be sure that it was a spiritual sign.

When he entered into the enclosed room where the others waited, out of nowhere fell a white feather from the ceiling, which fell in front of Balamcoatl, which he caught within his palm… the others just stared, not knowing what to make of this.

"Do you suppose that he will understand?" asked Regulus.

"No, not at this time," replied Mikael, the archangel who people on earth refer to as Michael.

"He must do the proper prayer. And then I will reveal myself to him. In his heart, he knows who he was and why he is on earth again at this time. But he doubts himself and still wonders if it is all true. Remember, Regulus, he is in human form."

Within the next few months two more white feathers mysteriously fell out of nowhere within enclosed rooms, each witnessed by Balamcoatl, Kolilkab and their students. Balamcoatl knew that they were a spiritual sign but did not know their significance or what they meant.

Seven months passed without incident except for the appearance of the three white feathers. Each summer, Balamcoatl and Kolilkab would conduct a 4-day *shugyo* experience for their apprentices. As a standard practice before the training, he would say prayers for health, safety, love and power for all those involved.

This time, however, he did a different prayer.

"Let our students see a sign of 'who I was' in my last incarnation. Let them see a sign knowing that I was _____."

He mentioned the name, as people would recognize it today. He then let go of any expectations about the prayer.

"He has asked for a sign. It is now time," said Mikael to Regulus.

The 4-day theme of the training was initiation, death and re-birth as well as fear. Their students would experience a 24-hour solitary quest, a 'death spiral' ceremony and an ancient baptism called bathing. After many changes in the schedule of the teachings and experiences, the day of the sun, Sunday, was finally determined to be the best day for the 'death spiral' experience. Sunday would be the darkest night—the night of the new moon.

This was during the month of the sun's guardian, the Lion. This period of time was also known as the moon of the regal one—the king. It was the month associated with the Sun Archangel known as Michael. Sunday was also his day of honor. Little did Balamcoatl realize that Sunday would also be the exact day that he was born 51 years ago at the 17th hour of the 3rd day of the 8th month of the Fire Dog—Lion year of the calendar utilized by the Eastern Dragon people; a calendar Balamcoatl was not familiar with.

The 'death spiral' is an ancient method from the Lands of the Condor to experience 'death in life,' and then a rebirth as the student exits a stone labyrinth of resurrection. Walking counter-clockwise into the spiral you feel as if you have descended into the underworld. This is an opportunity to face the demons of your past, forgive and ask forgiveness and then let go of any attachments to the past. In the center of the spiral, the student faces west and accepts their 'death.' Then facing east, the place of dawn and the rising sun, they accept their 're-birth' and reclaim their power as a luminous warrior.

Sunday dawned bright and very dry, little rain had fallen that spring and summer. Balamcoatl planned on constructing the death spiral early in the afternoon so that they could conduct the ceremony at dusk. In addition, he wanted to work on the issue of *phobos*—the Greek word for fear and the origin for the word phobia.

"I don't know if we can do the fear exercise tonight under these dry conditions," said Balamcoatl with a questioning look.

"I know," replied Kolilkab. "Is it absolutely necessary to have a fire?"

"No, but I would have to adapt the exercise. After fighting the image of their fear, they could bury it instead of burning it. But it would not have as strong of an impact on their *ku*[106]. Burning is the best, but if we can't have a fire then we'll have to have them bury their images," replied Balamcoatl.

"The exercise is important for their spiritual growth," said Kolilkab.

"Yes it is. Most people live their lives in fear. Controlled and inhibited by the unknown, they separate themselves from their hearts and nature. Fear is a reality but it is also one of the prime barriers to an accomplished life and to spiritual power," said Balamcoatl.

"We are taking them bathing Monday morning. Entering those fast-flowing waters in the dark, then submerging oneself, not once but four times, now that sure does bring up fear," replied Kolilkab. "I remember the first time that we went bathing."

"But bathing is necessary. As you know, hanging over everyone's head is the specter of death. It is encoded within the very blood that courses through our bodies. Fear spawns in the body and it is through the body that fear is released—the ultimate body/mind connection. The best way to neutralize this fear is to experience 'death in life' or symbolic death. Although this is partly a death of the old self or old life, it also is a step forward in conquering their fear of physical death," Balamcoatl paused for a moment as one of their students asked to speak to Kolilkab. After just a few minutes Kolilkab returned.

"She asked if we would go over the procedures for bathing tomorrow morning," said Kolilkab.

"I was planning on reviewing it at the mid-day meal," replied Balam-coatl.

At that moment they both looked up in unison at the noontime sky. It had been crystal clear and calm all morning long just as it had been over the past two days, but something seemed to be changing. Within a few minutes, the sky darkened into an ominous swirling bluish-black tempest. There was a pause of sound and movement as if a giant was holding its breath. And then… thunder, lightning and rain.

Torrents of rain fell as thunder boomed overhead and lightening struck all around them. Everyone ran to huddle underneath the confines of the cooking tarp, shaking and in awe. The intensity was otherworldly. People were scared at the suddenness and intensity of the wind and the rain, the thunder and the lightning.

"This is unbelievable," said Balamcoatl in a whisper to Kolilkab.

"I know… something is not right. This storm is not normal," replied Kolilkab.

"But what can it mean?" asked Balamcoatl.

"I don't know…."

"The land is now purified," Mikael said to Regulus. "I can now appear."

The land, which was now soaked through, allowed Balamcoatl and Kolilkab the opportunity to have a fire that night as part of their 'fighting the fear' exercise. In addition, the storm changed the timing of building the death spiral. It would now occur late in the afternoon not earlier as had been planned.

"Everything that we do is optional," explained Balamcoatl to the twelve apprentices who were sitting in a semi-circle by the southern edge of the death spiral facing him and Kolilkab.

"This is our first symbolic 'death-in-life' experience. It will definitely affect your *ku*. And your body will feel the change. Keep your mind strong and clear with no 'chatter' as you enter the spiral. Tomorrow morning before first light, you will experience a true old-time submersion baptism, not as membership in a church, but as a true experience of death and rebirth—a second birth. Are there any questions?"

Balamcoatl waited for any questions, and when there were none, he continued on, "The death spiral is now just stones arranged in four spirals. It needs to be 'opened,' activated like turning on a light switch, which I will do in a few minutes. If there are no further questions or concerns, please get prepared to enter the spiral."

At the last moment, an apprentice asked a question, "Balamcoatl, if at the last instant, we decide not to go into the spiral, do we still have to?"

"That's a good question, Kumac. No, you do not. If you feel uncomfortable, and I know that you were brought up very religiously with the priests doing the ceremonies not you, you do not have to enter; just let us know by shaking your head 'no.' And that goes for anyone else as well," replied Balamcoatl.

As everyone left to get ready for the experience, Balamcoatl had a feeling that this was not just any ordinary spiral. There was something different about it. He then let go of any attachment or anticipation and cleared his mind, preparing to enter and open the spiral.

Kolilkab had chosen two apprentices as birth guardians. They would stand at the mouth of the 'birth canal' of the spiral, which was also the entrance, and pull the 'new ones' into existence. The others would stand on the outside of the outermost spiral chanting a phrase linking heaven and earth, until it was their turn to enter and face their symbolic death. Each one who chose to enter the spiral must stand at the entrance praying and contemplating their desire to enter the spiral. If they chose to still enter, they must take their first step into the vortex with their left leg as a sign of intent and focused-will to 'let go of their old self.'

"Something is not normal," thought Balamcoatl as he stood at the entrance to the death spiral. "My song is coming...."

With that last thought, Balamcoatl's left foot stomped the ground inside the spiral and as his right leg caught up with his left, his spirit song[107] sprang from his lips, and he began walking the spiral with serpentine movements of his body. The response from the apprentices was immediate—fear and wonder became etched on their faces. One hour later....

"I never saw you open a spiral like that before... your song came out and your movements...," said Kolilkab.

"I know," replied Balamcoatl. "It must have scared people. I noticed that three didn't walk the spiral."

"Kumac was totally freaked out. I've talked to him and he's okay now. But you really pushed his major belief buttons. He said you looked like some type of demon. He also confided in me that he gets uncomfortable when he looks into your eyes before you do ceremony or a healing. He says you have a frightening look of 'non-attached intensity'—eyes not of this world," explained Kolilkab. "I assured him that it is your totally focused strong mind and intent."

"Is he okay with bathing tomorrow morning?" asked Balamcoatl.

"He said he's still willing to participate... just as long as he doesn't have to go into a death spiral," replied Kolilkab.

"Good. Now let's talk about tonight's fear exercise."

Hours slowly passed as the apprentices fashioned images out of wood of one of their fears. The fear was to be minor, one that they could let go of in the night's exercise. Darkness came around 9:00 o'clock when Balamcoatl lit the fire to begin the experiential exercise. Everyone sat on the ground in a semi-circle with the fire in the center of them and the West open so that each apprentice could approach the fire from the West—the black direction of fear and the direction of re-birth.

"One at a time, please approach the fire in a counter-clock wise manner, fight your fear, burn it and then return to your seat in a clock-wise way," Balamcoatl emphasized from his seated position in the north next to Kolilkab.

In turn, each apprentice approached the fire and laid their symbolic image of their fear before them. When ready, they fought their fear with a wooden sword and when successful, they tossed the remains into the fire. One after another, each approached the fire and fought their fear.

"They're not going-for-it, they're half-heartedly doing it," thought Balamcoatl.

When all were finished Balamcoatl looked around the semi-circle and each apprentice's head was hanging low staring into the fire.

"They know they didn't go-for-it. How am I going to tell them that they blew it? They squandered an awesome opportunity to release one of their fears." With these thoughts going through his mind, Balamcoatl decided to stand and talk more philosophically about releasing fear rather than giving a searing commentary on—'you blew it.'

He stood and began a more nurturing synopsis of the exercise, only stating a few things before….

"Uh-oh, my neck's twitching." Balamcoatl recognized the feeling that he always got when there were otherworldly energies around. But this time, it was different. He turned his head to look behind him into the woods. Everyone else was still seated on the ground staring into the fire. No one else was looking up.

This was the night of the new moon and the only light in the clearing was cast by the small fire. The night before Balamcoatl had stood in this same spot observing the dark woods, while the apprentices were on their vision quest; he was listening and making sure that everyone was all right. When he had turned off his flashlight, in the blackness of the night, he couldn't see more than a foot or so in front of him.

"What… no." These two short thoughts coursed through Balamcoatl's mind as he turned his head back around to see if there was some other light source coming from his front other than the small fire. And when he saw nothing that could explain what he just saw, he turned his head back around again in dis-belief—making sure he saw what he saw…. This all took less than a minute's time.

"Please stand and be quiet, we have visitors," said Balamcoatl as calmly as possible, all the while not knowing what he had seen.

As Kolilkab stood up next to her husband, looking at the 'lights,' Balamcoatl leaned over and whispered into her ear, "What is that?"

Without any hesitation Kolilkab said, "Why, they're Angels!"

And then Balamcoatl remembered his prayer for a sign of who he had been. It made sense, but he never expected a sign like this.

"A shooting star…," someone said as all looked up as it blazed across the night sky.

"Three crosses," said another.

"A white dove…," an apprentice exclaimed as it flew over their heads.

"Look at the stones of the death spiral…," another said. The stones had at least doubled and tripled in size; some were now the size of boulders. But the most unusual thing was the greenish otherworldly glow that surrounded each.

After this no further words were spoken. Time seemed to be suspended as Balamcoatl, Kolilkab and the twelve apprentices witnessed in awe a massive column of light a few feet off of the ground at least five feet wide and four or five times as tall. This light was in the north by the entrance to the death spiral. It was a light that was whitish and not of this world. Suspended higher up by it were two other columns of light not quite as bright or as large. The legends have always told that an archangel is always assisted by two helping angels. After an unknown amount of time had passed….

"We need to leave and go to bed now," whispered Kolilkab to Balamcoatl. "There are only a few hours left until we have to get up and go bathing."

"You're right," replied Balamcoatl.

He then turned and said to the others in a quiet voice, "It's only a few hours until we put you in the stream and baptize each of you. We all need to get some sleep, so please return to your tents; be respectful as you leave and give prayers, blessings and a thank you for this experience."

Balamcoatl and Kolilkab were the last to leave and return to the shelter where they were staying. Kolilkab slept soundly the few hours that they had, while Balamcoatl stayed awake. His mind was focused on the visitation and trying to figure out the identity of the archangel. The last doubt of who he was had left his mind; he again gave blessings for answering his prayer of giving a sign of his past incarnation. And right before he was going to wake his wife up to go bathing, he thought, "Will they figure it out… who I was, who I am and who I will be?"

Summer turned into fall as Balamcoatl finally had solved the mystery of the identity of the archangel. The archangel was Mikael, known to most as the archangel Michael. Balamcoatl had determined this through his research of the connection between him and the archangel:

1. The Archangel Michael's day is Sunday and the astrological sign is Leo.
2. He is the warrior archangel and the guardian of the 'mysteries.'
3. Mikael is the guardian of labyrinths (death spirals included) and the organizer of earth energies.
4. Mikael has always been connected with both water and lightning. And according to various prophecies, great events are often heralded by unusual weather conditions.
5. Mikael is known as the angelic psychopomp, the mediator between life and death, and the archangel of the shamans.
6. The celestial bees are under the supervision of Mikael. The bee is Balamcoatl's family aumakua.
7. And finally, Mikael assists the 'lightbringers' of the different Ages of humanity and is the messenger of the prophets.

It was late one fall afternoon during the 'month of balance,' when one of Balamcoatl's apprentices contacted him.

"Balamcoatl, you'll never guess what I have," said Kimo in an excited tone.

"While you were finishing the late afternoon building of the spiral, I took a picture of you in the center of it. When I got home I just threw the camera in my vehicle and just last week got around to getting the pictures developed. I knew something was up when the photo shop lady said, 'One of your pictures has caused quit a stir.' Guess what; I have a daylight photograph of the Archangel and the two assisting angels. They were observing us building the spiral... and no one ever suspected!"

Now that you have heard more of my tale, let me relate to you, my dear friend, a few of the teaching chronicles of the Archangel Mikael.

The Teaching Chronicles of the Archangel
Mikael as told to the Morning Star:

"I am your elder brother, Morning Star. You are on earth to bring a message once again. All of creation is equally important yet uniquely, intrinsically evolved. Evolution is the created choice only within the required destiny of creation. In different terms, when the created goes out of the evolutionary curve, we, the Archangels, enter the curve to re-establish the balance. This is not desirable for the majority of your race, but it is necessary and has happened before on your world. Your message may right the unbalance. However, your message goes directly against the materialistic hierarchal authoritarianism of all stratums of society from religion to multi-national corporations.

There are always great transformations during the change of Ages when your world leaves one, what you call constellation, and enters another one. But, after the procession of five Ages, the sixth Age is an enlightened age of great spiritual evolution, a leap as you might say in the soul of humanity and the soul of the earth. There is, however, the transition time between the ending of the darkness and the beginning of the light, the dawn in a manner of speaking. This is the end of time, a time of darkness where the established belief systems are held on to by the entrenched privileged, refusing to let go of the control inherent in their positions of power, wealth and illusion. The old structures of patriarchal hierarchal materialistic authoritarianism must perish to make way for the new enlightened age. However, these structures will not die of their own accord and in this is the chaos, the pain of birthing the light out of the darkness. Nevertheless this new age will be marked by truth and the revolutionary revelation of Divine Humanity as a guiding light against all forms of domination. It will not be an easy transition, Morning Star. Tell your people that they may go willingly into the new age or as you say, 'kicking and screaming,' but the new age will be birthed and the old structures will fall. If they kick and scream, we will have to become directly involved and many of humanity will not survive. It is best if they let go of their greed, fear and materialism; if not, then we will have to cleanse through the elemental movements of earth, wind, fire and water...."

"The other Archangels and I watch over your world as well as others that your race does not know. We are responsible for a part of creation that you recognize as the Milky Way. From your vantage point it is a 'river of lights' that stretches across the cosmos—it is your Cosmic Mother. It is your home in the great expanse that is the mind of God. And there are other sentient beings on these worlds unknown to you that call the Milky Way home. During these transition times I am only responsible for your world. Before me was the Archangel that you refer to as Sammael. Each Archangel is accountable, in your words, for the different periods of your race's evolution. I was here before at the last turning of the Age when you were also here, Morning Star. And we are both back again during this transition time. If your message is not heard and understood this time, there will be great destruction, as materialism and greed have replaced people's loving minds with the illusions of fear and separatism. Materialism, if not stopped, will destroy your race anyway; but what cannot happen is the destruction of the rest of the creatures of the earth. This would not be acceptable; therefore, we will have to intervene directly. This is not in the best interest of your race's evolution. Time is now; the future is not set."

"There was never a war in heaven between the forces of light and dark. This is a spiritually immature thought that projects human behaviors and emotions on heavenly events, which are only the resultant illusions of the human ego. When fear is intertwined into so called spiritual/religious knowledge, be wary and remember that fear controls and separates. It is only love that provides the freedom and connection of spiritual evolution. Love is unity, a oneness that stretches throughout the eyes and mind of God. There is no such entity as Satan that commands the forces of darkness. The only darkness is the destructive darkness within each human that allows the devastating rampage of materialism, power and greed, as well as the ability to harm and kill each other. This is the landscape where war, domestic violence, rape and the other stains on the soul hold sway.

Tell your race not to look for the dark without, but look to the darkness within; learn to control this damaging darkness of being. There is also a constructive darkness of redemption and germination that gives birth to the greatest potentiality that is implanted within the seed of the soul. However, humans must control the ruinous darkness, while growing the beneficial darkness, shine the light of love on both and then all will see through the illusions that are manifested within their caves of terror."

"There is much spiritual and religious ignorance and illusion on your earth. It causes separatism and pain. The majority of humanity is led down a rock-strewn path of darkness and domination, blindly believing the dogma and doctrine of immature gate-keeping religious systems of power and control. Some of your largest religious structures teach that 'man is made in the image of God.' This is arrogant, ignorant, immature and domineering. It immediately separates the rest of the earth and the rest of creation into a box of un-divine non-being. Humanity is a <u>reflection</u> of God, not made in the image. Thus, the earth and all its creatures are also a reflection of God, as well as the other worlds and all sentient beings in creation are a reflection of God. There is no one image; it is all a reflection.

Humans, in their fear, have a tendency to follow and to believe without searching their hearts, minds and intuition to determine their own truth. To challenge the established dogma is usually unheard of. But your message, Morning Star, brings a breeze of love and power to purify the stagnation of thought prevalent within society. The winds of change are coming and before long it will be a hurricane of truth destroying the seeds of mediocrity."

Enough has been said,
The Archangel Mikael

Epilogue

It is October of 2005.[108] Sherry and I have returned once again with a group of students to the land of the Feathered Serpent—a land not only of sun and sand, but also of jungles, jaguars, hummingbirds and mystery. It has been almost twenty years since Sher and I first set foot on these sacred lands of the Maya. As we returned time after time to the Yucatan Peninsula, we noticed the changes that had begun to slowly take place.

At first we saw the changes as gradual, just like the times when you feel the first whispers of a change of seasons. But then, we sensed a storm gathering on the horizon—a storm that would ravish these sacred lands and their sites all in the name of greed and materialistic gain.

In the early years before the immense changes, I encountered, experienced and witnessed the magical and incredible: my wife shape-changing into her Nagual; a spirit-man at Teotihuacan; secret caves of jaguars and 'virgin-water;' secret passages beneath pyramids hidden in the jungle and other adventures too numerous to list here. But a few will be told in my forth-coming book 'Further Teachings of the Feathered Serpent,' to be released during the fall of 2006.

In addition, I had also been drawn to the Maya sacred site of Tulum located on the cliffs overlooking the bluish-green Caribbean. Tulum spoke to my soul. It is a place of power—a portal to the Otherworld. A ceremonial site where the sky, the sea and the earth all meet in a playful operatic symphony of celestial music and wonder that carries one to other planes of power.

Over the years I would learn that both the bee and Venus were sacred to the people and priests of Tulum. In turn I would also learn of a secret and hidden 'back way' into Tulum. I had studied with a Maya *h-men* (shaman) and he had passed on this knowledge of entering Tulum at night by

181

the sea-born cliffs. This allowed us the opportunity to conduct teachings and ceremony at night in the ruins.

I feel that I don't need to go on and on about the spiritual and physical desecration of these sacred lands of the Maya and the other lands that I have talked about previously. The picture below says it all. The historical, secret and ceremonial path into Tulum from the sea has been destroyed. This is its replacement:

Even though humanity has adversely affected the earth and the sacred sites that I have discussed, do not lose hope. Notwithstanding that the sacred sites have been disrespected and in some cases desecrated, the sacred power is still alive, if only sleeping, waiting for the enlightened ones to awaken and to return.

I believe in the light, in the all encompassing love of creation. At the end of this Age, through these trying times, keep faith in yourself as a Divine Human—a Feathered Serpent. Maintain a strong mind, a fearless spirit and embrace your *Ollin* heart. I bless each of you on this journey.

Rev. Dr. JC Husfelt
The Morning Star
Ahzab Kab Ek—"the star that awakens Earth"

APPENDIX

Appendix 1

As a religion of heaven and earth, Divine Humanity believes that we are divine and we are human; not sinful and human, but divine and human. Humanity means not only the human race but all sentient beings (all existences such as flowers, dogs, trees, fish, worms and stars) throughout the universe.

Divine Humanity believes that the Divine and all existences have consciousness and interpenetrate non-dualistically (non-dual interpenetration - Oneness).

In the light of the past and the present unbridled destruction of the earth's biosphere, it is essential for all people to acknowledge that nature is divine—a living existence in which everything has life and consciousness shared in common with all human beings.

Divine Humanity, as a world religion of equality and simplicity, conveys a love for all forms of life and acknowledges everything in creation as divine as well as honoring its own unique intrinsic expression. Therefore, not only is every human being a divine human with an intrinsic human expression and the light, holy spark, of God within him/her, but all trees are divine as well as being a tree that has consciousness; in its intrinsic expression, the tree may provide food and shelter for us as well as for other creatures of the earth.

Divine Humanity is a personal religion and spiritual philosophy that is based on one's truth found within one's heart and mind. It is not based on faith, dogma or doctrine.

Divinehood/Feathered-Serpenthood

Divine Humanity believes in the attainment of Divinehood (in an archetypal context—Feathered-Serpenthood—a Sun of God) in our present incarnation in both the body and mind, just as we are here and now, in our untransformed, impure and imperfect state. However, this does not mean that we automatically awaken to our divinity and in the next breath attain Divinehood. It means that Divinehood lies innate within each of us until awakened—this is the hidden Divine Nature—Sun of God - the Holy Grail.

The process of attaining Divinehood follows the ageless and tested formula of initiation, ascetic (difficult) work and transmission, which in our case would be the awakening and attainment of Divinehood.

Initiation is the acceptance of Divine Humanity as one of our basic beliefs and a guiding principle in our life—the acceptance in the divineness of all things and their intrinsic worth and identity. This engenders love, compassion and respect for all things in the universe. This is the beginning of the realization that the divine and all things (sentient beings) interpenetrate non-dualistically (non-dual interpenetration—Oneness) and that all things have a consciousness.

Ascetic work is the core of Divinehood or Feathered-Serpenthood. It is the process of opening and awakening our heart/mind. I prefer to use the term Feathered-Serpenthood due to its archetypal imagery of the oneness or union of heaven (feathered) and earth (serpent). As well, it reflects my own experiences, initiations, ascetic training and transmissions of power from various indigenous cultures' elders/shamans. Feathered-Serpenthood (Divinehood) is a Fivefold Path embracing Three Noble Expressions—The Three Pillars of Light.

The Fivefold Path is structured as an earth/heaven medicine wheel or mandala that is anchored in the ability to 'let go' or detach from the emotional, mental and physical enemies such as stupidity, ignorance, arrogance, guilt, anger and fear, the mental illusion of ego and the spiritual separation of self:

1. The Serpent Path of the South
2. The Jaguar Path of the West
3. The Hummingbird Path of the North
4. The Eagle/Condor Path of the East
5. The Center—Divinehood/Feathered-Serpenthood

Appendix 2

Make Money? Catch Fish?

In 2002, I returned with my wife Sherry, to one of our most favorite islands, Maui. A few days after we had arrived, I went to see a friend who works at one of the major resorts in *Ka'anapali*. As I was walking through the hotel lobby, I passed a young woman coming in the opposite direction and caught the last four words of her conversation. They were: "…make lots of money." Those four words triggered this teaching.

Centuries ago on this island, in fact on any island in the South Pacific, four equivalent words of prosperity would have been: "…catch lots of fish!" Depending on the culture, both sets of words usually spelled wealth. At this point, you may be asking yourself, so where is the teaching? Don't they both have the same meaning?

Well, yes and no. Both spell wealth, but the spiritual teaching is in the answer—no; there is a huge difference between the two. A wealth based on fish cannot be accumulated nor can it ever be horded. The wealth magically, and practically, disappears when the fish spoils! Any excessive amounts of fish would naturally be shared not horded away. Such is not the case with money. It is accumulated and stashed away to satisfy one's personal inadequacy, sense of external materialistic power (false as it may be) and to reduce one's fear of life and its many unknowns. Fish, does not breed greed; money does, as the desire for it opens Pandora's Box to ethical and moral depravity and spiritual void-ness.

Fish-wealth brings status as it would contribute to the Hawaiian concept of *pono* (balance and harmony) and the well-being of the island's extended family (*ohana*), and the community. In contrast, money fractures communities into the 'haves and the have-nots.'

Possibly the biggest problem of all is that money and a capitalistic spirit separates and exploits, as well as, destroys nature and the environment. To improve the bottom line and their own wealth index, the welfare and protection of nature and the environment is disregarded by the greedy, materialistic mind-set of the corporate 'demi-gods' and their shareholders. To the corrupted ones and their false empires of bottom-feeders (bottom-line analogy), there is no concept of "the love of the land." On the contrary, their motto, belief and rallying cry is: "the love of money."

The CEO's and their fellow cronies reside in a lair of the man-made tower that in its creation ripped and tore the earth, replacing the magic of nature with the concrete and steel of dominance. This cavern of greed only separates their consciousness from the earth even more and blinds them to the paradise of natural beauty that provides a sanctuary and garden for creation's creatures.

Ironically, in our 21st Century culture, even though fish have an intrinsic value, while money does not—except in its illusion of value—money is still worshipped as a savior of humanity. Having no intrinsic value, unlike gold, has led to the ethical and moral problems plaguing our culture. In addition we have the "ethereal" money that appears magically in the world of stocks, options, hedge funds and futures, but has no intrinsic value what so ever.

Making money focuses on achieving external power. This outer power, in the minds of the weak, justifies the desire for wealth; the behaviors of lying, deceitfulness, deceptiveness, destructiveness to the environment and families; workers as commodities to be hired and fired and an ego that focuses on the 'I' not the 'we.'

However, catching fish from an outrigger canoe requires inner power. This is the power of spirit and heart that results in a harmonious partnership with the land, the sea, the sky and all the inhabitants of such. This inner power is reflected in the love, respect and prayers of thanks that are given to the ocean and to its creatures as the bounty taken is shared with all of the family and community. On the other hand, in the world of commerce and profit, even fishing may be despoiled. I am talking about commercial fishing. Being true to its name, it tends to over-fish, while turning a blind eye to any destruction and/or pollution of the oceans and the rivers of the world.

Please do not misunderstand me. I am not advocating a society of individual communities that grow their own food or fish the sea; nor, as you are well aware, am I supporting a Capitalistic society of destruction that spawns an inequality of the 'haves and the have-nots.' There is, however, the balance between the two, a point of harmony of humanity and nature where love resides for all—a spiritual egalitarianism.

Appendix 3

Chakra Awakening Meditation

Preparation—find a quiet place where you will not be disturbed (by ringing phones, interruptions, etc.) in your home or out in nature. Be as comfortable as possible and totally relaxed. If you are in your home and you have incense or sage, you may burn this, but it is not necessary. You may also put on a drumming cassette tape, or some other repetitive sound tape, such as bells or gongs. Again, this is not necessary; these are just aids to help you quiet the internal dialogue, or "chatter," within your mind, and to help you begin the meditation.

Sit down in a comfortable position and start doing slow deep breathing. Let your eyes gradually close. Continue deep breathing, slowly; visualize the air coming in through the top of your head and going out through your navel region. Feel yourself relaxing.

Meditation—now put your right hand over your left hand with your thumbs upward and slightly touching, forming a "flame." Place your hands at your first chakra. Staying in this position, identify with all of your senses every sound that you can hear. Hear your breathing; hear the wind. Identify all the different sounds.... Next, identify all the different feelings. What do you feel sitting here? Is the floor hard? Are your clothes soft? Identify what you feel.... Now, what do you smell? Identify the scents around you.... Lastly, what do you taste? Taste your upper lip, your lower lip. Identify all the tastes....

Now in your mind's eye, see yourself sitting here. You know how you are dressed -- just see yourself sitting here like that. Keeping that image of yourself sitting here, you now see a flame suddenly burst into appearance in your hands. It's just a little flame, right there in your hands at your first chakra. What does this flame smell like? You can smell a little bit of the flame burning. What is the sound of that flame? If you could get close enough to it, what would that flame, the essence of that fire, taste like? How does that flame feel?

You can still see the flame, right there at your first chakra. It's getting a little larger now. And as it gets larger, it activates and awakens your first chakra. The flame reaches your first chakra and it bursts open and starts swirling with brilliant red color. What does this feel like? Taste like? How does it smell? What sound does it make? And how does it look? The flame is swirling at your first chakra -- you can see it from the front to the back of your body.

And now that flame is going up a little higher. As soon as it reaches your navel, your second chakra, it bursts open into a swirling, orange-colored vortex of energy. What does it feel like? What taste would you associate with it? How does it smell? Does it make any sound?

Now the flame is moving up to your third chakra, in your solar plexus. You see it bursting open into a swirling yellow energy vortex. The flame is right there in front of that vortex, triggering it open. You see it swirling. How does that feel? What is its taste? Its smell? Its sound?

Now the flame travels up a little bit higher. It goes up, and hits your heart chakra, and bursts it open into this beautiful green, swirling vortex. See the green color that represents love, opening and swirling. How does it feel? How does it taste? How does it smell? What sound does it make? You see this vortex extending out from your body, to the front and the back, like a long tunnel of swirling, green energy, ignited by the flame.

And now the flame is coming up to your throat. As soon as it touches your throat, it opens up this blue, swirling energy vortex right at your throat level. You can see it swirling through your throat. How does it feel? What does it taste like? What does it smell like? Do you hear any sound?

The flame is traveling up now, past your lips, past your nose, past your eyes, up to your forehead. And now your sixth chakra, your third eye, is blown open, and you see a violet-colored energy-vortex swirling there.

In fact, you can now see, in your mind's eye, all of the vortexes that you have opened. You see them all much more clearly, because your third eye is opened. Identify each of them again. See how much clearer that red one is swirling; how much clearer that orange one is swirling; that yellow one; that green one; that blue one. See how much clearer they all are to you, now that you've activated your third eye. You have this swirling mass of violet energy in your forehead. And outside of your body, you can still see the flame that has ignited and opened up all of these vortexes of energy.

And now this flame is moving up again. Up and up, until it bursts out through the top of your head. This last vortex of energy, at your crown chakra, is so bright it's almost unbelievable. It's a pure white color, because of the white energy that is flowing down into it from the Heavens. This light flows right down through your body, right down to the bottom of your body, and into the Earth. Witnessing this light, you feel very strongly your connection between the Heavens and the Earth.

And now the flame is engulfing your body completely. You have all seven of these energy vortexes, all these beautiful colors, swirling up and down your body. Surrounding your whole body on the outside are these flames of light and fire. These flames are just engulfing your body completely. How does that feel? What does it smell like to have this much power, this much energy? What does it sound like? What do you see in your mind's eye? All these colors, all these energy vortexes swirling.... Now the flame is coming up from around your body, and it's forming a halo around your head. The purest white light of your crown chakra is coming through the middle of this halo. What does this look like? What does it feel like? How does it smell? Is there any sound?

Now the halo is coming down into the flame, and the flame is coming down, down to your third eye. It's coming down further now, down into your throat. The vortexes of energy at your crown and third eye are still swirling as this flame leaves them behind. Keep them swirling—only the flame is disappearing, because the flame is what ignited the vortexes; but you don't need the flame any more right now.

And so the flame keeps going down your body. Down past your throat to your heart, down to your solar plexus. It's down below your navel now; and down past your first chakra. It's all the way back down to your hands.

Conclusion—the flame is in the palms of your hands now. See the little flame right there again. Look at it, and lock it away in your body memory. Tell your subconscious to remember this experience. See all seven of your chakras swirling open at once. See all seven brilliant, beautiful colors. Feel the energy forces of Heaven and Earth coming through you, as all those chakra vortexes swirl.

And now the flame in your hands will slowly disappear. When it does, thank, bless, and love yourself. Then take a few deep breaths, and slowly open your eyes.

Appendix 4

Foundation Journey

Preparation—find a quiet place where you will not be disturbed (by ringing phones, interruptions, etc.) in your home or out in nature. Be as comfortable as possible and totally relaxed. If you are in your home and you have incense or sage, you may burn this, but it is not necessary. You may also put on a drumming cassette tape, or some other repetitive sound tape, such as bells or gongs. Again, this is not necessary; these are just aids to help you quiet the internal dialogue, or "chatter," within your mind, and to help you begin the journey.

Lie down in a comfortable position and start doing slow deep breathing. Let your eyes gradually close. Continue deep breathing, slowly; visualize the air coming in through the top of your head and going out through your navel region. …. Feel yourself relaxing.

Journey—identify with all of your senses every sound that you can hear. Hear your breathing; hear your heart beating. Identify all the different sounds.... Next, identify all the different feelings. What do you feel? Is the floor hard? Are your clothes soft? Identify what you feel.... Now, what do you smell? Identify the scents around you.... Lastly, what do you taste? Identify all the tastes....

Now in your mind's eye, see yourself in nature. It may be a garden setting or possibly a jungle one…. Whatever is special to you…. Look around, what do you see? Identify at least three things that you see…. Now, what do you hear? Identify at least three sounds around you…. Now, what do you smell? Identify at least three scents around you…. Now, touch at least three things…. Lastly, what do you taste? Identify all the tastes....

Now, identify the whole area…. And find a special place to sit and wait that is in your nature area. This may be under a tree or by a stream or even possibly by an ocean or sea. Feel the joy and happiness by being here in this special and sacred place.

Take your time being here…. This is a place of peace, oneness and rejuvenation…. It will become a place of transformation….

Conclusion—when you are ready to leave your special place, look around one last time and lock it away within your mind and body memory. Thank, bless and love this experience and tell your subconscious to remember this 'foundation journey.' Bring your consciousness back to this reality by using all of your senses. Feel the floor or ground beneath you…. Slowly move your body and gradually open your eyes.

As with all experiential exercises and journeys, it is best to lock the experience away within your subconscious, either by writing it down, or discussing it with another person, or both. You may also want to draw or sketch your special and sacred place in nature.[109]

Appendix 5

Ho'oponopono

There is a natural and harmonious order to the entire
universe. The three major forces are the God(s),
nature and man. The Hawaiian of old realized
that it was necessary that these forces be kept in "harmony"
and that they were all in some way interrelated.[110]

I consider the Hawaiian *Ho'oponopono* to be one of the best conflict
resolution practices ever developed. This makes sense when you consider
that it was developed by people living on an island in the wide-open ex-
panses of the Pacific. People living in such a close proximity to each other
stand the chance of self-destruction, if conflict is not resolved. Harmony
is essential for the well-being of the islanders.

The following is an over-view of the practice of *Ho'oponopono* and
may help you design a system that will fit your own circumstances, whether
at home or at work. The four phases below are taken from a book that I
would highly recommend—*Ho'oponopono*:

1. **Opening**—includes prayer and statement of the problem
    as well as outlining conflict resolution sequence.... set the
    proper climate then the *hala* or transgression is stated.
2. **Discussion**—all members involved share their thoughts
    and feelings in a calm manner and listen to all the others
    as they speak.... Most problems have many dimensions
    symbolized by knots in a fishing net, which refers to the
    members of the *ohana* (extended family).... These must

be discussed—shared…. Discussion of problem is led and channeled by the *kahuna* or leader…. Traditionally, the Hawaiians felt that allowing emotional expressions to escalate discouraged problem resolution…. There is an emphasis on self-scrutiny as participants share honestly and openly and in a way that avoids blame and recrimination…. If tempers flare, a cooling off period is called.

3. **Resolution**—enables the exchange of confession, forgiveness and release…. This is *mihi* or sincere confession of wrongdoing and the seeking of forgiveness…. Forgiveness must be given…. If restitution is necessary, then the terms of it are arranged and agreed upon…. This results in *kala*—mutual release…. *Kala* indicates that the conflicts and hurts have been released and are *oki* (cut-off).

4. **Closing**—the leader summarizes what has transpired, then gives spiritual and individual thanks for the sincere participation of all…. After this a meal is usually shared.[111]

Appendix 6

Monica's Story—Summer 2000

"I am reborn and I feel great. I didn't think that I would feel any different. Before going on the mountain I thought I was okay and that this experience would be fun. I really didn't think that much would happen and I was going to prove it. I had fun writing my obituary and reading the one my father wrote for me. I thought it was cool because I'm not afraid of dying.

Right! Then why did I cry like a baby through the whole ceremony? It surprised me and I tried to suppress it, but it kept bubbling out. And then I said to myself 'I hate saying Goodbye.' All the loneliness that I felt when I left home and came to the States, when I left my friends and family and when I said goodbye, came pouring out. All the times that I kissed my mother and father, sisters and brothers goodbye and held in the tears to appear strong knowing that I wouldn't see them again for years.

I cried last night. I mourned my grandmother, I mourned my father-in-law, I mourned, I cried and it felt good. I don't know if feeling proud of oneself is ego, but I felt proud of me especially when I shed my clothing for bathing. I died last night and it was hard, and I wanted to be reborn in the proper way. I wanted to experience the moment to its fullest. The old inhibitions were dead and the new brave me is here.

This morning as I sat under my spirit blanket and listened to Sherry sing her beautiful spirit song, I heard all around her an echo in harmony. While Sherry voiced her spirit or herself in the waters, I got the feeling that I need to do that. I need to let my voice be heard and not be afraid to express myself in anyway that I feel like. I used to hold it in so as not to appear different. No more!

What happens next? That is hard. To keep what I experienced here, and who I am here, and to be that person every day will take a lot of conscious effort. I will need to use all of my WILL and determination to move forward and not go backwards. I am reborn and can only go forward and I must remind myself of that every morning. I need to greet each day early and with celebration and enthusiasm. No more sleeping to escape life. I am reborn. In the fire, I cast the old me and I burned, and the new me came out of the waters fresh and unblemished. I have shed the wall that I built around myself. I thought it was my protection, but it was my prison. Now I am surrounded by the Truth and that is my protection and I am free."[112]

Appendix 7

Slaying the Dragon

Preparation—you will need to fashion an image that represents your Dragon of Materialism out of some type of flammable material. When making your image, it is best to be in a balanced state of mind and heart. You will also need to make a wooden sword that you will use to battle your dragon. In addition, please make an image of a feathered serpent. This is the transformation form of your Dragon of Materialism.

Because you will be burning your dragon, this ritual is preferably done outdoors, but can also be done indoors in a fireplace, if necessary. Prepare the fire ahead of time in a very respectful manner, in a spiritual way. Please conduct a fast or modified fast before this ritual.

Slaying the Dragon—conduct this ritual at sundown after washing/showering and dressing in different clothes than the ones that you wore during the day. One hour before sunset, sit alone and be in silence. Do deep and slow breathing to relax yourself… putting yourself in the present moment. You may also invite one of your spiritual guardians to come and join you for this ritual—you will know if one comes to you by feeling its presence.

Purify the area with herbs or incense; light the fire and sit and wait. After the fire burns for a few minutes, with words of offering, love and power, pour some of the perfume/scented oil, honey and the olive oil onto the fire as a gifting to the spirit of life and the spirit of the fire.

Let the fire burn. When you feel the time is right, approach the fire with your sword and the imagery of your dragon. Place your image before the fire. With full intent and power 'battle your dragon.'

Transformation—you have been successful. Pick up the remains of your dragon and burn them in the fire. Bring your image of the feathered serpent to the fire. Sit with it and feel the transformation. When you are ready, run the image of the feathered serpent through the flames of the fire to purify and to complete the transformation.

Completion—Offer a prayer of closure. Give the fire a gifting of the honey and some of your smudging herbs or incense. Bless, thank, and love this experience. Bless, thank, and love your guardian if one is with you.

Make sure the fire is totally out. Return the site to the original (even better) state. Return to your home, shower/wash and change clothes once again. Put your feathered serpent in a special place, remain quiet until bedtime; then sleep and dream.

Appendix 8

Death and Re-Birth

It's impossible to share in a book the procedures for a spiritual/religious ceremony such as bathing. These types of ceremonies must be orally taught as well as transmitted from teacher to student. Only a properly prepared teacher may conduct this type of ceremony.

However, I can give your guidelines to help facilitate the death of the old self and the birth of the new self as a Luminous Warrior. Let me caution you that it is best to only conduct this ritual after having actively practiced the work of the South and West for at least a year. When you feel that it is the right time, please conduct this ritual of 'death and re-birth.'

Preparation—you will need to have someone who is close to you (such as a spouse, parent or child) write your obituary for your death. This same person will assist you in your symbolic death and re-birth. For your re-birth, you will write your own new words of being and power. This is a statement of new being—a proclamation of the 'new you.'

Additionally, you will need a new natural fiber blanket—a spirit blanket, which will only be used for spiritual purposes—as well as a new set of spirit clothes, preferably white. These spirit clothes could be as simple as a white tunic. It is your choice. It would be best to conduct this ritual near a body of water—stream, lake or ocean.

Death and Re-birth—ideally, you would conduct this ritual in conjunction with the ritual, 'slaying the dragon.' Early in the morning after 'slaying the dragon,' you would awaken before first light and prepare for your ritual. Your assistant will witness your death and re-birth as well as reading your obituary.

If possible, it would be best to do this ritual with a minimum of clothing on (nude if appropriate). Sit on the earth in a quiet manner; breathe deeply and slowly let your eyes close. In your mind's eye, begin at a time in your past and see your life unfold from that moment on to the present day. When you are ready to 'die' to this old self, open your eyes and slowly lie down on the earth.

Your assistant will cover you from head to toe with your blanket. Let some time pass by. Your assistant will now read your obituary. Let more time pass by. When ready, give a pre-determined signal with your body and your assistant will lift the blanket off of you and pull you into a standing position. Please dress in your new spirit clothes.

To acknowledge your re-birth, and as an act of power, please read your proclamation of the 'new you.' When finished, celebrate with movement and laughter.

Completion—Offer blessings and a prayer of closure. Gift your assistant with a small token of appreciation. Return home and share a meal with family and friends.

Bibliography

Campbell, Joseph, *The Hero With A Thousand Faces*, Princeton University Press, Princeton, New Jersey, 1990

Carrasco, David, *Religions of Mesoamerica*, Waveland Press, Inc., Prospect Heights, Illinois, 1990

Chilton, Bruce, *Rabbi Jesus*, Doubleday, New York, 2000

Cook, Roger, *The Tree of Life*, Thames and Hudson Inc., New York, 1988

Eliade, Mircea, *Shamanism*, Princeton University Press, 1964

Emerson, Nathaniel B., *Unwritten Literature of Hawaii*, Charles E. Tuttle Company, Rutland, Vermont & Tokyo, Japan, 1965

Fenton, Roberta, *The Mayan Gods*, Dante, Mérida, Yucatán, Mexico, 2004

Fernández, Adela, *pre-hispanic gods of Mexico*, Panorama Editorial, S.A., Mexico, 1984

Florescano, Enrique, *The Myth of Quetzalcoatl*, The John Hopkins University Press, Baltimore and London, 1999

Freidel, David, Schele, Linda, Parker, Joy, *Maya Cosmos*, William Morrow and Company, Inc., New York, 1993

Gallenkamp, Charles, *Maya*, Penguin Books, New York, 1976

Gilbert, Adrian G, Cotterell, Maurice M., *The Mayan Prophecies*, Element Books Limited, Rockport, Massachusetts, 1995

Gutmanis, June, *Na Pule Kahiko*, Editions Limited, Honolulu, Hawaii, 1983

Harden, MJ, *Voices of Wisdom*, Aka Press, Kula, Hawaii, 1999

Jenkins, John Major, *Maya Cosmogenesis 2012*, Bear & Company Publishing, Santa Fe, New Mexico, 1998

Jenness, Diamond, *The Faith of a Coast Salish Indian*, British Columbia Provincial Museum, Victoria, Canada, 1986

Kane, Herb Kawainui, *Pele*, The Kawainui Press, Captain Cook, Hawaii, 1987

King, Serge, *Kahuna Healing*, The Theosophical Publishing House, Wheaton, Illinois, 1983

Lee, Pali Jae and Koko Willis, *Tales from the Night Rainbow*, Night Rainbow Publishing Co., Honolulu, Hawaii, 1988

McBride, L.R., *The Kahuna*, The Petroglyph Press, Hilo, Hawaii, 1983

Merrifield, Heyoka, *Sacred Art Sacred Earth*, Rain Bird Publishers, Inchelium, Washington, 1993

Miller, Mary, Taube, Karl, *The Gods and Symbols of Ancient Mexico and the Maya*, Thames and Hudson Ltd, London, 1993

Morris, Jr., Walter F., *Living Maya*, Harry N. Abrams, Inc., Publishers, New York, 1987

Nicholson, Irene, *Mexican and Central American Mythology*, The Hamlyn Publishing Group Limited, Middlesex, England, 1967

Pukui, Mary Kawena, Haertig, M.D., E.W., Lee, Catherine A., *Nānā I Ke Kumu 1 & 2*, Hui Hánai, Honolulu, Hawaii, 1979

Rank, Otto, Raglan, Fitzroy Richard Somerset, Dundes, Alan, *In Quest of the Hero*, Rodman, Julius Scammon, *The Kahuna Sorcerers of Hawaii, Past and Present*, Exposition Press, Smithtown, New York, 1979

Saunders, Nicholas J., *People of the Jaguar*, Souvenir Press Ltd, London, 1989

Shook, E. Victoria, *Ho'oponopono*, East West Center, University of Hawaii Press, Honolulu, Hawaii, 1989

Smith, Jonathan Z., *The HarperCollins Study Bible*, New York, 1993

Storm, Rachael, *Eastern Mythology*, Anness Publishing Limited, London, 2001

Tedlock, Dennis, *Popol Vuh*, Simon & Schuster, New York, 1996

Thunderhorse, Iron, Le Vie, Jr., Donn, *Return of the Thunderbeings*, Bear & Company Publishing, Santa Fe, New Mexico, 1990

Tolkien, J.R.R., *The Shaping of Middle-Earth*, Ballantine Books, New York, 1995

Van Buren, Elizabeth, *Lord of the Flame*, Neville Spearman Limited, Sudbury, Suffolk, England, 1981

Waters, Frank, *Mexico Mystique*, The Swallow Press Inc., Chicago, 1989

Feathered Serpent Medicine Apprenticeship

The Feathered Serpent Medicine Apprenticeship is an on-going comprehensive spiritual educational program working towards awakening and mastery of 'First Knowledge.' The Apprenticeship Program is offered in the greater Seattle area and the greater Long Island, New York area. To find out about the Apprenticeship Program as well as other offerings or to invite JC and Sherry Husfelt to your venue:

E-MAIL: spirit@divinehumanity.com
WEBSITE: http://www.divinehumanity.com

Endnotes

[1] "We tend to think of myth and history as being in conflict with each other, but the authors of the inscriptions at Palenque and the alphabetic text of the Popol Vuh treated the mythic and the historical parts of their narratives as belonging to a single, balanced whole....

To this day the Quiché Maya think of dualities in general as complementary rather than opposed, interpenetrating rather than mutually exclusive. Instead of being logical opposition to one another, the realms of divine and human actions are joined by a mutual attraction. If we had an English word that fully expressed the Mayan sense of narrative time, it would have to embrace the duality of the divine and the human in the same way the Quiché term *kajulew* or 'sky-earth' preserves the duality of what we call the 'world.' In fact, we already have a word that comes close to doing the job: *mythistory*, taken into English from Greek by way of Latin. For the ancient Greeks... this term became a negative one, designating narratives that should have been properly historical but contained mythic impurities. For the Mayans, the presence of a divine dimension in narratives of human affairs is not imperfection but a necessity, and it is balanced by a necessary human dimension in narratives of divine affairs." Dennis Tedlock, *Popol Vuh*, pp. 58-59

[2] In this context, a traditional Hawaiian High Priest

[3] Please see appendix for knowledge concerning Divine Humanity

[4] a certain type of spiritual power

[5] Hawaiian meaning 'foundation for seeking wisdom'

[6] *Seattle Times*, September 3, 2005, p. A13

[7] Nathaniel B. Emerson, *Unwritten Literature of Hawaii*, pp. 262-263

[8] These words are taken from the print *E Hoe Wa'a Me Ka Akahele* by nature photographers Paul & Victoria McCormick

[9] One of the four major *Akua* (gods) of old Hawaii; in this context, *Kane* represents the sun.

[10] *West Hawaii Today*, Thursday, September 15, 2005, p. 8A

[11] *USA TODAY*, Friday, September 16, 2005, p. 1D

[12] Charles Gallenkamp, *Maya*, p. 205

[13] Otto Rank, Fitzroy Richard Somerset Raglan, Alan Dundes, *In Quest of the Hero*, p. 184

[14] http://www.bluecloud.org

[15] Elizabeth Van Buren, *Lord of the Flame*, pp. 258 – 259

[16] Iron Thunderhorse & Donn Le Vie, Jr., *Return of the Thunderbeings*, pp. 99 - 100 & 128

[17] J.R.R. Tolkien, *The Shaping of Middle-Earth*, pp. 184 - 185

[18] Nathaniel B. Emerson, *Unwritten Literature of Hawaii*, pp. 262-263

[19] *National Geographic Global Warning*, September 2004 pp. 8-9

[20] http://www.talkorigins.org/faqs/flood-myths.html#Hawaii

[21] David Carrasco, *Religions of Mesoamerica*, p. 48

[22] Each Age is determined by locating the sun's position at the time of the Spring Equinox with each Age lasting approximately 2160 years. This is the time that it takes for the sun to "progress" backwards (our view from earth) through one constellation. However, the ancient Hebrews and Mayas determined their Ages by the conjunctions of Jupiter and Saturn.

[23] Adrian G Gilbert & Maurice M Cotterell, *The Mayan Prophecies*, p. 211

[24] Irene Nicholson, *Mexican and Central American Mythology*, pp. 74 - 75

[25] *Aztec Calendar booklet, Teotihuacan*

[26] Frank Waters, *Mexico Mystique*, pp. 119 - 121

[27] Dualism encourages and supports a battle between the dark and the light—good and evil; duality on the other hand recognizes the complimentarily interaction of the light and the dark—spirit and matter—as forces that make up the whole of existence that is held together and surrounded with another force, the unifying interpenetrating force of creation—the Oneness or the love/light/consciousness of God—this is the spiritual/religious philosophy of radical non-dualism.

[28] Heyoka Merrifield, *Sacred Art Sacred Earth*, p. 95

[29] Frank Waters, *Mexico Mystique*, p. 126

[30] Dr. JC Husfelt

[31] Adela Fernández, *pre-hispanic gods of Mexico*, p. 78

[32] http://uts.cc.utexas.edu/~sparta/topics/alamo.htm

[33] Dr. JC Husfelt

[34] Rachael Storm, *Eastern Mythology*, p. 202

[35] Reminiscent of the Celtic life-sustaining cauldron—one of the forms of the Holy Grail

[36] L.R. McBride, *The Kahuna*, pp. 61 - 62

[37] MJ Harden, *Voices of Wisdom*, pp. 48 - 49

[38] Julius Scammon Rodman, *The Kahuna Sorcerers of Hawaii, Past and Present*, p. 152

[39] Kerry Hull, http://www.famsi.org/reports/99036/section05.htm

[40] http://www.pbs.org/holomaipele/myth1.html

[41] Mary Kawena Pukui, E.W. Haertig, M.D. & Catherine A. Lee, *Nānā I Ke Kumu 2*, pp.121 - 122

[42] June Gutmanis, *Na Pule Kahiko*, p. 5

[43] Herb Kawainui Kane, *Pele*, pp. 5 & 6

[44] http://belize1.com/BzLibrary/trust646.html

[45] Enrique Florescano, *The Myth of Quetzalcoatl*, p. 1

[46] *The Mayan Gods*, pp. 36 - 39

[47] David Freidel, Linda Schele, Joy Parker, *Maya Cosmos*, p. 211

[48] Mary Kawena Pukui, E.W. Haertig, M.D. & Catherine A. Lee, *Nānā I Ke Kumu 2*, p.123

[49] Serge King, *Kahuna Healing*, pp.132 - 133

[50] Diamond Jenness, *The Faith of a Coast Salish Indian*, pp. 47 & 57

[51] *Ibid*, pp. 46 – 47

[52] Mary Kawena Pukui, E.W. Haertig, M.D. & Catherine A. Lee, *Nānā I Ke Kumu 1*, pp.38 - 39

[53] Diamond Jenness, *The Faith of a Coast Salish Indian*, p. 37

[54] Another spelling for *nagual*

[55] Mary Miller and Karl Taube, *The Gods and Symbols of Ancient Mexico and the Maya*, p. 172

[56] Walter F. Morris, Jr., *Living Maya*, p. 158

[57] http://kms.kapalama.ksbe.edu/projects/2003/plants/tileaf/

[58] Joseph Campbell, *The Hero With A Thousand Faces*, p. 217

[59] Pali Jae Lee and Koko Willis, *Tales from the Night Rainbow*, pp. 18-19

[60] Roger Cook, *The Tree of Life*, p. 22

[61] People of Izapa, a prominent Mesoamerican ritual site active during the first century CE

[62] John Major Jenkins, *Maya Cosmogenesis 2012*, pp. 51, 61, 121 and 125

[63] *Ibid*, XXXIX

[64] Pali Jae Lee and Koko Willis, *Tales from the Night Rainbow*, p. 47

[65] The number of younger Americans turning to prescription drugs to get a good night's sleep is soaring, as is the money being spent to keep from tossing and turning…. Among adults ages 20 to 44, use of sleep aids doubled from 2000 to 2004, and spending among the age group for a restful night jumped 190% over that period…. The numbers were even more startling among children ages 10 to 19: Use of sleep aids was up 85% and spending was up 223% over 2000 levels. Michelle Healy, *USA Today*, October 18, 2005, p. 5D

[66] E. Victoria Shook, *Ho'oponopono*, p. 7

[67] *Ibid*, p.1

[68] How are you?

[69] Friend, buddy

[70] Divine power – Life force

[71] All right

[72] Goddess of the moon—*Hina-i-ka-malama*

[73] Goosebumps

[74] Ok

[75] Spirit, ghost

[76] Go for it

[77] House

[78] Dirty look

[79] Caucasian

[80] Feather cloak

[81] Feather helmet

[82] High priest

[83] Venus as Morning Star

[84] Irene Nicholson, *Mexican and Central American Mythology*, pp. 74 - 75

[85] JC Husfelt, D.D.

[86] Nicholas J. Saunders, *People of the Jaguar*, p. 112 & p. 128

[87] MJ Harden, *Voices of Wisdom*, p. 53

[88] David Freidel, Linda Schele, Joy Parker, *Maya Cosmos*, p. 433

[89] *ibid*, pp. 202 & 204

[90] *ibid*, pp. 411 & 413

[91] "… all the ecstatic experiences that determine the future shaman's vocation involve the traditional schema of an initiation ceremony: suffering, death, resurrection." Mircea Eliade, *Shamanism*, p. 33

[92] "a Christian theological term denoting divine gifts without which human salvation would be impossible." Jonathan Z. Smith, *The HarperCollins Dictionary of Religion*, p. 392

[93] "the belief that human beings require deliverance. A distinctive trait of some religions, it is a notion almost entirely absent in others…." *Ibid*, p. 954

[94] "the ritual process of purification, the procedure for making a person, place, or thing sacred." *Ibid*, p. 957

[95] Jesus and Mary Magdalene

[96] http://essenes.net/Mikveh.htm

[97] Bruce Chilton, *Rabbi Jesus*, p. 46

[98] *Ibid*, p. 48

[99] *Ibid*, pp. 48-49

[100] *Ibid*, pp. 49-50

[101] *Ibid*, p. 60

[102] I was taught and passed on the power and medicine of this tradition by Vince (Stogan).

[103] http://essenes.net/Mikveh.htm

[104] *Ibid*

[105] The only time that Christians seem to do any ceremony or ritual before dawn is once a year at Easter. Even Peter, the supposed 'rock' that Christianity is built on, supposedly practiced pre-dawn ocean bathings.

[106] Subconscious

[107] An individual's unique song of power; it is composed of vocalizations not words and only attained through rigorous spiritual and mental training. This leads to mastering the power of the 'mindsong.' The most powerful songs are the ones of long dead shamans—this is the song that Balamcoatl carried.

[108] Our journey was sandwiched between hurricanes Stan and Wilma.

[109] Please contact Dr. Husfelt if you would like him to personally design journeys for you based on this 'foundation journey.'

[110] *Ho'oponopono*, Shook, p. 6

[111] Ibid, pp.10 - 12

[112] Monica McCormack-Sheehan

About the Author

JC Husfelt, D.D., the Morning Star - *Ahzab Kab Ek*—"the star that awakens Earth," is a master shaman, a master of the healing arts, a martial arts master, and a 'teacher of teachers.' JC is the founder of Divine Humanity and the One Earth Church, family head of Tenchijinho and a spiritual lineage holder. He, as well, has been passed on the power and authority of various shamanic lineages.

JC, philosopher and visionary, is the author of *I Am A Sun Of God And So Are You*. Before he totally left the mundane life, JC was a teacher and wellness consultant with clients such as L.L. Bean, NCR, The President's Council on Physical Fitness and Sport and the United States Senate.